PRAISE FOR

Stories, Images, and Magic from the Piano Literature

A fascinating tapestry of tales, letters and comments from the composers themselves, from their colleagues and friends as well as from well known performers who consistently confront the challenge of making choices that are authentic, imaginative and inspiring.

Leon Fleisher
Andrew W. Mellon Chair in Piano
Peabody Institute of the Johns Hopkins University

A most stimulating read. Neil Rutman, himself a brilliant pianist, has succeeded in creating an invaluable tool for both teachers and performers. Much more than a reference book, it will Inspire the reader to deeper exploration and understanding of the music at hand.

Anton Nel
Long Endowed Chair in Piano
University of Texas at Austin
Artist Faculty at Ravinia and Aspen

A true gold mine of information, this book is a must-read for every pianist, and for every music lover. Insight of this kind is priceless.

Antonio Pompa-Baldi
Concert Pianist
and Distinguished Professor of Piano
Cleveland Institute of Music

Stories, Images, and Magic from the Piano Literature

Neil Rutman

Torchflame Books
An imprint of Light Messages

Copyright © 2015, by Neil Rutman
Stories, Images, and Magic from the Piano Literature
Neil Rutman, DMA
www.neilrutman.net

Published 2015, by Torchflame Books
an Imprint of Light Messages
www.lightmessages.com
Durham, NC 27713 USA
SAN: 920-9298

Hardcover ISBN: 978-1-61153-172-5
Paperback ISBN: 978-1-61153-149-7
Ebook ISBN: 978-1-61153-148-0

Cover design by Gunnar Bartlett

Contents

List of Illustrations

Acknowledgements

Compiling the entries in *Stories, Images, and Magic from the Piano Literature* was a painstaking process of researching hundreds of books—both obscure and readily available. Sorting through the legion of images which would be included in the final draft, as well as deciding which composers would be researched, required insight and discrimination. Tim Purkiss, Director of Interlibrary loan at the University of Central Arkansas, was a patient and invaluable colleague in not only locating my scores of requests, but finding obscure volumes that otherwise would have been overlooked. I would like to thank Patricia Stroh, Curator of the Ira. F Brilliant Center for Beethoven Studies, for locating and elucidating many sources relating to Beethoven. I am grateful to Phillip Bailey and Horst Lange, Professors of Languages at the University of Central Arkansas, for their fine respective French and German translations of previously untranslated texts. I thank my dear teachers, Ellen Mack of the Peabody Institute and Aiko Onishi, for their hours of proofreading and their patience with my many requests for advice. Their insight into which images to include and which to discard was invaluable.

I am also indebted to my editors, Wally Turnbull and Taylor Kennemar. Wally Turnbull, at Light Messages Publishers, has been a source of continued insight and meaningful suggestions throughout the editing process. He is a man of unending patience and professionalism, for which I thank him.

Aiko Onishi has been the driving force behind this anthology. Her imaginative artistry and love of musical imagery has been a positive energy in my musicianship for decades. Twenty years of patient prodding and persuasion that this book should be written has finally paid off, for which I thank her.

Chapter 1
Stories, Images, and Magic from the Piano Literature

Stories, Images, and Magic from the Piano Literature is written with one purpose in mind: to stimulate the imagination of pianists as they study and perform the great works of the piano literature. This book brings together for the first time under one cover, for the delight and edification of the musician, a plethora of programmatic, poetic, or imaginative musical images and stories on piano works from the classical literature. Many images originate with the composers themselves, the pens of their acquaintances or contemporaries, while others derive from pianists and authors of distinction from later generations, as well as from translations of poetry on which a piano work is based.

The imageries compiled are not meant to substitute for serious study of tonal architecture, structure, and technical competency and finesse. *In der Nacht* by Schumann is not about Leander swimming to his beloved Hero through stormy seas, even though composer Robert connected this story to the piece in an 1838 letter to his future wife, Clara Wieck.[1] *In der Nacht* is not program music. Such anecdotes, however, do stimulate the imagination of the performer. They act as catalysts for ideas, pianistic nuances, ways to touch the keys, emotional reactions—of intimacy or vigor—during the process of re-creation and study, and are not without benefit during performance. Most performers are aware of the emotional and imaginative casualties that may ensue from endless hours of technical practice and over-long familiarity with a score. As Alfred Cortot reminds us, the image itself is neither necessary for the audience to know nor essentially connected to

---

1 *Early Letters of Robert Schumann*, ed. EDITOR. (London: George Bell and Sons, 1888): pp. 274-75.

the architecture of the piece, but it *is* essential in unlocking the imagination of the student and performer during the learning process.

The use of imagination in the process of interpretation was sublimely discussed by the great pianist Dinu Lipatti in a lecture given at the Geneva Conservatoire:

> What can I tell you about interpretation? I can only recapitulate, perhaps very imperfectly, the method which guides us, in stages to the TRUTH. First one should try to consider the complete emotional content of a work by playing it a great deal various ways before ever trying to play it technically. When I say 'playing it a great deal' I mean above all playing it 'mentally' as the work would be performed by the greatest of interpreters. The imagination is here required. Having lodged in our mind the impression of perfect beauty given by this mental preparation – an impression continually renewed and revivified by repetition of this performance in the silence of the night, we can go on to the actual technical work....
>
> Finally...the cold, clear headed detached being who has conducted the practice work on the material on which the music is made takes part in the complete performance together with the *imaginative* artist, full of emotion, of spirit, of life and warmth. It is the artist who has recreated it in his mind and imagination and who has now discovered a new and greater power of expression.
>
> Forgive me for expressing myself so badly on something so solemn.[2]

How could he ask us to forgive him for such eloquent expressions?

Imagination always takes the artist on the inevitable journey from absolutes to the illusive. In the beginning interpretation causes us to think in the absolute and objectively decipher the information notated in the score into notes, rhythms, and fingerings. On another more subjective level we interpret the shape of each phrase, the nuance, and the structure of the work as a whole. But the layer of applying our *imagination*—the images conjured by perceiving the feeling or mood of a piece through picture, story or verbal suggestion—is more elusive, subjective, and fascinating, yet always necessary. It is a crucial layer of musical preparation. It is hoped that this anthology might invigorate that layer.

The images and stories included range from the Baroque to about 1950, or from the repertoire that is most commonly performed by the modern pianist. Pianistic thought of the Romantic Era encouraged the marriage of literature, art, and programmatic images, and there is naturally an

---

2   *"Dinu Lipatti – The Teacher." The Pianist Magazine*, 28 (1983): 23, 25.

abundance of imagery from the nineteenth and early twentieth centuries. Sadly earlier eras offer fewer direct quotes from the composers themselves. But it would be impossible to convince me that the most imaginative and original of eighteenth-century composers—Scarlatti, Haydn, and Mozart, for example—did not often conceive of music in terms of descriptive and emotional imagery. The absence of recorded imageries from earlier eras may be due to the fact that, as with many things from more distant centuries, they were simply not written down or have not survived.

In compiling the images I have toned down, but not completely turned off, my filter of scholarly criticism. Authentic stories and images by the composers are of unquestioned interest and value, as are the accounts of their images left by dependable contemporaries. I have also included imageries penned by later pianists of distinction such as Alfred Cortot, Marguerite Long, and Edwin Fisher, to name but a few. Occasionally these artists will record an historical incident without citing their source, which I have always made an attempt to locate. An example is the story related by Alfred Cortot that Mendelssohn wrote the *E minor Fugue, Op. 35, no. 1* by the bedside of his dying friend, Hanstein. Cortot gives no source for this story but simply relates it in an offhand manner. Further research traced this romantic image by Mendelssohn's friend, Julius Schubring, to the London *Musical Times* of 1866, thus validating Cortot's original image. Furthering this idea, we know that commentators like Anton Schindler were not always reliable witnesses, and that Cortot lived in an era when most musicians felt Beethoven's *Immortal Beloved* was Therese Malfatti, and wrote accordingly. Yet I have carefully selected Schindler's remarks on Beethoven—many of which have accepted historical integrity—or the images of Cortot, Long, Brendel or Fischer, not to stir up controversy among historians as to which can be documented or not, but because they lead the interpreter's imagination to wonderful places.

By far the greatest challenge in compiling this anthology was deciding which composers to include or overlook, and which images to retain or discard. The sheer number of images for some composers dictated their own chapters, and by and large the composers chosen are those whose piano works are the most important or oft played. Reaching verdicts on which images or stories to include was inevitably a more subjective choice, though much thought went into the perusal of each one. I have avoided the puerile and sentimental while retaining those which have historical integrity and potential for implementation in effectual teaching and performing.

The piano works occur in alphabetical order in each chapter and are referred to by the title most commonly used in the English-speaking world.

For example, Schumann's *Waldszenen* and *Davidsbündlertänze* are rarely called "Forest Scenes" or "The Band of David Dances" and are thus listed in the original language. On the other hand the *Capriccio sopra la lontananza del suo fratello dilettissimo* by Bach is usually referred to by the English translation "Capriccio on the Departure of His Beloved Brother." In listing titles easy recognition rather than lingual consistency is a priority. Most of the images are entered without comment. There are a few exceptions when editorial elucidation clarifies a concept, identity of some obscure person, or mythological or literary allusions. I have retained all original spellings, punctuations, and italicizations, and enclosed all images cited within quotation marks. Longer quotes have been blocked and indented for ease in reading. Quotations are followed by a four letter key and a number which correspond to the page number and reference publication listed in the bibliography.

I regret that many of my favorite piano works are not to be found in *Stories, Images, and Magic from the Piano Literature,* but the realization that the research could be endless, that there is always yet another image waiting to be revealed in the future, has caused me finally to put a temporary conclusion to my research.

So if there be errors, or if I might be reproached or misunderstood for attempting to spark an emotive and imaginative interpretation of music, let us remember the words of Scarlatti in the preface to his *Sonatas*: "Therefore, show yourself more *human* than critical, and your Pleasure will increase… Live happily."[3]

Neil Rutman
San Francisco, 2015

---

3   Scarlatti, Ralph Kirkpatrick. *Sonatas*. (Princeton: Princeton University Press, 1981): 104.

Chapter 2
Bach

General Observations:

According to Bach's first biographer, Johann Nikolaus Forkel (1749-1818), Bach "regarded his musical parts as so many persons engaged in conversation. If there are three, each of them on occasion may be silent and listen to the other until it finds something relevant to say itself." BACF 98.

Work: Capriccio on the departure of his beloved brother, BWV 992 (1704)

According to Albert Schweitzer, "The nineteen year old Bach may have written *Capriccio sopra la lontananza del suo fratello dilettissimo* (Capriccio on the departure of his beloved brother) for the family leave taking. It begins with an arioso, inscribed 'Cajoleries of his friends, who try to deter him from his journey'; then comes an Andante, meant to be 'a representation of the diverse accidents that may befall him in foreign lands'; the 'general lamentation of his friends' is depicted in a passacaglia-like adagissimo on a descending chromatic theme suggesting that of the Crucifixus in the B minor Mass; in the following movement 'the friends, seeing that it cannot be otherwise, come and say farewell'; thereupon the 'Aria of the Postilion'; and a 'fugue in imitation of the postilion's horncall' ends the delightful work." BACS 343-344.

Work: Chromatic Fantasy and Fugue, BWV 903 (ca. 1720)

Forkel recorded in his 1802 biography of Bach, "I have taken considerable pains to discover a similar piece of music by Bach, but without success. The Fantasia is unique and unequalled. Wilhelm Friedemann sent it to me from Brunswick inscribed with these words by a mutual friend: 'Anbey kommt an etwas Musik von Sebastian, sonst genannt: *Fantasia chromatica*; bleibt schon in alle Saecula.'" ["Attached you will receive some music by Sebastian, otherwise called: *Fantasia chromatica*; it remains beautiful in all centuries." – Trans. Horst Lange]. BACF 127.

Work: Goldberg Variations, BWV 988 (published 1741)

"An amusing example of Bach's homey humor occurs at the end of his *Goldberg Variations*: the last variation is based on a quodlibet, a medley of popular tunes. The words [to one of them] are *Kraut und Ruben/Haben mich vertrieben*....: 'Cabbage and turnips have driven me away- if you'd cooked me better grub, I'd have stayed at home.'" LIVE 13.

Editor's note: The quodlibet is composed of a medley of several tunes, only two of which are remembered, "I have so long been away from you, come closer, come closer," and "Cabbage and turnips have driven me away, had my mother cooked meat, I'd have opted to stay."

Work: The Suites and Partitas

Editor's note: Insights into moods and gestures of the Suite's dance movements come from the relatively unknown 1835 Peters edition of the *Partitas* edited by Friederich Griepenkerl, Bach's "great-grand pupil," whose views came from an oral tradition transmitted via his teacher Forkel, and from Bach's contemporary Mattheson. In the Preface to this edition Griepenkel provided detailed description of each movement and its corresponding character. Many of them are cited below.

Allemande

From editor Alfred Dürr we read, "The allemande was traditionally regarded as a rather serious dance; in his *Musikalisches Lexicon* (Leipzig, 1732), Johann Gottfried Walther wrote that the allemande "must be composed and likewise danced in a grave and ceremonious manner." Likewise, in *Der Vollkommene Capellmeister* (Hamburg, 1739), Johann Mattheson described the allemande as "a serious and well-composed harmoniousness in arpeggiated style, expressing satisfaction or amusement, and delighting in order and calm." BAAD Foreword.

Courante

The *New Encyclopaedia Britannica* states, "The Courante...originated as an Italian folk dance with running steps, thus the derivation from the verb 'correre', or to run. As a court dance it was performed with small, back-and-forth, springing steps, later subdued to stately glides. Each couple held hands to move forward and backward or dropped hands to face each other or turn." BACO 681.

Friederich Griepenkerl writes, "The Courante has very strict rules as a dance. However, if merely played, it is allowed greater freedom so long as its uninterrupted figuration does justice to its name, that is, rapid and lively. A rapid allegro is well suited to it. Matheson says: 'The courante has something hearty, desirous, cheerful, which is all found by hope.'" BACG 85-87.

Aria

Discussing the Aria Griepenkerl writes, "Where this name occurs in old instrumental compositions it designates a short, cantabile, piece with a striking melody which is often much embellished, as in the suites of Handel. Its character is calm serenity and its movement is that of our andante." BACG 85-87.

Gavotte

Griepenkerl writes, "Its movement is moderately gay, its character exultant joy. It has a hopping, not a running nature, yet it is pleasing. The second gavotte is usually called a musette...the quavers that occur in it must be slurred, not detached. It is based on a continuous or continually reoccurring bass note, as on the bagpipes or the hurdy gurdy. Its nature is soft ingratiating song with naïve rustic simplicity." BACG 85-87.

Sarabande

Griepenkerl writes, "The Sarabande, originally a Spanish dance...requires a slow movement...Its character is a certain grandeur in the expression of all the more profound feelings of sublimity, dignity, and majesty. Religious texts could often be added to some of J. S. Bach's sarabandes. Everything that is pretty must carefully be avoided, and for this reason it cannot tolerate runs." BACG 85-87.

Minuet

Griepenkerl writes, "The character of the minuet is decent, moderate gaiety with noble simplicity and without affectation, which is the reason why quavers are its fastest notes." BACG 85-87.

Passepied

Griepenkerl writes, "The passepied is similar in character to the minuet, though it is more lively... Charming frivolity is its main character, which at times reaches to a temperate, noble, and charming gaiety. Mattheson says: 'the passepied does not have the fervor, passion, or heat of the Gigue...Its movement is usually a rapid allegretto or a moderate tempo.'" BACG 85-87.

Loure

From Griepenkerl we read, "The Loure is a short piece full of gravity, dignity, indeed grandeur, coupled with noble reticence. It is in 3/4 time and the movement is slow.... The Loure in 6/4 time is played twice as fast as the one in 3/4." BACG 85-87.

Bourée

The *New Encyclopedia Britannica* states that the Bourée is a "French folk dance with many varieties, characteristically danced with quick, skipping steps. The dancers occasionally wear wooden clogs to emphasize the sounds made by their feet. Notably associated with Auvergne, bourrées are also danced elsewhere in France and in Vizcaya, Spain." BOEN 432.

Gigue

In discussing the gigue, Griepenkerl's 1835 edition suggests the following, "The Gigue (giga), as music for dancing, is a small, gay piece in 6/8, 12/8, or 12/16… Mattheson is of the opinion that there are four kinds of gigue, which he characterizes as follows:

1. Normal English gigues have a heated and fleeting fervor, a passion that soon evaporates.

2. Loures and slow and dotted gigues have a proud and puffed up nature, which is why the Spaniards love them.

3. The canaries must be very eager and fast, and at the same time sound rather simple.

4. Italian gigues, which are played on the violin, force themselves, as it were, to be extremely fast and fleeting, though in a flowing, not a furious manner, rather like the swiftly moving arrow of a stream." BACG 85-87.

Work: Two-Part Inventions, BWV 772-786

Bach's charming, but rarely read, introduction to the *Two Part Inventions* is translated as follows:

"Honest guide, by which the lovers of the keyboard, and particularly those desirous of learning, are shown a plain way not only to play neatly in two parts, but also, as they progress, to treat three obbligato parts correctly and well, and, at the same time, to acquire good ideas and properly to elaborate them, and most of all to learn a singing style of playing, and simultaneously to obtain a strong foretaste in composition." BACB 210.

Work: Well-Tempered Klavier, Books I and II, BWV 846-893 (1722, 1742)

Gerber,[4] in his Dictionary, says that Bach composed the First Part of the *Well-Tempered Clavichord* (sic), "at a place where time hung heavily on his hands and no musical instrument was available. There may be some truth in this. Gerber's father had been Bach's pupil in the early Leipzig years, so that

---

4　Ersnt Ludwig Gerber (1746-1819) was a composer and the author of the famous dictionary *Historisch-biographisches Lexikon der Tonkünstler.*

the tradition may quite well be based on some remark of Bach's, especially as we know that Gerber was studying the *Well-Tempered Clavichord* (sic) at the time, and Bach himself played it to him thrice." BACS 332.

In reviewing Czerny's edition of Bach's *Well-Tempered Klavier*, Robert Schumann for the most part made favorable comments on Czerny's tempo indications and introductory remarks.   Regarding Czerny's expression marks Schumann wrote that he approved of, "his [Czerny's] indications for shading of each piece; the latter instructions we consider especially desirable, for nothing can be more tiresome or contrary to the meaning of Bach than to drone out his fugues or to restrict one's representation of his creations to a mere emphasis on the successive entries of the principal theme [subject]. Such rules are suited to students.   But most of Bach's fugues are character pieces of the highest type; some of them truly poetic creations, each of which demands its individual expression, its individual lights and shades.   A Philistine accentuation of the entries of the fugues subject is far from sufficient." SCMM 89.

Editor's note: While pianists today shun the Czerny edition of the *Well-Tempered Klavier*, in its day its intent was forward-looking.   Schumann was quite right to point out that instead of submitting to scholastic and pedantic interpretations, the Bach fugues require poetry, shaded expression, and individual characters.

Work: Prelude no. 8 in E-flat minor, Well-Tempered Klavier, Book 1

Paul Badura Skoda implies a connection between the sudden death of Bach's beloved first wife, Maria Barbara, while he was away on business and the heart-wrenching despair of this prelude.   He writes, "There can be little doubt about the affection of this prelude.   It depicts intense pain, and is expressed with an unrestrained passion that rarely occurs in Bach's music... We can only guess at the emotions that led to the composition of this exceptional work.   In his lectures on Bach, Wilhelm Fisher suggested that the sudden death of Bach's first wife, Maria Barbara, which must have affected him deeply, may have been the event that prompted him to write this piece. (Maria Barbara, to whom he had been married for thirteen years, died suddenly on July 7, 1720 while he was away from home on a visit to Carlsbad with the Prince of Cothen, and was buried before he returned)." BACB 214-215.

Editor's note: As is often the case, scholars are divided as to whether this prelude was written in the summer of 1720 or in 1721-22.   While there is evidence for both dates, one should be circumspect in conclusively connecting the composition of this prelude with the death of Maria Barbara.

Nevertheless, Fisher's theory is not far-fetched, and it causes one to ponder the prelude in a new and certainly compelling light.

Work: Fugue no. 4 in C-sharp minor, Well-Tempered Klavier, Book 1

Editor's note: A handful of the Fugues from the *Well-Tempered Klavier* are profoundly solemn and mystical in nature, and often referred to as 'Passion' Fugues. The C-sharp minor, D-sharp minor, B-flat minor, and B minor Fugues from Book 1, and the F-sharp minor fugue from Book II are in this category. They are full of imagery and Bach, who is generally not associated with programmatic or literary stimuli, musically depicts the Passion of Christ—and simultaneously his own heartfelt religious view—by incorporating religious symbolism and numerology into these Fugues.

Timothy Smith wrote a lengthy yet insightful look into the pathos and mood of the C-sharp minor fugue. I extract a large portion of the article here to underline the affection of a work such as this. Subsequent fugues are analyzed in less depth, but the imagery and emotional meaning is clear— certain fugues held a sublime spiritual meaning for Bach. He was able to condense and represent in these keyboard works the most sublime, painful, and fervent thoughts about which authors and theologians have written for centuries. The entire article by Mr. Smith is well worth reading. Portions of Timothy Smith's article follow:

> "In this unusual work Bach has used musical and mathematical symbols to express religious belief...In this analysis we shall consider how the fugue represents a lament, Christ's passion, the sign of the cross, and a crown.
>
> **A Lament**
> ...Please listen to the high voice of mm. 70-73 and mm. 101-105. Yes, they are very much alike. In both passages the high voice descends chromatically from c# to g#... I have called these two passages *lamenti*, a word that the Italians of Bach's day used to describe descending chromatic melodies in general. Obviously this fugue is a lament. But what has Bach lamented?
>
> ...Let us begin by considering two other compositions where Bach used the same lament.
>
> The first is the *Crucifixus* of his Mass in B Minor, where the choir sings "He was crucified under Pontius Pilate." Here Bach has repeated the lament thirteen times! In fact this is all the bass line does- it continually laments. In Bach's *Crucifixus* the object of his lamentation is obvious- the one being crucified was Jesus.

The other composition is a little known canon for five voices that Bach wrote for Johann Gottlieb Fulda…Fulda's canon, like the *Crucifixus*, uses the same laments.

The lament in the Fulda canon is especially important for what Bach wrote beneath it: *Symbolum Christus Cornonabit Crucigeros*. Translation: "This is a symbol of Christ who will crown those who carry his cross." So the laments of both the *Crucifixus* and canon are associated with the Crucifixion of Jesus.

Christ's Passion
A second reason for the importance of this lament is that it descends five semitones. These are the intervals between the six pitches c#- b#- b-a#-a-g#.

Prelude and Fugue in C-sharp minor, WTC, Bk. 1, mm. 70-73.
Tovey Edition.

What are more significant about five tones than any other number? Lutherans of Bach's day associated five with the wounds that were inflicted upon Jesus by the nails in his hands and feet, and a soldier having thrust a spear into his side.

When marks resembling Jesus' wounds have been impressed upon a person, or a work of art such as this fugue, Christians called them *stigmata*. As a symbol of unassuming meekness, stigmata are a reminder to accept suffering without complaint….

When music has this particular connotation we call it *passion music*. But we do not mean passion in the sense that we use it today. The Latin root, *passio*, means suffering. It is the same root from which we get compassion.

Christians place a great emphasis on Jesus' passion…This is done because suffering and compassion are at the center of Christian belief… Because the suffering of Jesus is considered to be the model, Christians reflect upon his passion in order to become more compassionate people.

Johann Sebastian Bach was fully committed to this belief. This dimension to his personal life is beyond dispute. He himself suffered greatly. Both of his parents died when he was ten. His wife Maria Barbara died and was buried while he was required to be out of town because of his employment. Ten of his children did not survive adulthood.

By now you must think we have ranged pretty far afield from this fugue. But I have not forgotten that we were discussing the *Well-Tempered Klavier*. It is only now that we are ready to continue that discussion. We began it by observing that there is sadness in this fugue. Now we know why. We may not be interested in the religion of Bach, but if we are interested in his music then we ought to acknowledge how it was influenced by his faith...

Why for example does this fugue, like the Fulda canon, have five voices?...Of the 48, only this and the fugue in B flat minor (WTC I) are in five voices.

But if five voices seem coincidental, you may be more curious to know why the subject of this fugue is so short. In fact it is the shortest in Book I of the *Well-Tempered Klavier*. Had you noticed that it has five pitches? No other fugue has a five note subject.

Does it seem plausible that there is a relationship between the five voices, five toned subject, and five semitone lament that we discovered earlier. The crimson thread that seems to tie all of this together is the passion of Jesus. And that is one reason why I have called this fugue passion music.

The Sign of the Cross
The subject of this fugue quotes the Advent chorale *Nun Komm der Heiden Heiland* (Come Saviour of the Heathen). Both melodies move from the starting pitch *do* down to *ti* and then cross above the starting pitch to *me* and descend twice (*re-do*) to the starting position. The melody is universally recognized to be *chiastic*. This word comes from the Greek letter Chi, a Christological symbol since Roman times. Athanasius Kircher, a near contemporary of J. S. Bach, had described the *chiastic* melody as a *circulatio* (circle)....

When Bach set the word *Kreuz* (cross) to music he often assigned the *circulation* melody to it...At other times he assigned the motive to *Jesum* or *Christus*. Interestingly Bach's own name in musical tones is a variation of a *circulation*....

So the subject of this fugue is the melodic sign of the cross. For this reasons I shall call it the cross motive. Notice that the cross motive contains an unusual and almost painfully dissonant interval between its 2nd and 3rd pitches. This is the interval of the diminished fourth (d4). Of all the subjects in the *Well-Tempered Klavier* this is the only one that employs the d4, an interval that, if not composed carefully, would draw red marks from your composition teachers. Bach's reason for using this dangerous interval was to communicate anguish and distress.

A Crown

Now I need to tell you about Bach's monogram: a seal that he used on his correspondence and legal papers. The monogram contains his initials JSB in florid calligraphy. Its superimposed mirror BSJ creates numerous crosses. These crosses are representations of the letter X (Chi), the first letter in the Greek spelling of Christ. In some of his manuscripts Bach substituted X for the word *Kreuz* (cross). Above the chi symbols there is a crown. Within the crown there are five jewels.

Bach's monogram bears a strong resemblance to the inscription that he wrote on Fulda's canon: "Christ will crown those who carry his cross." The monogram makes its crosses by superimposing Bach's initials JSB upon their retrograde BSJ. This symbolizes Bach himself carrying the cross. It also explains the crown.

We have now come to the heart of this fugue. Bach has signed his name three times: once in m. 41 (HCAB), a second time in m. 48 (BACH), and a third time in m. 64 forward (BACH #2). The first two signings are especially significant; they mark something. The marking is symbolized by the rhetorical device, known as *chiasmus,* where a motive is represented forward and later backward. In Bach's day (as even today) this type of framing was engineered to draw attention to what falls between. The Germans even have a word for what falls between; they call it the *Herzstuck (oomlaut)* or "Heart Piece." So the most important part of this Fugue lies between Bach's two signature motives. That passage begins in m. 41.

So mm. 41-43 is the passage of which I wrote emanates from Bach's heart. I'm able to make this observation because these measures fall between the *chiasmus* that Bach created by signing his name backward HCAB and forward BACH.

So here is what is so important about the *Herzstuck* of mm. 41-43 and why it comes from Bach's heart. The melodic inversion of the lament is Bach's musical symbol for a crown that has been generated out of the cross. We can be very confident of this interpretation. The evidence for it is found in the canon that Bach wrote for Fulda. Remember that Fulda's canon also contains a five semi-tone lament in the leader voice and the inscription "Christ will crown those who carry his cross…"

In the beginning I wrote that this analysis would decipher the meaning of the lament. Here is what it means. The five descending semitones represent Christ's passion and his cross. The five ascending semitones of its retrograde (m. 41) represent the crown that Christ gives to those who carry his cross: *Christus Coronabit Crucigeros*. In essence this fugue and Fulda's canon are both musical representation of Bach's personal creed." BATS

Work: Fugue in D-sharp minor, Well-Tempered Klavier, Book 1

Badura-Skoda writes of this fugue, "It is probably no accident that this subject displays an affinity to Luther's chorale 'Aus tiefer not schrei ich zu Dir' (Out of the depths I cry unto Thee), which in turn goes back to earlier sacred melodies. In the Baroque doctrine of figures this sequence of intervals and semitone notation (fifth minor sixth fifth) was termed 'pathopoietic' (causing suffering')." BACB 223-224.

Alfred Cortot[5] writes, "The theme of the fugue is a Gregorian theme, used already by Vittoria for a motet. The words of the latter are, 'O you who pass by, see if there is any sorrow like to My sorrow.'" COMI 28.

Work: Fugue no. 10 in E minor, Well-Tempered Klavier, Book 2

Eugenie Schumann recounts lessons she had with her mother, Clara, on this little fugue: "The study was followed by the Bach fugue in e minor from vol. I of the *Wolhltemporierte Klavier*. I learnt strict legato and the subtle shading of rhythm in this. My mother took endless trouble with the first few bars; but when these had been mastered, the fugue became easy, and I soon learnt to play it well enough to make it a pleasure to myself." SCEU 97.

Work: Fugue no. 14 in F-sharp minor, Well-Tempered Klavier, Book. 2

Badura-Skoda suggests, "As in the majority of short slurs, the first note of a pair should be emphasized (strong), whereas the second should diminish slightly. It may be safely assumed that such articulation should be applied to unmarked notes of this kind as in the *F-sharp minor Fugue* of WTC 1.

---

5   Alfred Cortot (1877-1962) was a renowned Franco-Swiss pianist and influential pedagogue and writer. He is widely regarded as one of the greatest pianists of the twentieth century.

Prelude and Fugue in F-sharp minor, WTC Bk. 1, mm. 18-20.
Tovey Edition.

That these chains of sighs are symbols of pain can be deduced from various vocal works, such as the chorus "So ist mein Jesus nun gefangen" (Thus my Jesus is now captured) in the St. Matthew Passion, bars 27-30, at the words, "Mond und Licht ist vor Schmerzen untergegangen" (Moon and light have disappeared because of their pain)." BACB 110.

Editor's note: The Well-Tempered Klavier contains several more fugues which can be interpreted with this type of religious imagery—the B-flat minor (wherein the subject incorporates the cross motive) and the B minor (here the chromatic sighs of the subject act like a lament) fugues from Book 1, to name just two. The evidence of the C-sharp minor fugue from Book 1 cited earlier testifies that Bach worked with imageries of a deep emotional nature.

Chapter 3
Bartók

Work: Fifteen Hungarian Peasant Songs (1914-1917)
Ballad. Andante

This work follows the story of Angoli Borbála, a tragedy describing the death of a young woman whose lover leaves her after she discovers she is expecting his baby. When the lover returns finding his beloved already dead, he drives his dagger into his own heart—graphically depicted by the harsh and dissonant chords in the last two bars. BARP 90.

Work: Kossuth (1903)

This piano transcription would follow the same story as Bartók's own program notes for the original orchestral work at its premiere in 1904, "The leader [of the Hungarian revolution against the sovereignty of the Austrians and the Hapsburg dynasty] was Louis Kossuth. As Austria saw, in 1849, that the war was going against her, she concluded an alliance with Russia. A crushing blow was inflicted upon the Hungarian Army, and the hope of an independent Hungarian kingdom was shattered—apparently forever." BARP 17.

Work: Mikrokosmos (1926-1939), Volume VI, *"From the Diary of a Fly"*

Bartók describes the climactic section ("Agitato," ms. 49) as, "the desperate sound of a fly's buzz, when getting into a cobweb" and subsequently ("con gioia, leggero," m/ 59) when "he escapes." BARP 144.

Work: Mikrokosmos, Book VI, *"Six Dances in Bulgarian Rhythm"*

Referring to the Bulgarian Dances, Bartók's son, Peter, wrote, "How foreign to Western ears such rhythms can be I learned through painful experience while recording some of these dances, as orchestrated by Tibor Serly, with the New Symphony Orchestra in London. The rhythm of one of these dances was a simple 3 + 3 + 2/8. We tried this dance (about two minutes long) for a whole afternoon, but the excellent musicians stubbornly managed to stretch out the shorter beats until the measures became close to 3+3+3/8. The phenomenon was not unexpected as I remembered my father's observation: to educated Western musicians these rhythms can be difficult to comprehend, even though they come natural to Bulgarian peasants." BARK 166.

Work: Out of Doors Suite (1926)
Musiques Nocturnes (The Night's Music)
The random appearance of various nocturnal sounds makes memorization of this piece very difficult. Mária Comensoli, a piano student of Bartók, was astonished when she first played *The Night's Music* by memory (as required at Bartók's lessons) and Bartók remarked, "Are you playing exactly the same number of ornaments that imitate the noises of the night and at exactly the same place where I indicated them? This does not have to be taken so seriously, you can place them anywhere and play of them as many as you like." BART 148.

According to Bartók's son Bela Jr., "the present example took its origins from [the vicinity of Vésztö]; in it my father perpetuated the chorus of frogs heard in the peaceful nights on the Great Plain." BARP 107.

Work: Romanian Folk Dances (1915)
Joc cu Bâtă (Dance with Sticks)
According to Bartók this is a "young men's solo dance, with various figures, the last of which—as a consummation—consists of kicking the room's ceiling!" BARP 75.

Brâul (Waistband Dance)
Bartók suggests, "This dance is performed at gatherings in the spinning house, generally only by girls, sometimes by young men and girls. They hold each other, their arms clasped tightly around each other's [waists], and form a circle..." BARP 76.

Buciumeana (Butschum [Translyvania])
This work is described by Bartók as one in which "the used melody is the more important part of the work. The added accompaniment and eventual preludes and postludes may only be considered as the mounting of a jewel." BARP 76.

Work: Sonata for Two Pianos and Percussion (1937)
Peter Bartók's recollection of the first Budapest performance of this work in 1938 suggests that an occasional discreet conducting of the work does no

harm to its execution. He wrote, "My father and mother were to play the chamber work with two percussionists. At the (probably final) rehearsal things still did not go well. My father kept stopping to correct this or that in the playing of the complex percussion parts; there were explanations and furthers trials; finally he declared that the piece had to be taken off the program... My father could not allow a less than satisfactory introduction of the piece to the Hungarian audience. What saved the program was Ernest Ansermet's offer (he conducted the orchestral portion of the concert) to sit in as a conductor of the sonata." BARK 188.

Editor's note: During a performance of this work my pianistic partner and I sighed with relief when one of the percussionists (at a point where he has little to play) was able to discreetly conduct a particularly awkward passage in the first movement.

Work: Sonatina (1915)

According to Bartok in a 1945 radio interview, there are two themes in the first movement representing "dances played by two bagpipe players, the first by one and the second by another." The second movement would have been originally played on a violin's lower string to make it "more similar to a bear's voice," and the last movement contains "two folk melodies played by [unaccompanied] peasant violin players, danced during Christmas time by a man wearing an animal costume with a moveable beak." BARP 73-74.

Chapter 4
Beethoven

General Observations:

Carl Czerny records the following, "His [Beethoven's] improvisation was most brilliant and striking. In whatever company he might chance to be, he knew how to produce such an effect upon every listener that frequently not an eye remained dry, while many would break out into loud sobs; for there was something wonderful in his expression in addition to the beauty and originality of his ideas, and his spirited style of rendering them." BEET 185.

Editor's note: The following exhaustive list of adjectives was meticulously extracted by pianist and author Kenneth Drake from Carl Czerny's *On the Correct Performance of Beethoven's Pianoforte Works*. Czerny used these adjectives throughout his treatise to describe the moods found in the piano works of Beethoven. Those with an asterisk are the terms used more frequently than others. This interpretive vocabulary holds a special interest given Czerny's intimate acquaintance with Beethoven's own playing of these works, and it may have been used by Beethoven himself to describe various moods and characters.

unruly	serious*	tragic	teasing
weighty	fantastic	humorous	pathetic
lulling	firm	intimate*	bewitching
determined	fleeting	complaining	religious
brilliant*	joyous	strong	roaring
singing	pious	noisy	peaceful
capriciously	tender*	lively*	touching
chorale-like	witty	light	gentle*
delicate	good-natured	charming	jocose

dramatic	powerful*	virile	flattering
exalted	sparkling	marked*	dejected
simple*	expressively*	melancholy	speaking
elegant	graceful	merry	stormy
mournful	shrill	murmuring	agitated
energetic	grand	mischievous	profound
resolute	serene	naïve	dreamy
lofty	heroic	unaffected	sensitive

BEEK 19-20.

Work: Concerto no. 4 in G major, Op. 58 (1805-1806)
Second Movement
From Czerny we read, "In this movement one cannot help thinking of an antique tragic scene, and the player must feel with what intense, pathetic expression his solo is performed, in order to contrast with the powerful and austere orchestral passages, which are, as it were, gradually withdrawn." BEEZ 100.

It was German theorist Adolf Bernhard Marx (rather than Liszt) who first began to connect the Orpheus program—that of Orpheus calming the Furies—with the Fourth Piano Concerto in his 1850 biography of Beethoven. CONC 69.

From Michael Sternberg we read, "Pathos? Grief for the lost Eurydice? Orpheus? Virgil? Ovid? Gluck? I don't know. The confrontation of stern orchestra and pleading, persuasive piano fits the Orpheus legend well, and the idea that Beethoven might have had this scene in mind is not implausible: he did, after all, tell his friend Karl Amenda that the slow movement of his Quartet, Opus 18, no. 1, depicted the tomb scene in Romeo and Juliet." CONC 70.

Work: Concerto no. 5 in E-flat major, Op. 73 (1809-1811)
Second Movement
According to Czerny, "When Beethoven wrote this Adagio, the religious songs of devout pilgrims were present in his mind, and the performance of this movement must therefore perfectly express the holy calm and devotion which such an image naturally excites." BEEZ 103.

Work: Sonata in E-flat major, Op. 7 (1796)
Czerny wrote, "In a new edition of the Sonata in f minor, Op. 57 (which Beethoven considered his finest), the work has been subtitled 'Appassionata.' for which it is really too grandiose. The title would suit the Sonata in E flat, Op. 7, much better, for Beethoven was in a very impassioned frame of mind when he wrote it." BEEZ 12.

According to Fritz Spiegel, "Beethoven was constantly inspired (i.e., not commissioned) by beautiful women to write compositions for them; and Beethoven's pupil Carl Czerny (1791-1857) reported to Frimmel that he was 'seriously in love' with a pupil, Anna Louise Babette, (Barbara), Countess Keglevich. To her he dedicated his Piano Sonata op. 7 in about 1796. (It was at one time nicknamed 'The In-Love Sonata')." LIVE 18.

According to Edwin Fischer, "The Sonata, Op. 7 in E-flat major, which the publisher called *Grande Sonate,* was dedicated in 1797 to the Countess Babette de Keglevics, who later became Princess Odescalchi. This lady seems to have aroused Beethoven's interest in a high degree. This did not, however, prevent him from giving her lessons every morning in his dressing gown and slippers. As soon as it appeared the sonata was called the *Verleibte (The Enamoured).* It is a spirited work, sustained by a strong feeling for nature." BEEF 43.

Work: Sonata in D major, Op. 10, no. 3 (1798)
Second Movement
Anton Schindler[6] wrote that Beethoven said of this movement that the music was "suggesting through nuances of dynamic shading the mental state of a person in a deeply depressed mood." BEES 406.

The noted Swiss pianist Edwin Fischer wrote, "The Largo e mesto is said to have been composed under the impact of reading the description of Klërchen's death in Goethe's Egmont." BEEF 40.

---

6 Anton Schindler (1795-1864) was an associate, secretary, and early biographer of Beethoven. Schindler is nowadays considered an inconsistent witness for many facts connected with Beethoven, and many of his comments may not have occurred when or with whom he stated. In *Beethoven and His World* Clive Brown wrote, "On the whole, Schindler's credibility, though somewhat eroded, survived largely intact until the 1970s, when it was dealt a fatal blow by the discovery that more than 150 of his entries in the surviving conversation books had been made after Beethoven's death. The purpose of these falsifications has been shown to be essentially self-serving: to bolster his claim of having enjoyed a relationship with Beethoven that was both intimate and mutually respectful; to lend authenticity to his pronouncements concerning Beethoven's intentions regarding certain compositions; and to obtain ammunition for use in his personal feuds." That being said, Schindler's quotes entered here seem to the editor to have a ring of musical truth. If they were not said in the context recorded or were subsequently embellished, the pianist can separate historical accuracy from the value of imaginative imagery.

From Carl Reinecke's fascinating 19th-century study, The Beethoven Pianoforte Sonatas, Letters to a Lady, we read, "I should like still to point out to you the relationship between the first motive and the wonderful piece from the music to Egmont, 'Clärchen's Tod bezeichnend' ('expressive of Clarchen's death'):

BEER 28.

Work: Sonatas, Op. 14

According to Schindler this is how Beethoven analyzed these sonatas,

> First of all he declared that when he wrote the Sonatas, op. 14, about 24 years earlier, the spirit of the times was more poetic than it was "now" [1823]. In the earlier period listeners automatically recognized in the two sonatas, op. 14, a struggle between two principles, or a dialogue between two persons because that was quite obvious. The two principles are described as "pleading" and "resisting." In the second sonata, this dialogue, as well as its significance, is expressed more tersely, and the opposition of the two voices (the two principles) is even more noticeable than in the first sonata. Right from the beginning, the opposition of the two is evident in the contrary motion; at the end of the exposition the two voices (or principles) come somewhat closer together, and their mutual understanding can be felt in the cadence of the dominant immediately following. Unfortunately, right after this, the struggle begins again.

In an insightful footnote to these words of Schindler, Konrad Wolf makes the following observation,

> This report was ignored and finally forgotten because Beethoven's first German biographer, Adolf Bernhard Marx, objected to it… In recent history only Williams S. Newman has even mentioned it. Even though this exchange probably did not take place in this form, there is much inner truth to it. As Peter Stadlen has stated, the fact that so many of Schindler's reports proved to have been put in later by Schindler himself, to give his statement the ring of authenticity, does not necessarily mean that their musical substance is inaccurate. In this instance, it is most

likely that at some time or other Beethoven said exactly what Schindler attributes to him." WOLF 116

Editor's note: They are certainly interesting images to share with students who frequently study these easier Beethoven Sonatas.

Work: Sonata in A-flat major, Op. 26 (1800-01)
Third Movement
Czerny used the term *tenuto* in referring to the chords in the Funeral March of Op. 26, "As a funeral march on the death of a hero this movement must be played with a certain serious bigness, which emerges not only from the slow stride of the tempo but also from a heavy touch on the chords in the strictest tenuto, by means of which the full voiced quality of these chords is apparent in every degree of *piano* and *forte*." VOLL 49-50.

Liszt remained in Paris throughout the epidemic [the Parisian cholera epidemic of 1832]. He was a frequent visitor to the home of Victor Hugo, where he used to play the *Marche funèbre* from Beethoven's Sonata in A-flat major "while all the dead from cholera filed past to Notre Dame in their shrouds." LIS1 151.

Work: Sonata in C-sharp minor, Op. 27, no. 2 (1801)
Czerny said according to Beethoven the Adagio was like "a night scene, where a plaintive voice sounds from a great distance." VOLL 51.

Reinecke writes in his 1901 recollections *The Beethoven Pianoforte Sonatas, Letters to a Lady*,

> The performance by Liszt of this movement, and of the Allegretto which follows, is to me never to be forgotten, although nearly sixty years lives between. You can gauge from this how great the impression was, although (or perhaps *because*) the rendering was so thoroughly plain and genuine. Just as Beethoven has shunned writing between the Adagio, with its depth of feeling, and the Presto, raging along in stormy passion, a Scherzo, but rather a plain tuneful movement which forms a golden bridge from the first to the last movement, so also did Liszt avoid, in the execution, everything that could sound Scherzo-like. He played the movement like a dialogue which begins with a question, avoiding any sharp accent. A highly gifted performance certainly does not allow of being satisfactorily explained and described, but you will understand me. BEER 51.

Alan Walker documents the effects of an impromptu performance of this sonata by Franz Liszt,

The group had moved into Legouvé' s[7] drawing room, which possessed a piano, only to discover that there were no lights and that the fire had burned low. Goubaux brought in a lamp while Liszt seated himself at the piano. "Turn up the wick," said Legouvé, "we can't see," whereupon he accidentally turned it down, plunging the room into almost total darkness. Doubtless prompted by the gloom, Liszt began playing the Adagio of Beethoven's Moonlight Sonata while everyone remained rooted to the spot. Occasionally the fire's dying embers spluttered and cast strange shadows on the wall as the music unfolded its mournful melody. The experience was too much for Berlioz, who could not master his emotions. As Goubaux lit a candle, Liszt pointed to his friend, who had tears streaming down his cheeks. LIS1 182.

Here is a captivating and relatively unknown observation on this sonata from Edwin Fischer, who wrote,

> From various facts that have come to my knowledge I have conceived a different theory of the origin of the work which I should like to mention here without claiming any historical authenticity for it... There is in Vienna a manuscript of Beethoven's which contains a few lines from Mozart's *Don Giovanni* in Beethoven's undoubted hand: the passage after Don Giovanni has killed the Commendatore. Underneath Beethoven has transposed the passage into C sharp minor, and the absolute similarity of this with the first movement of Op. 27, No. 2 is quite unmistakable. In particular the postlude is note for note as in Mozart. At the time one of Beethoven's aristocratic friends died and was laid out in state in his palace. One night Beethoven is said to have improvised as he sat by the corpse of his friend; is it so unlikely that Beethoven was reminded of the similar scene in *Don Giovanni* and that this was the reason for the striking similarity which we have mentioned? In any case, there is no romantic moonlight in this movement: it is rather a solemn dirge. BEEF 62-63.

Work: Sonata in D major, Op. 28 (1801)
Second Movement
Czerny wrote, "This Andante, which Beethoven himself was very fond of playing, is like a simple narration,—a ballad of former times,—and must be so interpreted." BEEZ 41.

Work: Sonata in G major, Op. 31, no. 1
Of the second movement Edwin Fischer wrote,

> Have you ever come across an old country-house in the middle of an old-world park with a murmuring fountain? When the great venetian

---

7   Ernest Legouvé (1807-1903) was a distinguished French dramatist.

blinds are opened the light floods into a world long since vanished—a world of faded carpets, furniture of all periods, with an old spinet and a smell of withered rose-leaves. The atmosphere of such an old house fills one with nostalgia for a past in which there was still time to exchange sweet secrets with the flowers and listen to birdsong at eventide.

This is the kind of feeling I get in the second movement, with its ornaments, trills and its *adagio grazioso*. May Beethoven not have been looking back to the past quite deliberately for once? When the opening theme, which is reminiscent of Haydn's *Mit Wilrd' und Hoheit angetan*, appears in the bass it must be played softly and transparently, not clumsily. BEEF 71.

Work: Sonata in D minor, Op. 31, no. 2 (1802)

From Fischer: "Read Shakespeare's 'Tempest,'" Beethoven said when asked to explain the meaning of this sonata. It must be admitted, however, that this remark does not help us very much—it merely tells us that nature's demons, wind and water, have a hand in this movement." BEEF 72.

The source for connecting Shakespeare's *Tempest* with Opp. 31 and 57 is the following recollection by Anton Schindler: "One day when I was telling the master of the great impression that Carl Czerny's playing of the D minor and F minor sonatas opp. 31 and 57 had made upon the audience, and he was in a cheerful mood, I asked him to give me the key to these sonatas. He replied, 'Just read Shakespeare's Tempest.' It is, therefore, to be found in that play. But where? Questioner, it is for you to read, to ponder, and to guess." BEES 406.

Edwin Fischer wrote, "Referring to the second subject's sequel (bars 55 ff.) Beethoven said: 'The piano must break!'" BEEF 73.

According to Czerny the six sixteenth notes distributed between the two hands must follow each other with the utmost equality in order to imitate, in some degree, the gallop of a horse. He continued, "Beethoven extemporized the theme for this Sonata in 1803, as he once saw a horseman gallop by his window. Many of his best works were produced under similar events. With him, every sound, every motion was music and rhythm." BEEZ 45.

Czerny related the same story in an alternate version: "During the summer of 1803 he was staying in the country in Heiligenstadt near Vienna. One day he happened to see a rider galloping past his window. The regular rhythm of the hoof beats gave him the idea for the theme of the Finale of his Sonata in D minor, Op. 29 no. 2 [Op. 31, no 2]." BEEZ 12.

Edwin Fischer's take on the famous origin of this movement is more romantic, though perhaps embellished. He writes, "There is an interesting story that Beethoven composed the last movement in the twilight as he saw a rider galloping past through the mist.

Sonata in d minor, Op. 31, no. 2, third movement, mm. 1-4. Tovey Edition.

Perhaps that explains the notation of the left hand with its implied rhythm which reproduces the fall of a horse's hooves. BEEF 73.

Work: Sonata in C major, Op. 53 (1803)

Edwin Fischer wrote, "The French call this sonata *L'aurore,* and the title suits it very well. The first movement in particular has the radiance of dawn, an 'aura' which reminds us of Goethe's 'Ganymed ';[8] and perhaps it is more than a coincidence that a bird-call in Schubert's setting of that poem repeats exactly a certain figure in this sonata. But even without any such poetic interpretation, the work is obviously a masterpiece on its purely musical merits." BEEF 79.

Fischer also wrote, "The fact that the Prestissimo [third movement] is reminiscent of the duet *O namenlose Freude* from *Fidelio* suggests the kind of execution required." BEEF 81.

Work: Sonata in F major, op. 54 (1804)

From Fischer we read, "The second movement, *Allegretto,* is a piece which, if well played, can easily hold its own alongside the last movements of other early sonatas. One may imagine oneself on the bank of a river which passes by in changing patterns, long, calm waves alternating with eddies—but the element of water, the symbol of ever-renewed life, is always present." BEEF 81.

---

8   "Ganymed" is a poem by Johann Wolfgang von Goethe, in which the character of the mythic youth Ganymede is seduced by God (or Zeus) through the beauty of Spring. The poem was set to music by both Schubert and Wolf.

Work: Sonata in F minor, Op. 57 (1805)
First Movement

Speaking of the first movement Cortot said, "The second subject, presented in A flat major, is...noble, welcoming, generous, it makes us think of Prospero in *The Tempest*. In the passage in A flat minor which follows the appealing trills and the descending lament by which these are extended we should see, on the contrary, Caliban, or the incarnation of evil forces in general. Sombre, hostile, this part should suggest an inexorable rhythm, and tremendous power." COMI 108-109.

According to Cortot Beethoven used to say, "'If they knew what I am thinking about when I write they would be terror struck.' Questioned on the meaning of the *Appassionata* he replied, 'Read *The Tempest*.' This phrase instructs us as to what he wished to say in this instance. But when we are ignorant of his intentions do not let us say, 'He meant nothing.' That is the opinion of a lazy or indifferent person." COMI 108.

Editor's note: See Anton Schindler's account of the connection between Shakespeare's *The Tempest* and this sonata and Op. 31, no. 2 on page 25.

Third Movement

Czerny says that, "Perhaps Beethoven (who was ever fond of representing natural scenes) imagined to himself the waves of the sea in a stormy night, whilst cries of distress are heard from afar:—such an image may always furnish the player with a suitable idea for the proper performance of this great work." BEEZ 50.

Perhaps the inordinate length of the last movement of the *Appassionata* caused Czerny to caution that the movement "should be only rarely stormy, picking up tempo and strength first with the repeat of the second half and continuing then into the close." VOLL 62.

Work: Sonata in E-flat major, Op. 81a (1810)

Czerny wrote, "The Lebewohl or "Farewell" Sonata bears the imprint of the turbulent political events of 1809, when Napoleon's armies invaded Austria and occupied Vienna after bombarding the city. Many of Beethoven's friends fled from Vienna, including his student and patron the Archduke Rudolph, to whom the sonata is dedicated. Beethoven entered the dates of the Archduke's departure and return into the score and allowed the emotional progression of "farewell-absence-return" ("Lebewohl-Abwesenheit-Wiedersehen") to determine the basic character of the three movements." BEEZ 119.

Edwin Fischer wrote, "The coda [of the first movement] is particularly poetic—the posthorn vanishing in the distance and the beloved friend disappearing in a cloud of dust, yet the realm of absolute music is never abandoned." BEEF 91-92.

In a letter to Breitkopf and Haertel, Vienna, 9 Oct. 1811, Beethoven wrote, "I have just received *Das Lebewohl*, etc., I see that you really have other copies with French title. But why? *Lebewohl* is something very different from *Les Adieux*; the first is said in a heartfelt manner to a single person, the other to a whole assembly, to whole towns." BEEL 122.

Speaking of this Sonata Cortot wrote, "The Sonata Opus 81a, called *Les Adieux*, is dedicated to the Archduke Rudolph. We are in the year 1809. The Archduke is fleeing before the invasion, and Beethoven is certainly affected by the departure of his friend, disciple, and protector. But someone else is going away—Therese von Brunswick. It is not difficult for us to believe that this departure caused Beethoven still deeper and sharper pain." COMI 112.

Editor's note: Cortot lived in an era when Therese von Brunswick was generally considered to be the *Immortal Beloved* of Beethoven. More recent research has shifted much opinion toward Antonie Brentano as the keeper of this title. It is one of those inaccuracies which does not diminish Cortot's observational genius.

Edwin Fischer gave a supercharged interpretation of the Finale by writing, "After the introduction to the Finale, which stands for the first embrace of the reunited friends…" BEEF 93.

Work: Sonata in E minor, Op. 90 (1814)
A. C. Kalischer writes, "Schindler has given an interesting clue to the contents of this Sonata. The composer is said to have told Count Lichnowsky, to whom it is dedicated, that he wished to set to music the love story with his wife (formerly a dancer). As superscriptions the count was to put 'First movement: struggle between heart and head,' and over the second movement: 'Intercourse with the beloved.'" BEEL 163-164.

Work: Sonata in A major, Op. 101 (1816)
According to Schindler Beethoven characterized the first and third movements as "Impressions and Reveries." BEES 424.

Work: Sonata in B-flat major, Op. 106 (1819)
Of the third movement Edwin Fischer says,

'The Appassionato e con molto sentimento' which Beethoven requires seems to contradict the mezza voce, but the contradiction is only apparent, since when we have something to say that comes from the depths of the soul, we lower our voices to a whisper.

'The mausoleum of the collective anguish of the world' was Lenz's description of this movement; but it is in fact a passionate argument with God which ends in submission and humility, after the gift of heavenly consolation has been received. Metaphors and words are only upsetting here, however, and the statement that "Music begins where language ends" is nowhere more applicable. "Holy peace, how beautiful, how glorious. Here is God, here rest to serve Him," Beethoven wrote inshi sketchbook. BEEF 106.

A similar idea written by Beethoven in a sketchleaf (Vienna A45) for op. 106 expresses his feelings about his stay in Mödling in the summer of 1818 when he was working on op. 106; more specifically, about the Brühl valley. The quote is:

Ein kleines Hauss allda so klein, dass man allein nur ein wenig Raum hat /
Nur einige Täge in dieser göttl. Briel [i.e. Brühl] /
Sehnsucht oder Verlangen /
Befreiung o. Erfüllung

A little house there so small that alone one has just a little space
Only a few days in this divine Brühl
Longing or desire
Liberation or fulfillment

(Trans. by Horst Lange) BESK 353.

Editor's note: The A45 sketchleaf on which this is written contains mostly sketches for the last two movements of op. 106, but also for the second movement.

Cortot says of the slow movement, "At times we think of the immensity of cathedrals. Beethoven, then absorbed in working at the *Mass in D*, allowed the religious feeling to invade his piano music. Even the melodic contour of the *Benedictus* appears here." COMI 118-119.

Speaking of Hans von Bülow's[9] lessons with Liszt and the latter's performance of the *Hammerklavier*, Alan Walker writes, "The lessons lasted for two hours a week, and Bülow was never charged a penny for them... Especially fascinating to Bülow were Liszt's unexpected solutions to difficult

---

9   Hans von Bülow (1830-1894) was a distinguished and influential German virtuoso pianist, conductor, and composer. His early editions of the piano works of Beethoven were extremely influential in pianistic thought in the early twentieth century.

technical problems, some of which he recorded for posterity. Towards the climax of the great fugue from the *Hammerklavier* Sonata, for example, Beethoven demands a violent crescendo followed by a series of awkwardly placed trills:

Sonata in B-flat major, Op. 106, fourth movement, mm. 377-381.

Liszt's solution, recommended by Bülow, produces a greater climax and makes the trills "speak" more effectively. It is not nearly as difficult as it looks, and it does not harm Beethoven's musical thought.

Sonata in B-flat major, Op. 106, fourth movement, mm. 378-381.

LIS2 173.

Work: Sonata in E major, Op. 109 (1820)

According to Edwin Fischer, "The work has the charm and luminosity of an old sweetheart met again after twenty years, with the noble features but spiritualized and more transparent." BEEF 108.

Editor's note: While one should not read too much into it, Fischer's allusion to a sweetheart may not be too far off. Op. 109 was dedicated to Maximiliane Brentano, and many modern scholars feel that Maximiliane's mother, Antonie Brentano, was Beethoven's "Immortal Beloved." Whatever the verdict on that subject, the respectful and nostalgic words of this dedication truly come from the heart of Beethoven.

The Dedication paragraph for Op. 109
Vienna, December 6, 1821

> A dedication!!!—Now this is not one of those which are abused wholesale. It is the spirit which holds together the noble and better people on this globe and which time can never destroy. This is the spirit which speaks to you now and which still brings back to me the years of your childhood as well as your beloved parents, your most excellent and intelligent mother and your father, so truly endowed with good and noble qualities, always concerned with the well-being of his children. At this moment I am in the Landstrasse- and see you all before me. And while I think of the wonderful qualities of your parents, I have not the least doubt that you are inspired to be like them, and will be more so with each passing day. The memory of a noble family can never be erased from my heart. May you sometimes think kindly of me.
>
> My most heartfelt good wishes. May heaven forever bless you and all of yours.
>
> > Devotedly and eternally,
> > Your friend
> > Beethoven
>
> BBAL 175.

Work: Sonata in A-flat major, Op. 110 (1821)

First Movement

Cortot reflects, "The exact date of completion of Sonata Opus 110—Christmas Day 1821—also leads to reflection. Is there not something here that resembles Faust's conception of Easter? Here Nativity and there Resurrection. But the idea of the Resurrection animates this Sonata too. In the second fugue do we not find traced in Beethoven's hand the direction—*poi a poi de nuovo vivente* ("little by little coming to life again")? Dominating the close of this composition, then, is the feeling of a man, who, after much inward conflict, at last seizes with enthusiasm a truth, a visible certitude." COMI 123.

Second Movement

It has been said that the humorous character of this movement is betrayed by Beethoven's use of two German folks songs, *Unsa katz had katzln ghabt* or *Our cat did kittens have* (ms. 1-8) and *Ich bin luderlich,* or *I am slovenly* (ms. 17-33). While there is no evidence that Beethoven actually modeled his melodies on these songs there is one good thing about these alleged resemblances coming to light, for the lyrics, when inserted into the music, do serve to highlight the humor of the music. After all, this second movement is a terribly boisterous and funny movement:

Ou-r cat did kittens have,
THREE AND SIX-TY DID SHE HAVE!
Ou-r cat did kittens have,
THREE AND SIX-TY DID SHE HAVE!
THREE AND SIX-TY,
THREE AND SIX-TY,
THREE AND SIX-TY DID SHE HAVE!
I am slovenly,
You are slovenly,
We are all of us slo-ven-ly.
I am slovenly,
You are slovenly,
All of us are slo-ven-ly . . .

BEJC

Editor's note: The great Swiss pedagogue and member of the Eastman School of Music Piano Faculty from 1929 to 1982 Cecile Genhart took this imagery a step further, envisioning the second movement as a German beer drinking song. For her the sudden fortissimos in mm. 36 and 39 where the drinkers suddenly raising their mugs in the tavern with a shout of "Yo, Ho!"

Work: Sonata in C minor, Op. 111 (1822)

Edwin Fischer wrote, "The two movements of this work symbolize this world and the world to come. Thus, the relentless figuration of the first movement in which Beethoven expressed life's hard struggle should be chiselled out with steely fingers, whilst the Arietta, which represents the transcendental, should be played with a touch so dematerialized as not to seem to be of this world... Be completely conscious of the relative unimportance of details; be conscious of the eternal laws that rule the stars, and then your hands and fingers will become "magnetic" and conjure up a transcendental light from wood and strings." BEEF 116.

From Robert Schumann in the *Neue Zeitshcrift fur Musik* of 1840: "The grandeur of Beethoven's thirty second piano sonata represents the opening of the gates of heaven." QUOT 13.

Cortot writes, "[W]e may admit that Beethoven came very close here to the Hindu version of the soul's destiny. To the suffering and pain...succeeds in the second part of the sonata…the feeling of Nirvana, of being merged in non-existence, or rather reabsorbed into the Universal Soul." COMI 128.

Work: Piano Trio in D major, Op. 70. No. 1 (1808)

Czerny said, "The character of this Largo, which must be played very slow, is ghastly awful, like an apparition from the lower world. During it, we may not unsuitably think of the first appearance of the Ghost in Hamlet." BEEZ 7.

Work: 33 Variations on a waltz by Anton Diabelli, Op. 120 (1823)

Editor's note: Despite the *Diabelli Variations* being a non-programmatic work of sublime architecture, they have inspired flights of fancy and imagination in some of the finest pianists. Performing any work in a Theme and Variation form demands prompt, continuous switching from one character to another, which character must be immediately caught and clearly defined. Perhaps to assist the interpreter in these quick mood transformations and as a humorous exercise Czerny, Hans von Bülow, Wilhelm von Lenz, and Alfred Brendel have all given descriptive titles to the variations. I cite below those of Alfred Brendel as the most compelling, with a sprinkling of a few others.

Bibliographic Source for the following images of Brendel and von Lenz is BEBR 125-126. Other sources are cited as they appear.

Theme
Brendel's satirical title for the theme is *Alleged Waltz.*

Variation 1
Alfred Brendel gives the title of *March: gladiator, flexing his muscles.* He refers to its character as "serious but slightly lacking in brains."
Wilhelm von Lenz called it *The Mastodon and the Theme —a fable.*

Variation 2
Brendel entitled it *Snowflakes.*

Variation 3
Brendel entitled it *Confidence and nagging doubt.*

Variation 4
Brendel entitled it *Learned Ländler.*

Variation 5
Brendel entitled it *Tamed goblin.*

Variation 6
Brendel entitled it *Trill rhetorics (Demonsthenes braving the surf).*
Wilhelm von Lenz called it *In the Tyrol.*

Variation 7
Brendel entitled it *Sniveling and stamping.*

Variation 8
Brendel entitled it *Intermezzo (to Brahms).*

Variation 9
Brendel entitled it Industrious nutcracker. Like Variation No. 1, he characterizes it as "deeply serious but slightly lacking in brains."

Variation 10
Brendel entitled it *Giggling and neighing.*

Variation 11
Brendel entitled it *Innocente' (to Bülow).*

Variation 12
Brendel entitled it *Wave Pattern.*

Variation 13
Brendel entitled it *Aphorism (biting).*

Variation 14
Brendel entitled it *Here He Cometh, the Chosen.*
Von Bülow comments, "O imbue this wonderful number with what I should like to call the 'high priestly solemnity' in which it was conceived, let the performer's fantasy summon up before his eyes the sublime arches of a Gothic cathedral." BEBU 61.

Variation 15
Brendel entitled it *Cheerful Spook.*

Variation 16 and 17
Brendel entitled it *Triumph.*

Variation 18
Brendel entitled it *Precious memory, slightly faded.*

Variation 19
Brendel entitled it *Helter-skelter.*

Variation 20
Brendel describes this variation as "hypnotic introspection" and offers as a title Inner *sanctum.*
Suggesting the title *Oracle*, von Bülow recommends "an effect suggestive of the veiled organ-registers." BEBU 67.

Variation 21
Brendel entitled it *Maniac and moaner.*

Variation 22
Brendel entitled it *'Notte e giorno faticar' (to Diabelli).*
Czerny writes of this variation, marked "energetic and with lively humour," that "This Variation is a parody on Leporello's 'Keine Ruh bei Tag und nacht' and Beethoven wrote it down one day in an ill-humour, as he was so frequently desired by the Publisher to accelerate the completion of the work." BEEZ 64.

Variation 23
Brendel entitled it *The virtuoso at boiling-point (to Cramer).* He characterizes Nos. 23, 27 and 28 as "one-track minds in an excited state."

Variation 24
Brendel entitled it *Pure Spirit.*

Variation 25
Brendel entitled it *Teutscher (German dance).*

Variation 26
Brendel entitled it *Circles on the Water.*

Variation 27
Brendel entitled it *Juggler.*

Variation 28
Brendel entitled it *The rage of the jumping-jack.*
Von Bülow says of this variation, "This Variation ... must be hammered out with well nigh raging impetuosity... More delicate shading would not be in place – at least in the First Part." BEBU 76.

Variation 29
Brendel entitled it *Stifled sighs (Konrad Wolff).*

Variation 30
Brendel entitled it *Gentle grief.*

Variation 31
Brendel's title for this variation is To Bach (to Chopin).

Variation 32
Brendel entitled it *To Handel.*

Variation 33
Brendel entitled it *To Mozart; to Beethoven.*

Chapter 5
Brahms

Work: Ballades, Op. 10, no. 1 "Edward" (1854)

    The musical architecture of this narrative, dialogue-like work of Brahms closely follows the story of this grisly ballade of murder, deceit, guilt, and confession:

Edward
(Anonymous Scottish Ballad)

"Why does your <u>brand sae</u> drop wi' <u>blude</u>,   (sword) (so) (blood)
Edward, Edward? Why does your brand sae drop wi' blude,
And why sae sad <u>gang</u> ye, O?" –   (go)
'O I hae kill'd my hawk sae gude,
<u>Mither</u>, Mither; O I hae kill'd my hawk sae gude,   (Mother)
And I had nae <u>mair</u> but he, O'.   (more)

"Your hawk's blude was never sae red,
Edward, Edward; Your hawk's blude was never sae red.
My dear son, I tell thee, O" –
'O I hae kill'd my red-roan steed,
Mither, Mither; O I hae kill'd my red-roan steed,
That erst was sae fair and free, O'.

"Your steed was <u>auld</u>, and ye hae got mair,   (old)
Edward, Edward; Your steed was auld, and ye hae got mair;

Some other <u>dule</u> ye <u>dree</u>, O". –   (grief) (bear)
'O I hae kill'd my father, dear,

Mither, Mither;
O I hae kill'd my father, dear,
Alas, and wae is me, O'

"And whatten penance will ye <u>dree</u> for that,   (do)
Edward, Edward; Whatten penance will ye dree for that?
My dear son, now tell me, O". –
'I'll set my feet in yonder boat,
Mither, Mither; I'll set my feet in yonder boat,
And I'll <u>fare</u> over the sea, O'.   (far)

"And what will ye do wi' your tow'rs and your <u>ha</u>',   (hall)
Edward, Edward? And what will ye do wi' yor tow'rs and your ha',
That were sae fair to see, O?"

'I'll let them stand till they doun <u>fa</u>',   (fall)
Mither, Mither; I'll let them stand till they doun fa',
For here never mair <u>maun</u> I be, O'.   (must)

"And what will ye leave to our <u>bairns</u> and your wife,   (children)
Edward, Edward?
When ye gang <u>owre</u> the sea, O?" –   (over)
'The <u>warld's</u> room; let them beg through life,   (world's)
Mither, Mither; The warld's room; let them beg through life;
For them never mair will I see, O'.

"And what will ye leave to your <u>ain</u> mither dear;   (own)
Edward, Edward? And what will ye leave to your ain mither dear,
My dear son, now tell me, O?" –
'The curse of hell frae me sall ye bear,
Mither, Mither; The curse of hell frae me sall ye bear;
<u>Sic</u> counsels ye gave to me, O!'   (such)

BRAB Foreword.

From *The Etude Magazine* of 1912 Mark Hambourg writes,

The old Scottish Ballade "Edward" is blood curdling and dramatic to a degree; and the well-known vocal setting of it by Johann (Carl Gottfried) Loewe (1796-1869), is in the form of a dialogue between mother and son; the mother questioning the son about the blood she sees upon him. He at first answers that he has killed his hawk; then that he has killed his horse; and at last confesses that it was his father he killed. The mother continues to ply him with questions as to what penance he will do, and what will become of his family and lands if he flees the country, as he says he must. Finally, she asks what will become of herself, if he leaves her. Here, in a great climax of horror, he turns upon her with curses, saying that it was she who persuaded him to murder the father. BRJJ 15.

Recalling a piano lesson on the Brahms *Ballade* by Hans von Bülow, Harriette Bower wrote in the *Etude Magazine* in 1912,

> One day, a young artist was playing a *Ballade* of Brahms, the one founded on the sinister poem of Edward. The opening of this Scotch *Ballade* is sad, sinister, and mysterious, like the old Scotch story. The master insisted on great smoothness in playing it – the chords to sound like muffled but throbbing heartbeats. A strong climax is worked up on the second page, which dies away on the third to a pianissimo of utter despair. From the middle of this page onto the end, the descending chords and octaves were likened to ghostly footsteps while the broken triplets in the left hand accompaniment seem to indicate drops of blood. Toward the end of the second page the notes descend far down in the bass. The player was hastening to turn the leaf (page). "Stop!" cried von Bulow, from the other end of the room. "We have been in the deepest dungeon and on the other side of that page comes a ray of sunshine; you must make a pause there, between the dark and the light, it is very effective." BRJJ 16.

Work: Concerto no. 1 in D minor, Op. 15 (1858)

Jan Swafford writes, "The explanation for the realism and immediacy is that in his mind the beginning of the Concerto evoked the tragedy that preceded its inspiration by a few days; Robert Schumann's leap into the Rhine. Like the 'Edward' Ballade of the same year, this is Brahmsian program music, the tragedy this time not literary, but real... The idea that the opening of the First Piano Concerto pictures Schumann's leap into the Rhine is the suggestion of biographer Max Kalbeck, which he said he got directly from Joachim." BRAJ 169.

Editor's note: The First Piano Concerto had a long gestation period. The 1858 composition date listed above is the traditional *completion* date. The commencement of this work indeed reached back to the time of Schumann's suicide attempt.

In a letter to Clara on December 30, 1856, Brahms referred to the sublime slow movement of the D minor Concerto as a "gentle portrait" that Brahms told her he was painting of her. BRLI 197.

Editor's note: In the autograph of this movement Brahms underlaid the text "Benedictus que venit in Nomine Domini" (Blessed is he that cometh in the name of the Lord) to the opening melody in the violins and violas.

Clara Schumann
Inspiration for "The Gentle Portrait"

Connection with Max Klinger[10]

Editor's note: The connection between music and the visual arts interested Brahms from the beginning of his career: even during his first stay in Dusseldorf he had gone out of his way to meet painters. He made himself knowledgeable about the prints of several artists, and was something of a collector. The sculptor, painter, and engraver Max Klinger was in turn greatly inspired by Brahms's music, and based many of his works on it. Best known is a singular collection entitled *Brahms-Fantasy Opus XII*, a cycle of forty-one drawings, etchings, and lithographs based on five songs and the *Schicksalslied, Op. 54*. The graphic images are not illustrations: they are, as the titles suggest, independent fantasies on the music and texts. The work appeared in 1894; Klinger was obviously in touch with Brahms before the work was published. While the art is not connected with the solo piano pieces, Brahms's positive reactions to Klinger's surreal and erotic art

---

10   Max Klinger (1857-1920) was a German Symbolist painter, sculptor, and printmaker. His adulation of the music of Brahms inspired him to create a series of surreal illustrations, greatly admired by the composer.

are *unusually* explicit and favorable to the imaginative interaction between visual and aural art in Brahms' mind. They are also a reminder that *absolute music* did not necessarily mean absolute abstraction.

Letters by Brahms follow, clearly indicating Brahms' enthusiastic reaction to Klinger's artistic response to his music.

Phantasien opus XII, 'Evocation'
Illustration by Max Klinger

Johannes Brahms in a letter to Max Klinger, Vienna, March 1886, wrote,

Highly esteemed Sir,

I should have told you long ago how pleased I was with the thought of seeing your fantasies in the title-pages of my compositions. The whole style of your art—your rich and fantastic invention which is at the same time of such splendid earnestness, of such momentous depth, leading then to ever further musings and imaginings—seems to me to be very appropriate for announcing music...

The individual sketches which Simrock showed me at the time interested and pleased me enormously— as does all of your work which has come my way. Specific ones, like the page for *Feldeinsankeit*, or just the curiously beautiful fantasy for the Cello Sonata, have never relinquished their hold on my memory.

Brahms Phantasien, Opus XII, 'Accorde'
Illustration by Max Klinger

Well, to my thanks for everything you give us, I could now simply add my specific thanks for the first printed title-pages of my new songs…

If you knew how very dear to my heart other creations of yours are to me and what beautiful vistas your sketches have afforded me, I am sure you would gladly pardon these immodest lines of

> your
>
> greatly and sincerely devoted
>
> Joh. Brahms

BRAL 632-633.

Johannes Brahms in a letter to Max Klinger, Vienna, 29 December 1893, writes,

Dear, most honoured Sir,

…Perhaps, it has not occurred to you to imagine what I must feel as I contemplate your pictures. I see the music, along with the lovely words—and then quite imperceptibly your wonderful drawings carry me further; looking at them, it seems as if the music resounded into the infinite and expressed all I could have said, more clearly than the music can but nevertheless just as enigmatically and portentously. At times I could envy you, that you with your pencil can be clearer; at other times I feel pleased that I don't need to be so, but must conclude in the end at all art is the same and speaks the same language...

With my heartfelt gratitude and devotion,

J. Brahms

BRAL 710.

The Piano Pieces

Brahms's short piano pieces are listed here not in their alphabetical, but in their chronological order.

Work: Fantasien and Drei Intermezzi, Op. 116 and 117 (1892)

The summer of 1892 in the Austrian spa town of Ischl produced the piano pieces Opp. 116 and 117. From Maria von Bülow we read,

> Brahms said he wrote them because there were so many women pianists at Ischl- there were, indeed, a number of talented young women who summered in the musical and fashionable resort (the lovely Ilona Eibenschütz[11] among them), but he also probably had Clara in mind, whose musicianship was intact even if her pyrotechnical abilities were not. According to Hans von Bülow, Brahms referred to Opp. 116 and 117 as "the Lullabies of my sorrows". Perhaps the illness and death among so many of those close to him must have been very much on his mind [after all, this was late middle age for Brahms]. Ottilie Ebner must be added to the list of the seriously ill; and that summer, her sister and mother died. Each incident was marked by a sympathetic letter from Brahms. BRVB 395-404.

Editor's note: For a thorough account of this period see Hans Joachim Hinrischen, *Hans von Bülow: Die Briefe an Johannes Brahms* (Tutzing, 1994), 22 ff).

Jan Swafford writes,

> In 1892 he was working on little piano pieces that would become the *Seven Fantasies of Opus 116* and the *Three Intermezzos on Opus 117*. In connection with these works, it may have been that summer when his future biographer Max Kalbeck experienced a peculiar vision. He was visiting Ischl and went walking on a warm early July morning. Emerging from the woods and rushing toward him he saw what he took to be a peasant or maybe the owner of the property, coming to shoo

---

11 Ilona Eibenschütz (1872-1967) was a Hungarian pianist and friend of Brahms for whom he privately premiered his piano pieces, op. 118 and op. 119.

him away. Then Kalbeck realized it was Brahms, with hat in one hand and his coat in the other dragging on the ground, running through the dewy meadow as if a demon were after him. Wild eyed, weeping, and gasping and sweating, Brahms brushed past Kalbeck and disappeared in the distance, apparently without seeing his friend at all.

Another day Kalbeck came to visit Salzerugerstrasses and noticed the door to the musicroom open. From inside came pealing piano music, stopping and starting, passages repeated over and over with tiny changes. Kalbeck realized that Brahms was composing or revising a piece. But as the music changed and grew under the composer's hands, there rose an accompaniment of the "strangest growling, whining, and moaning, which at the height of the musical climax changed into a loud howl." Unlikely as it seemed, Kalbeck decided that Brahms must have gotten himself a dog. Hearing the scrape of a piano stool, he went in to find Brahms alone in the room, his face red and beard glistening with tears. Embarrassed, Brahms wiped his face with the back of his hand and slowly returned to his usual joking self.

There may have been more to these episodes than the artistic ecstasies Kalbeck assumed... This summer in Ischl, rather than the lash of the muse, Brahms wailing may have come from all the illness and death weighing on him. Some of it may have gotten into the music as well—such as the *Three Intermezzos for Piano* that he called "cradle songs of my sorrows." BRAJ 579-580.

Swafford further comments on these late pieces by stating, "The inspiration for this flood of pieces in Opuses 116-119 of 1892-3, twenty in all...we can trace to matters both personal and "purely" musical. The beauty of playing and person of young Ilona Eibenschütz likely had something to do with them. It was the gently beautiful, lilting intermezzos of Opus 117 that Brahms declared "three cradle songs of my sorrows." Maybe all the pieces with their delicate lyricism are love songs to lost women in Brahm's life, to Ilone and Clara and Agathe, and Hermine and Alice, to Elisabet for whom he wrote the rhapsodies of Opus 79, and to all others known and unknown to history." BRAJ 586-587.

Work: Intermezzo in E-flat minor, Op. 118, no. 6

Editor's note: The Swiss poet Joseph Viktor Widmann[12] was so moved by this work when first published that he wrote a now-forgotten poem elucidating his imagery of the piece. The poem deals with death and life's strivings. I unearthed this poem in 2013, entitled "Op. 118 Intermezzo in E-flat minor," in its original Gothic format from a German publication of

---

12 Joseph Viktor Widmann (1842-1911) was a Swiss journalist and writer.

1904. As Styra Avins writes, Brahms references the poem in a letter to Fritz Simrock, Vienna, 8 May, 1896: "It occurs to me to send you a few poems. The one by Widmann is from '93…" BRAL 733. The original poem by Widmann follows with the translation.

op. 118. Intermezzo Es-moll
von *.*

Die träge Welle leckt den müden Strand,
Und unterm Meeresnebel gähnt der Wind
Verschlafen hin zum blassen Küstensaum. —·
Und regungslos am blassen Küstensaum,
Als hielt' die Schildwach' er am eignen Grab,
Ein Sterbender des Daseins Forb'rung löscht.
Das Meer des Lebens hat ihn ausgespie'n.
Ihm raunt der Tod ins Ohr: „Du welker Tor,
Sieh deiner Tage stolz geträumten Traum
Zerrinnen in der nächt'gen Wellen Schaum!
Er schwindet, nur der Irrtum bleibt zurück."
Der Greis erbebt. Die letzte Träne rinnt,
Sein Sterbeseufzer wird zum Hülfeschrei:
„Laß Gott, mein Gott, nicht Wahn die Tugend sein!
Wofür, o Herr, hätt' ich entsagt? gekämpft?
Das Opfer dürft' den Opfernden verhöhnen?"
Jäh stockt das Wort im Morgenrosenglanz,
Der leuchtend sich der dunklen Nacht vermählt;
Der Himmel flammt, entzückt. Das Meer erbebt.
Von Osten schallt mit schwellender Gewalt,
Hinbrausend ob der Wogen Orgelton,
Ein Siegesjubelsang. Posaunend wirft
Der Sturm sein schmetterndes Hallelujah
In donnernden Akkorden ehern drein:
„Niemals, o Mensch, war eine Tugend Wahn,
Die zur Vollendung Korn für Korn gereift,
Das Laster nur hat sich allein gelebt!"
Der Alte lächelt, nickt und zieht hinab
An Todes Hand ins ew'ge Land des Schweigens.
Die Welle leckt am nächtlichen Gestade
Den müden Strand. Und unterm Nebel zieht
Der Wind verschlafen hin zum Küstensaum. —

BRAK 552

Op. 118 Intermezzo in E-flat minor

The languid wave is lapping at the tired beach,
And under ocean fog the wind is yawning
Half-sleeping toward the pale edge of the coast.
And at the pale edge of the coast a dying man,
(Stock-still, as if his own grave's somber sentinel)
Extinguishes the great command to be.
The sea of life has spit him out, and death
Is whispering in his ear: "You withered fool,
See how the proud ambition of your life
Is pounded in the waves' eternal strife.
It fully perishes; error alone abides."
The old man trembles, sheds a final tear,
His sighs of death grow into cries for help:
"Dear God, let virtue not be an illusion!
Why did I then renounce and fight?
The sacrifice, o Lord, must never spite
Or cruelly mock the one who sacrificed!"
He pauses, for the rosy gleam of dawn
Appears and lovingly conjoins the night.
The sky, enraptured, is aflame. The ocean trembles.
And from the east above the organ of the waves
With e'er increasing power now rings out
A cheerful song of victory. With thundering chords
The trombones of the unrelenting storm
Join in and add a blaring Hallelujah:
"O mortal man, if seed by seed a virtue
Has slowly grown and ripened toward perfection,
It never was, nor will be, an illusion.
It's vice alone that lives for its own sake."
The old man smiles, he nods and follows death
Into the land of everlasting hush.
The wave is lapping at the tired beach.
Under the fog the languid wind is moving
Half-sleeping toward the pale edge of the coast.

Trans. Horst Lange

Work: Intermezzo in B minor, Op. 119, no. 1

Brahms wrote to Clara in May 1893 of this piece, saying, "I'm tempted to copy out a small piano piece for you because I'd like to know how you get along with it. It is crawling with dissonances! These are deemed appropriate and can be explained—but maybe you don't like their taste, in which case I wish they were less appropriate but appetizing, and to your taste. The little piece is exceptionally melancholy and to say "to be played very slowly" isn't saying enough. Every measure and every note must sound ritardando, as though one wished to suck melancholy out of each and every note. With a wantonness and contentment derived from the aforementioned dissonances. God Almighty, this description will surely whet your appetite!" BRAK 707.

Clara's written response to Brahms's description of the piece was, "You must have known how enthusiastic I would be when you were copying out that bittersweet piece which, for all its discords, is so wonderful. No, one actually revels in the discords, and when playing them, wonders how the composer ever brought them to earth. Thank you for this new, magnificent gift!" Later Clara called the B minor a "gray pearl." BRAJ 586.

Work: Variations on a theme by Robert Schumann, Op. 9 (1854)

Jan Swafford writes that after Clara wrote her set of variations on a theme from Schumann's (*Bunte Blätter* (Mottled Leaves) in 1854 Brahms immediately began writing his own set of variations on the same theme. Julius Otto Grimm, who was very close to Johannes in those days, christened the Schumann Variations "Trost-Einsemkeit," "Consolation and Loneliness." On the manuscript he signed some of these variations *B* for Brahms and *Kr* for Kreisler. Here is an echo of Schumann and his alter egos, Florestan and Eusebius. BRAJ 112-113.

Swafford writes of the tenth variation, "This is the most lyrical of the set and at the head of the manuscript of no. 10 stands the Romantic subtitle 'Fragrance of Rose and Heliotrope.' That heading disappeared in the first edition. Poignantly at the end of that rose and heliotrope variation, veiled in the middle voice, Clara speaks by way of a theme she had originally written for her *Romance, Op. 3*." BRAJ 123.

Chapter 6
Chopin

Work: Ballades
The poems of Mickiewicz[13]

The connection of the Ballades of Chopin with the poems of Mickiewicz originates with an 1841 review on the *Second Ballade* by Robert Schumann in which he wrote, "I recollect very well that when Chopin played the ballade here, it ended in F major; now it closes in a minor. At that time he also mentioned that certain poems of Mickiewicz had suggested his ballade to him. On the other hand, a poet might easily be inspired to find words to his music; it stirs one profoundly." SCMM 143.

Editor's note: An informative footnote to this quote by Dorota Zakrzewska in *Alienation and Powerlessness: Adam Mickiewicz's "Ballady" and Chopin's Ballades* reads, "The key sentence of this excerpt, dealing with Mickiewicz's poems as inspiration for Chopin's Ballades is mistranslated here; in the original version of Schumann's review it reads *Er sprach damals auch davon, das er zu seinen Balladen durch einige Gedichte von Mickiewicz angeregt worden sei* (Gesammelte Schriften über Musik und Musiker, vol.II, 32), which should be translated as "he was inspired to write his Ballades by some poems of Mickiewicz." This difference is of crucial importance, since it indicates that the Ballades in general (or at least the First and Second Ballades as the only compositions written up to date) were inspired by Mickiewicz's poetry instead of the Second Ballade only."

The distinguished French pianist Alfred Cortot wrote,

---

13 Adam Bernard Mickiewicz (1798-1855) was a Polish national poet, dramatist, essayist, publicist, translator, and political activist. A leading Romantic dramatist, he has been compared in Poland and other parts of Europe to Byron and Goethe.

According to Robert Schumann who reports it as first-hand knowledge from the mouth of Chopin himself, the Ballades were inspired by a reading of the poems of Adam Mickiewicz, Chopin's fellow countryman and friend, banished by the Russians from that Poland whose glories and national aspirations the poet sang too boldly for their liking. In their translation into music, it would certainly be idle to look for an accurate paraphrase of the texts which had struck Chopin's imagination. It is the burning spirit of patriotism animating Mickiewicz's eloquence which he retains far more than its argument or imagery.... Notwithstanding, the interpreter would be depriving himself of one of his most precious resources, if he did not attempt to probe beneath the expressive magnificence of the musical language, and, in spite of it being sufficient unto itself, there discover the secret of the impression which first gave birth to it. In this we feel we shall help him by reproducing here, after the version provided by Laurent Ceillier in his commentaries on our series of concerts given in 1924, the brief account of the four poems which, according to tradition, suggested to Chopin the conception of his immortal works. CHOC Introduction.

Work: 1st Ballade "Conrad Wallenrod" (1835-1836)

Cortot writes, "The prose ballad which was the source of inspiration of this composition, is the last episode of the fourth part of Conrad Wallenrod, a historical legend taken from the chronicles of Lithuania and Prussia (1828). In this episode, Wallenrod, coming in from a banquet, elated with drink, speaks warmly of an exploit in which the Moors took vengeance on their oppressors, the Spaniards, by infecting them in the course of hypocritical effusions, with the plague, leprosy, and the most ghastly diseases, which they themselves had voluntarily contracted beforehand. To the stupefication and horror of his fellow guests, Wallenrod, gives it to be understood that he, the Pole, could also, if he would, breathe death upon his adversaries in a similar fatal embrace." CHOC Introduction.

Work: 2nd Ballade "The Switez" (or the Lake of the Willis) (1836-1839)

Cortot writes, "This lake, "as smooth as a sheet of ice, in which by night, the stars gaze upon their own image," is situated upon the site of a town formerly besieged by the Russian hordes. In order that they might escape the shame which threatened to befall them, heaven granted that the earth should suddenly be laid open, and swallow up the young Polish maidens, rather than that they should be delivered into the hands of the conquerors.

Transformed into strange mysterious flowers, thenceforward they have adorned the shores of the lake. Woe be unto him that touches them!" CHOC Introduction.

Work: 3rd Ballade "Ondine" (1841)

Cortot writes, "This is the picture of feminine seduction. Beside the lake, the youth swears eternal felicity to the maiden whose form he has scarcely discerned. She, having doubts about the man's constancy, flees despite the lover's protest, only to reappear in the enchanting guise of a water fairy. Scarcely has she tempted the youth, when he succumbs to her magic spell. As a punishment he is now swept down into the watery abyss and condemned to pursue the elusive nymph with everlasting cries, and never attain her." CHOC Introduction.

Work: 4th Ballade "The Three Budrys" (Lithuanian Ballade) (1842-1843)

Cortot writes, "The Three Budrys—or the three brothers—are sent away by their father, to far distant lands, in search of priceless treasure. Autumn passes, then winter.

The father thinks that his sons have perished in war.

Amidst whirling snow storms, each one, however, manages to return: but one and all bring back but a single trophy from their odyssey—a bride." CHOC Introduction.

Work: Concerto in E minor, Op. 11 (1830)
Second Movement

In a letter written to his friend Tytus Wojciechowski on May 15, 1830, Chopin wrote, "The Adagio of my new *Concerto* is in E major. It is not meant to be loud, it's more of a romance, quiet, melancholy; it should give the impression of gazing tenderly at a place which brings to mind a thousand dear memories. It is a sort of meditation in spring weather, but by moonlight. That is why I have *muted* the accompaniment." CHOT 88-89.

Work: Concerto in F minor, Op. 21 (1829-1830)
Second Movement

Chopin at nineteen was in love, or thought he was, with a younger singer, Constantia Gladkowska. He never told Constantia, but confided in Titus Wojciechowski that she inspired the Adagio of the F minor Concerto by writing, "I have found my ideal whom I have served faithfully, though without saying a word to her, for six months." CHOM 34-35.

From Berlioz we read, "This Andante transports the audience into an ecstatic calm;…the last note drops like a pearl in a golden vase, and the audience absorbed in its contemplation, hold back the applause for a few moments: they are listening still. It is like having watched the half tints of the evening twilight dissolve harmoniously, and then staying motionless in the darkness, the eyes still fixed on the point in the horizon whence the light has just vanished." CHOE 67.

Work: Études, Op. 10 (completed 1832)

Étude no. 3 in E major

Frederick Niecks[14] recorded that Chopin remarked to his pupil, Adolf Gutmann, that he had never in his life written another such beautiful melody; and on one occasion when Gutmann was studying it the master lifted up his arms with his hands clasped and exclaimed, "O, my fatherland! (O, ma patrie!)" CHOE 68.

Work: Études, Op. 25 (1836)

Étude no. 1 in A-flat major

According to Kleczynski,[15] "[I]t was said that Chopin explained to one of his pupils the manner in which this study should be executed. 'Imagine,' he said, 'a little shepherd who takes refuge in a peaceful grotto from an approaching storm. In the distance rushes the wind and the rain, while the shepherd gently plays a melody on his flute." CHOE 69.

In his old age Liszt gave an impromptu performance of some Chopin Etudes, and at this event on August 10, 1883, Carl Lachmund[16] recorded in his dairy,

> Sitting at ease as if comfortable, and with his hands in anything but a conventional position, he began the beautiful A flat Etude, the first from Chopin's Op. 25. Oh, how convincingly every melody note as he intoned it, spoke to one's heart and how beautifully the rippling accompaniment shaded its emotional meaning. This he followed with the second, in the relative key of f minor... Both etudes he played with that same quiet ease of phrasing that always impressed one in his playing, and there was an entire absence of any show of virtuosity or of dynamic extremes, so often heard in the playing of great piano virtuosos. His

---

14 Frederick Niecks (1845-1924) was a German musical scholar and author. In 1888 he published his magnum opus, *Frederic Chopin as Man and Musician*, with a German edition coming out in 1889. This was the first comprehensive biography of Chopin.

15 Jan Kleczyński (1837-1895) was a Polish pianist, composer, journalist, and chess master.

16 Carl Lachmund (1853-1928) was an American classical pianist, teacher, conductor, composer and diarist. He was a student of Franz Liszt for three years, and his detailed diaries of his time with Liszt provide an invaluable insight into that composer's teaching methods and some aspects of his character.

apparent disregard of metric times, without disturbing the symmetry of rhythmic balance, which lent the Lisztian charm to his phrasing, was to me most characteristic and wonderful. He had finished. No one could find words. We knew not what to say or do. LIS3 233.

Étude no. 2 in F minor
According to Robert Schumann, "Again one in which his individuality impresses itself unforgettably; so charming, dreamy, that it could be the song of a sleeping child." CHOE 70.

Editor's note: Schumann's description of this étude has always seemed extraordinary to me, and a bit incongruous. Perhaps it is the way we are accustomed to hearing pianists play it today.

Étude no. 3 in F major
According to Robert Schumann, "Here the concern was more with bravura, but of the most pleasant kind, and in this respect too Chopin deserved the highest praise." CHOE 70.

Étude no. 7 in C-sharp minor
Charles Rosen says of this Étude, "the so called Cello Etude, is derived from the *scena* in the third act of Bellini's *Norma,* with a melody originally destined for cello, but then altered to the full cello section." ROSE 344.

Work: Trois nouvelles études (1839)
There is a recollection from Arthur Friedheim[17] about Liszt, "seating himself for no apparent reason at the piano one day in Weimar and playing a single solitary piece very softly. It was Chopin's A flat major study, the second of the *Trois nouvelles études.* Although everybody in the room was used to the ethereal sounds Liszt could draw from the keyboard, Friedheim reports that the performance seemed to come from mystical regions where time and space are merged. Tears flowed freely that day." LIS3 503.

Work: Fantasy, Op. 49 (1841)
In discussing the fervent patriotism of Op. 49 Theodor Adorno wrote, "A listener must stop up his ears not to hear Chopin's *F Minor Fantasy* as a kind of tragically decorative song of triumph to the effect that Poland was not lost forever, that some day … she would rise again." CHAD 164.

Mieczyslaw Tomaszewski alluded to Adorno's comment above by writing, "We can indeed speak of intuition in Adorno's case, since when

---

17   Arthur Friedheim (1859-1932) was a Russian-born pianist, conductor and composer who was one of Franz Liszt's foremost pupils.

he wrote those words, in 1962, it was not yet known that the Fantasy was composed on motives from one of the most popular Polish insurrectionary songs, namely "Litwinka" by Karol Kurpiński. "Litwinka" was sung by the whole of Poland and the whole of the Great Emigration – the community of exiles who fled Poland in the wake of the November Uprising… "Litwinka" is merely alluded to in the F minor Fantasy. It is present in that work, but in a discreet way." CHFN.

Work: The Mazurkas

Editor's Note: It is documented that Chopin played his Mazurkas with great rhythmic freedom and, to many of his contemporaries, even altered the meter. Could we ever get away with interpreting them that way today? Regardless of one's opinions their rendition is enhanced when adding what the American pedagogue Frank Mannheimer required, "an ethnic flavor."

In relation to this freedom Hallé recounted the following interaction with Chopin:

> It must have been in 1845 or 1846 that I once ventured to observe to him that most of his Mazurkas … when played by himself, appeared to be written, not in 3/4, but in 4/4 time, the result of his dwelling so much longer on the first note in the bar. He denied it strenuously, until I made him play one of them and counted audibly four in the bar, which fitted perfectly. Then he laughed and explained it was the national character of the dance which created the oddity. The more remarkable fact was that you received the impression of 3/4 time whilst listening to common time. Of course this was not the case with every Mazurka, but with many. CHOE 72.

From Hector Berlioz we read,

> There are unbelievable details in his Mazurkas; and he has found how to render them doubly interesting by playing them with the utmost degree of softness, piano in the extreme, the hammers merely brushing the strings, so much so that one is tempted to go close to the instrument and put one's ear to it as if to a concert of sylphs or elves. CHOE 71.

From Liszt we read of the Mazurkas, "These productions which he loved to hear us call 'paintings on the easel.'" CHOE 71.

Editor's note: Liszt's fanciful description of Chopin's *Mazurkas* which follows, and later the *Polonaises* and *Polonaise-Fantasie*, from his rarely read book *The Life of Chopin* transports us to another era of musical thought and a florid style of writing to which the twenty-first-century reader is not accustomed. Nevertheless, one should consider that as Liszt *knew* Chopin and certainly heard him *play* these works, his expressions carry weight.

Liszt writes,

> An exceeding variety of subjects and impressions occur in the great number of his Mazourkas. Sometimes we catch the manly sounds of the rattling of spurs, but it is generally the almost imperceptible rustling of crape and gauze under the light breath of the dancers, or the clinking of chains of gold and diamonds, that maybe distinguished. Some of them seem to depict the defiant pleasure of the ball given on the eve of battle,… we hear the sighs and despairing farewells of hearts forced to suppress their tears… We sometimes catch the gasping breath of terror and stifled fears; sometimes divine the dim presentiments of a love destined to perpetual struggle and doomed to survive all hope, which, though devoured by jealousy and conscious that it can never be the victor, still disdains to curse, and takes refuge in a soul-subduing pity. In others we feel as if borne into the heart of a whirlwind, a strange madness; in the midst of the mystic confusion, an abrupt melody passes and repasses, panting and palpitating, like the throbbing of a heart faint with longing, gasping in despair, breaking in anguish, dying of hopeless, yet indignant love. In some we hear the distant flourish of trumpets, like fading memories of glories past, in some of them, the rhythm is as floating, as undetermined, as shadowy, as the feeling with which two young lovers gaze upon the first star of evening, as yet alone in the dim skies.

Upon one afternoon, when there were but three persons present, and Chopin had been playing for a long time, one of the most distinguished women in Paris remarked, that she felt always more and more filled with solemn meditation… She asked him what was the cause of the involuntary, yet sad veneration which subdued her heart while listening to these pieces [mazurkas], apparently presenting only sweet and graceful subjects:—and by what name he called the strange emotion enclosed in his compositions… he replied: "that her heart had not deceived her in the gloom which she felt stealing upon her, for whatever might have been his transitory pleasures, he had never been free from a feeling which might almost be said to form the soil of his heart, and for which he could find no appropriate expression except in his own language, no other possessing a term equivalent to the Polish word: ZAL!"[18] As if his ear thirsted for the sound of this word, which expresses the whole range of emotions produced by an intense regret, through all the shades of feeling, from hatred to repentance, he repeated it again and again. CHFL 79-82.

---

18 'Zal' has been interpreted as heart-rending sadness, nostalgia, or despair.

Work: Mazurka in A minor, Op. 17, no. 4 (1833)

According to Wilhelm von Lenz,[19] "Even in Chopin's presence we called it the 'mourner's face' (Das Trauergesicht)—he was quite happy about this name." CHOE 74.

Work: Mazurka in B-flat minor, Op. 24, no. 4 (1835)

Referring to the unisons in this Mazurka, Lenz recalled Chopin saying, "'They're the women's voices in the choir,' he would say, and they were never played delicately enough, never simply enough. One was barely allowed to breathe over the keyboard, let alone touch it." CHOE 75.

Work: Mazurka in D-flat major, Op. 30, no. 3 (1837)

"It seems like a Polonaise for a coronation festivity," someone said to Chopin. "Something like that," was his reply. CHOE 75.

Work: Mazurkas, Op. 33 (1838)

Mazurka no. 2 in D major

Aleksander Michalowski[20] recorded the following, "Despite her advanced years, Princess Czartoryska gave into my pleas and played a few Mazurkas, among others the well known Mazurka in D major. I was struck by the way she interpreted its main theme. At first she played it in a brash, forthright way, with no subtly of nuance. It was only toward the end of the piece, at the theme's second reappearance [bar 74 to the end], that she played it with a soft caressing touch, utterly subtle and refined. When I asked her about this contrasting treatment, she replied that Chopin had taught it to her that way: in this piece he wanted to present the contrast between the "tavern" and the "salon." That is why he wanted the same melody played so differently: at the beginning it was to evoke the popular atmosphere of the tavern, and, towards the end, the refinement of the salon." CHOE 75.

Mazurka no. 4 in B minor

Lenz recalled that "This piece is a Ballade in all but name. Chopin himself taught it as such, stressing the narrative character of this highly developed piece. At the end a bell tolls a heavy bass carillon G-C-G-C- and the sudden arrival of the final chords sweeps away the cohort of ghosts, Chopin would say." CHOE 75.

---

19 Wilhelm von Lenz (1809-1883) was a Baltic German Russian official and writer, and was a friend of many mid-century Romantic composers, including Franz Liszt, Frederic Chopin, and Hector Berlioz.

20 Aleksander Michałowski (1851-1938) was a Polish pianist and pedagogue with a speciality for teaching and writing on the works of Chopin.

Not directly connected with this Mazurka, but in keeping with its Ballade-like nature and Chopin's reference to ghosts, George Sand saw in Chopin, "all the superstitious fancies of Slavic poetry. Polish, he lived in the nightmare world of legends. Ghosts called to him and embraced him, and... he would thrust their emaciated faces away from his own, and struggle under the grip of their icy hands." COGS 446.

Work: Mazurka in B major, Op. 41, no. 3 (1839-1840)
Lenz recalled, "Chopin used to say that this piece opens with a chorus of guitars and that it is particularly difficult to render because of the tangle of groups of dancers changing direction at every moment." CHOE 76.

Work: Mazurka in F minor, Op. 68, no. 4 (published 1855)
His creativity was almost over: he composed only two Mazurkas (*Mazurka Op. 67, no. 2 and Op. 68, no. 4*) in 1849, the latter being, according to Fontana, "the last inspiration Chopin put on paper... he was already too ill to try it at the piano." CHOM 197.

Work: Nocturne in G minor, Op. 15, no. 3 (1830-1833)
According to Kleczynski, it was originally to be called, "After a representation of the tragedy of *Hamlet.* Afterwards Chopin abandoned this notion saying, 'Let them guess for themselves.'" CHOE 79.

Work: Nocturne in G major, Op. 37, no. 2 (1838-1840)
From Schumann we read, "Chopin played the G major Nocturne for Mendelssohn, who then gave a very poetic description of it. It was like a vision opening up of a garden peopled by beings walking in silence amidst fountains and strange birds; by this Mendelssohn wanted to convey the music's sense of complete envelopment." CHOE 65.

Work: Nocturne in F-sharp minor, Op. 48, no. 2 (1840-1841)
According to Gutmann, Chopin told him that the middle section (bars 57-100) should be played like a recitative. "A tyrant commands" (the first two chords), he said, "and the other asks for mercy." CHOE 81.

Work: The Polonaises
Liszt wrote with extraordinary passion and detail on the emotional character of the Polonaise. In a portion of his account he observes,

> While listening to some of the POLONAISES of Chopin, we can almost catch the firm, nay, the more than firm, the heavy, resolute tread of men bravely facing all the bitter injustice which the most cruel and relentless destiny can offer, with the manly pride of unblenching courage. The progress of the music suggests to our imagination such magnificent groups as were designed by Paul Veronese, robed in the

rich costume of days long past: we see passing at intervals before us, brocades of gold, velvets, damasked satins, silvery soft and flexile sables, hanging sleeves gracefully thrown back upon the shoulders, embossed sabres, boots yellow as gold or red with trampled blood, sashes with long and undulating fringes, close chemisettes, rustling trains, stomachers embroidered with pearls, head dresses glittering with rubies or leafy with emeralds, light slippers rich with amber, gloves perfumed with the luxurious attar from the harems…

…The Polonaise is without rapid movements, without any true steps in the artistic sense of the word, intended rather for display than for the exhibition of seductive grace;… By a rare exception this dance was designed to exhibit the men, to display manly beauty, to set off noble and dignified deportment, martial yet courtly bearing. "Martial yet courtly:" do not these two epithets almost define the Polish character? In the original the very name of the dance is masculine; it is only in consequence of a misconception that it has been translated in other tongues into the feminine gender. CHFL 37-39.

Work: Polonaise in F-sharp minor, Op. 44 (1841)

Transporting us to another era of musical thought and expression Liszt writes,

His GRAND POLONAISE in F SHARP MINOR, must be ranked among his most energetic compositions. He has inserted in it a MAZOURKA… The principal motive is a weird air, dark as the lurid hour which precedes a hurricane, in which we catch the fierce exclamations of exasperation, mingled with a bold defiance, recklessly hurled at the stormy elements. The prolonged return of a tonic, at the commencement of each measure, reminds us of the repeated roar of artillery—as if we caught the sounds from some dread battle waging in the distance. After the termination of this note, a series of the most unusual chords are unrolled through measure after measure. We know nothing analogous, to the striking effect produced by this, in the compositions of the greatest masters. This passage is suddenly interrupted by a SCENE CHAMPETRE, a MAZOURKA in the style of an Idyl, full of the perfume of lavender and sweet marjoram;… This improvisation terminates like a dream, without other conclusion than a convulsive shudder; leaving the soul under the strangest, the wildest, the most subduing impressions. CHFL 58-60.

Work: Polonaise in A-flat major, Op. 53 (1842)

Of the celebrated octave passage in this Polonaise Liszt said to a student, "What I wish to hear is the canter of the horses of the Polish cavalry before they gather force and destroy the enemy." LIS3 229.

During a Master Lesson recorded in the *Etude Magazine* in 1928, Mark Hambourg stated, "Our present *Polonaise in A Flat, Op. 53* sometimes bears the title of 'The Heroic', and there is an anecdote associated with it that when Chopin played it through for the first time the room seemed to him to fill with the spectres of the warriors he had evoked (for the Polonaise in A-flat is a true war song) and that he rushed away, struck with terror, before the creations of his own fancy!" BRJJ 43.

Editor's note: Read the similar experience in connection with Chopin's performance of the B-flat minor Sonata.

Work: Polonaise-Fantasie in A-flat major, Op. 61 (1846)

Liszt writes, "Despair has giddied the brain like a draught of Cyprus wine which gives a more instinctive rapidity to all our gestures, a keener point to all our words, a more subtle flame to all our emotions, and excites the mind to a pitch of irritability approaching insanity. Such pictures possess but little value for real art. Like all descriptions of moments of extremity, of agonies, of death rattles, of contractions of the muscles, where all elasticity is lost, where the nerves, ceasing to be the organs of the human will, reduce man to a passive victim of despair; they only serve to torture the soul. Deplorable visions, which the artist should admit with extreme circumspection within the graceful circle of his charmed realm!" CHFL 60-61.

Editor's note: Reduced to its essentials, it seems to me that Liszt senses the *Polonaise-Fantasie's* intensity and sensitivity—"torture the soul," "victim of despair," "approaching insanity,"—and that Chopin is, according to Liszt, giving us the extreme edge of what one can bear on a regular basis.

Work: Preludes, Op. 28 (1835-1839)

George Sand has depicted in her memoirs the state of hyper-sensitivity in which many of the *Preludes* were written in Majorca. While many today view her florid accounts with slight skepticism, it must be remembered that she not only wrote with the style of a novelist, but was there, and a witness to these events. She wrote,,

> The monastery had been full of phantoms for him even when he felt well… Once when my children and I returned from our nocturnal prowling among the ruins we found him, at ten o'clock, sitting at the piano as pale as death, with haggard eyes and hair standing almost on end. It took him quite half a minute to recognize us. Then immediately he made an effort at laughter and played us the sublime things that he had just composed— and at the same time revealed to us the terrible, nerve-wracking ideas that had forced themselves on him in his hour of loneliness, grief and terror.

In such circumstances he composed the finest of his short pieces which he modestly called *Preludes*. They are the works of a master-hand. Many of them suggest a vision of deceased monks and the sound of funereal changes accompanying them to the cemetery. Others are melancholy and tender. They came to him in the hours of sunshine and good health, while the children were laughing under the window, and guitars twanging far off, and birds singing in the wet trees. And little pale roses bloomed against the snow. Still others are of a bleak sorrow that charms your ear while breaking your heart. SAND 170-171.

Editor's note: The Chopin *Preludes* are universally loved as impeccable sketches of pure music at its most concise, elegant, and dramatic. The descriptive titles given to each of the *Preludes* beginning with Hans von Bulow, continued until after 1945 by Alfred Cortot, and those few given by George Sand, mostly lost, are both little known and, perhaps, not welcome to the twenty-first-century pianist. While the descriptions of Alfred Cortot may seem to some at times overly poetic and certainly unknown to Chopin, they are, nevertheless, the products of one of the greatest pianistic minds of the twentieth century. Men of the intellectual and artistic stature of Cortot would be the first to admit that their titles are, at best, only appendages to the interpretation of the *Preludes*. Nevertheless, a little seasoning from the musical thinking of previous generations can do no harm to the imagination of the serious twenty-first-century musician.

According to George Sand's daughter Solange, who stayed with the composer at the monastery in Majorca when the preludes were written, "My mother gave a title to each of Chopin's wonderful Preludes; these titles have been preserved on a score he gave to us." CHSO 224-238.

Editor's note: That titled score is lost.

According to Jean Jacques Eigeldinger, "But Solange did record her mother's allusion to names of the preludes, apparently without assigning these names to the prelude numbers. It is believed that "*Quelles larmes au fond du cloître humide?*" ("What tears [are shed] from the depths of the damp monastery?") corresponds to prelude No. 4, "*Quelle marche funèbre*" ("What funeral marches") corresponds to no. 20, "Quelle marche triomphale" ("What triumphant marches") corresponds to no. 9, "Quelles melancoliques gouttes de pluie tombant une à une... ("What melancholy raindrops falling one by one") corresponds to no. 15. CHSO 224-238.

The source for the following titles of the Preludes is the Preface to Cortot's Edition of the Preludes (COPR Preface), and the source for the images paired with these titles comes from a first-time translation by Phillip Bailey of a 1934 French journal article by Cortot (CHCO).

Prelude no. 1 in C major

"Attente fiévreuse de l'aimée…" which translates to "Feverish anticipation of the lover." Cortot writes, "Or, if you prefer, an anachronistic transposition of the scene imagined much later by Wagner which shows us Isolde waving her scarf to hasten the coming of Tristan." COPR Preface, CHCO 252.

Prelude no. 2 in A minor

"Méditation douloureuse; la mer déserte, au loin…" which translates to "A painful meditation; the distant, deserted sea…" Cortot continues, "a similar Tristanesque vision,—the third act,—the hero dying and the horizon without hope." COPR Preface, CHCO 252.

Prelude no. 3 in G major

"Le chant du ruisseau…" which translates to "The stream's song…" Cortot continues, "Banal title, but perhaps all the more appropriate to characterize the murmuring freshness of this lively waving of the left hand, supporting with its chatty buzzing the élan of an innocent and spontaneous melody." COPR Preface, CHCO 252.

Prelude no. 4 in E minor

"Sur une tombe…" which translates to "On a grave…" "This prelude was played at the funeral of Chopin, at the Madeleine, October 30, 1849. I was not, however, inspired by this circumstance in defining this poignant sentiment. The music alone in its inconsolable distress irresistibly commanded, at least for me, this desolate epigraph." COPR Preface, CHCO 253.

Prelude no. 5 in D major

"L'arbre plein de chants…" which translates to "The tree full of songs…" Cortot continues, "Here is one of the happy poems that George Sand has spoken to us about, which were born in Chopin's imagination in moments of sun and health." COPR Preface, CHCO 253.

Prelude no. 6 in B minor

"Le mal du pays…" which translates as "Homesickness…" Cortot continues, "Heimweh, as the Germans say, is more expressive and in these melancholic notes, I cannot but hear the same voice of Chopin evoking the distant fatherland. This prelude was also played at the church during his burial." COPR Preface, CHCO 254.

Prelude no. 7 in A major

"Des souvenirs délicieux flottent comme un parfum à travers la mémoire..." which translates to "Delightful memories float like perfume through my mind..." Cortot continues, "Too long an epigraph no doubt for such a short piece, which is enlivened by an indefinable mazurka rhythm evoking the happy times of adolescence." COPR Preface, CHCO 254.

Prelude no. 8 in F-sharp minor

"La neige tombe, le vent hurle, la tempête fait rage; mais en mon triste coeur, l'orage est plus terrible encore..." which translates to "The snow falls, the wind howls, and the storm rages; yet in my sad heart, the tempest is worse still..." Cortot continues, "Liszt pointed out that this prelude was capable of recalling the nightmarish impression described by George Sand. But it is more likely that she had in mind no. 15, and I will come back to that later." COPR Preface, CHCO 255.

Prelude no. 9 in E major

"Voix prophétiques..." or "Prophetic voices..." Cortot continues, "Finis Poloniae..."[21] "These are brazen voices, prophetic and solemn, shouting out in protest the indomitable pride of a people thought prematurely to be enslaved. It is in this sense of wild and bitter irony that one should understand the quote which I have attached to this prelude." COPR Preface, CHCO 255.

Prelude no. 10 in C-sharp minor

"Fusées qui retombent..." which translates as "Falling rockets [fireworks]..." Cortot continues, "Golden arrows in space, twinkling nebulae which disappear in a calm eddy of casual chords." COPR Preface, CHCO 256.

Prelude no. 11 in B major

"Désir de jeune fille..." which translates to "A young girl's desire..." Cortot continues, "And what melodic form better than this one could describe so much the modesty, chaste restraint, and delicate tenderness?" COPR Preface, CHCO 256.

Prelude no. 12 in G-sharp minor

"Chevauchée dans la nuit..." which translates to "A gallop in the night..." Cortot continues, "Nervous rhythms inflame by the incessant

---

21 Translates as "The end of Poland." This is a historic headline commonly attributed to Polish General Kosciusko who, after his defeat by the Russians at the battle of Battle of Maciejowice on October 10, 1794, realized that his country would soon be dismantled.

stubbornness of an imaginary horse pawing the ground, which disappear in the distance of a ghost-like vision." COPR Preface, CHCO 256.

Prelude no. 13 in F-sharp major

"Sur le sol étranger, par une nuit étoilée, et en pensant à la bien-aimée lointaine…" which translates to "On foreign soil, under a starlit night, and thinking of my beloved faraway…" Cortot continues, "Con morbidezza…, (with morbidness) such should be the indication for the feeling of this short Nocturne which suggested to me this epigraph: "On the foreign soil, under a night of stars, and thinking of my beloved faraway." COPR Preface, CHCO 257.

Prelude no. 14 in E-flat minor

"Mer orageuse…" which translates to "The stormy sea…" Cortot continues, "A vision of terror symbolized by eddies of threatening sound, which growl and unfurl in a gripping unison. 'At night we heard the sea without seeing it,' as Victor Hugo said, in another musical and evocative phrase." COPR Preface, CHCO 258.

Prelude no. 15 in D-flat major

"Mais la morte est là, dans l'ombre…" which translates to "But death is there, in the shadows…" Cortot continues, "This is the most famous of the preludes, the one that one customarily designates as being inspired by George Sand's story: 'The drip of water.' I had in the past interpreted it under the inspiration of the melancholic story by Anderson, whose poetic content had appeared to me to suit just as much George Sand's anguished tale the dramatic character of this gripping page, 'a young mother falls asleep cradling her child, and in a nightmare sees him brought to the scaffold. She wakes up but her tears still flow.' I have since tried to summarize the perhaps too precise anecdotal character of this moral of the story in a more precise way; 'But death is there, in the shadows.'" COPR Preface, CHCO 258.

Prelude no. 16 in B-flat minor

"La course à l'abîme…" which translates to "Race to the abyss…" Cortot continues, "Spurred on by the persistence of an inexorable rhythm in the pale light of the flashes of sounds that tear up the keyboard, Faust and his phantom war horse rush head long to meet their justice-loving destiny." COPR Preface, CHCO 259.

Prelude no. 17 in A-flat major

"Elle m'a dit, 'Je t'aime…'" which translates to "She told me, 'I love you…'" Cortot continues, "And all the confessions, all the ups and downs, all the ecstatic moments seem to flourish in the form of an intoxicating song that loses itself in the mystery of the night, punctuated by the distant vibrations a bell one hears in a dream." COPR Preface, CHCO 259.

Prelude no. 18 in F minor

"Imprécations…" which translates to "Imprecations…" or "Divine Curses…" Cortot continues, "We know this wild feeling which animates these sonorous lamentations. The two Etudes said to be revolutionary, have taught us its inflamed origin. The fit of indignation which inspires the musician, there as here, is no doubt only the echo of the news of the taking of Warsaw by the Muscovites."

Prelude no. 19 in E-flat major

"Des ailes, des ailes, pour m'enfuir vers vous, o ma bien-aimée!…" which translates to "Wings, wings, that I may flee to you, o my beloved!…" Cortot continues, "And perhaps here no other commentary is needed, for the music is more ardent in its quivering flight than any words which might seek to define it." COPR Preface, CHCO 260.

Prelude no. 20 in C minor

"Funerailles…" which translates to "Funeral ceremony…" Cortot continues, "The slow recession of a tearful funeral cortege, toward the anguished mystery of the unknown. Then the soul-wrenching vibration of the last chord, which seems to seal the weight of eternity on a half-opened tomb." COPR Preface, CHCO 260.

Prelude no 21 in B-flat major

"Retour solitaire à l'endroit des aveux…" which translates to "Solitary return, to the place of confessions…" Cortot continues, "Melancholic evocation of a vanishing happiness, disabused reverie cradled by the swaying of distant bells. Nella maggiore dolore…" COPR Preface, CHCO 26.

Prelude no 22 in G minor

"Révolte…" or "Revolt…" Cortot continues, "Revolt against destiny, against suffering, against oneself. The seething of a tortured soul which does not want to accept its defeat." COPR Preface, CHCO 261

Prelude no. 23 in F major

"Naiades jouant…" which translates to "Playing water fairies…" Cortot continues, "A trickling of crystalline sonorities from which surge forth troubling, enigmatic, this mysterious dissonance of the last measure that seems to prolong beyond the silence, the slow fading of a captivating dream." COPR Preface, CHCO 262.

Prelude no. 24 in D minor

"Du Sang, de la Volupté, de la Mort" which translates to "Of Blood, of Sensuality, and of Death." Cortot continues, "In borrowing from

Maurice Barrès to describe this last prelude, the title of his book *On Blood, Sensuality, and Death*, I'm well aware of having made a too audacious leap of poetic license and having subjected Chopin's thought to the concept of too modern a sensibility. And yet no words better than these seem to me capable of defining the flights of passion, tenderness, and despair which characterizes with their gripping alternating reversals the last page of this collection, where we have just read, transposed in sublime sonorities, all the emotions of the human heart." COPR Preface, CHCO 26 2.

Prelude in B minor, Op. 28, no. 6

In his charming 1900 book entitled *Chopin, the Man and his Music*, James Huneker quotes George Sand as remarking about this prelude, "It precipitates the soul into frightful depression." CHJH 225.

Hans von Bülow's title for this prelude, "Tolling Bells," may originate with its performance at Chopin's funeral. CHFL 207.

Prelude in D-flat major, Op. 28, no. 15

Speaking of this prelude and implying the hypersensitivity under which many of the preludes may have been conceived, George Sand wrote the following account, which is often mistakenly abridged. I include it here in its entirety:

> There is one especially, which he composed on an evening of lugubrious rain and which depresses the heart to a frightening degree. We had left him well enough, that morning, Maurice and I, and visited Palma to buy necessities for our encampment. It took us six hours to travel three leagues through torrents swollen by ceaseless rain and reach the place where the floods were deepest. It was already pitch dark and we were shoeless and we were abandoned by our driver.[22] We hurried back, braving unheard of dangers, because our invalid would be anxious for us; as indeed he was, but his anxiety had turned into a sort of quiet despair. We found him sobbing while he played this wonderful prelude. When we entered he rose, uttered a loud cry and said confusedly in a strange tone: "Ah, I knew that you were dead!" After recovering his spirits and becoming aware of our plight, his retrospective views of our dangers made him ill. Then he declared that while waiting for us he had seen it all in a dream, and not distinguishing dream from reality, had calmed and as it were lulled himself by playing the piano, persuaded that he too was dead. He saw himself drowned in a lake, with heavy drops of cold water falling rhythmically on his breast.

---

22 Robert Graves annotates this sentence by writing, "In other words, the driver would not abandon his bogged mule and carriage to escort her home" (Sand 171).

I made him listen to the noise of the water dropping at regular intervals on the cell roof;[23] but he denied having heard it and even grew vexed when I described the phenomenon as "mimetic harmony." He protested violently, and with justice, against the puerility of imitating in music the stimuli of the outer ear. His genius was informed by the mysterious harmonies of Nature, which he translated into sublime musical equivalents, but not by any slavish transcription of external sounds. That evening's prelude was full of rain drops beating on the charterhouse roof, but they were transformed by his imagination and singing gift into tears falling from the heart. SAND 171.

Editor's note: While this famous story is engrossing it must be remembered that many of the *Preludes* were composed prior to this trip to Majorca. If George Sand is a reliable witness in this case, and there is no reason to believe that the essentials of her story are not true, then the scene she describes was one in which Chopin may have been selecting, filing, and *polishing* the Preludes, perhaps not actually composing them. It is certainly a reminder of the ultra sensitive ear and acute imagination with which Chopin composed.

Prelude in A-flat major, Op. 28, no. 17

According to Ignacy Paderewski,[24] "Madame Dubois said that Chopin himself used to play that bass note in the final section (in spite of playing everything else diminuendo) with great strength. He always struck that note in the same way and with the same strength, because of the meaning he attached to it… He proclaimed it, because the idea of that Prelude is based on the sound of an old clock in the castle which strikes the eleventh hour… Madame Dubois said that Chopin always insisted that the bass note should be struck with the same strength, no diminuendo, because the clock knows no diminuendo. That bass note was the clock speaking." CHOE 83.

According to Alfred Cortot, this prelude "[R]ecalls Mendelssohn's Song without Words. When someone had spoken of this very Prelude, in front of Mendelssohn, the latter answered, 'I like it. I cannot tell you how much or why, unless it be, that it is something that I could never have written myself.'" COPR Preface.

Prelude in E-flat major, Op. 28, no. 19

---

23 Robert Graves also comments, "This proves to have been impossible: it must have been the rain dripping from the roof into the garden."

24 Ignacy Paderewski (1860-1941) was a much-lionized and brilliant Polish pianist, pedagogue, and later the first Prime Minister of Poland of the Second Polish Republic in 1919.

A fascinating reference from Cortot appears in the Preface to his student edition of the Chopin Preludes, in which he says, "Edgar Poe [Edgar Allan Poe] felt that the infinite beauties of the 19th prelude (E flat major) could not fail to move a sensitive listener to tears." COPR Preface.

Prelude in C minor, Op. 28, no. 20

According to Jane Stirling, "I had played what I had always called 'La Priere' (the prayer), the Prelude in c minor... Those chords (played by Chopin) sounded more celestial than of this earth, and contained an aspiration that extended into eternity." CHOE 83.

Work: Scherzo in B-flat minor, Op. 31 (1837)

According to Wilhlem von Lenz Chopin said of the opening measures of this work, "'It must be a question,' taught Chopin; and it was never played questioningly enough, never soft enough, never round enough (tombe), as he said, never sufficiently weighted (important). 'It must be a house of the dead,' he once said [...In his lessons] I saw Chopin dwell at length on this bar and again at each of its reappearances. "That's the key to the whole piece,' he would say.... Chopin was just as exacting over the simple quaver accompaniment of the cantilena, as well as the cantilena itself. 'You should think of [the singer] Pasta, of Italian song!- not of French Vaudeville,' he said one day with more than a touch of irony." CHOE 84-85.

Work: Sonata in B-flat minor, Op. 35 (1839)

Third Movement

George Marek wrote in his biography of Chopin,

> When he played the "Funeral March" Sonata in Manchester, a curious incident occurred. He had played the first movement and the Scherzo when he suddenly rose from his chair and disappeared. What was wrong? Had he forgotten the music? Had he suffered a coughing attack? He reappeared almost immediately and finished playing the Sonata. The Manchester Guardian commented on the incident. The explanation is contained in a letter to Solange of September 9, 1848, "A strange adventure befell me when I was playing my Sonata in B flat minor before some English friends. I had played the Allegro and Scherzo more or less correctly. I was about to attack the March when suddenly I saw arising from the body of my piano those cursed creatures which had appeared to me one lugubrious night at the Chartreuse (Majorca). I had to leave for one instant to pull myself together, after which I continued without saying anything. CHOM 210-211.

La Mara (Ida Marie Lipsius)[25] relates the following, "While performing for Napoleon III and his wife in Paris Liszt sat down at the piano and began with his recently composed *Trovatore* paraphrase. After he had finished, the empress asked him to play the Funeral March from Chopin's B-*flat minor Piano Sonata*. As he was playing, she began to weep and was forced to withdraw into an adjoining room. Liszt finished the mournful dirge, and there was an embarrassed silence while the emperor went to inquire after his wife. Apparently the music had aroused in her some powerful memories of her dead sister, and she was unable to contain her emotions." LIS2 541.

Franz Liszt wrote,

> It would be impossible to pass in silence the Funeral March inserted in the first Sonata, which was arranged for the orchestra, and performed, for the first time, at his own obsequies. What other accents could have been found capable of expressing, with the same heart-breaking effect, the emotions, the tears, which should accompany to the last long sleep, one who had taught in a manner so sublime, how great losses should be mourned? We once heard it remarked by a native of his own country: "these pages could only have been written by a Pole." All that the funeral train of an entire nation weeping its own ruin and death can be imagined to feel of desolating woe, of majestic sorrow, wails in the musical ringing of this passing bell, mourns in the tolling of this solemn knell, as it accompanies the mighty escort on its way to the still city of the Dead. The intensity of mystic hope; the devout appeal to superhuman pity, to infinite mercy, to a dread justice, which numbers every cradle and watches every tomb; the exalted resignation which has wreathed so much grief with halos so luminous; the noble endurance of so many disasters with the inspired heroism of Christian martyrs who know not to despair;—resound in this melancholy chant, whose voice of supplication breaks the heart. CHFL 27-28.

According to Cortot, Schumann, who only half understood this Sonata, nevertheless recognized its enigmatic beauty, and said of it, "The image of a sphinx bars its entrance, and also seals its exit." COMI 146.

Finale (Fourth Movement)

Of this movement Chopin remarked in a letter to Julian Fontana on August 8, 1839, "The left hand and right hand gossip in unison." CHHE 181.

Work: Waltz in A minor, Op. 34, no. 2 (1831)

---

25 Ida Marie Lipsius (1837-1927), alias "La Mara," was a German writer and music historian.

According to Frederick Niecks,[26] "One day when Stephen Heller—my informant—was at Schlesinger's music shop in Paris, Chopin entered. The latter, hearing Heller ask for one of his waltzes, inquired of him which of them he liked best. 'It is difficult to say which I like the best,' replied Heller, 'for I like them all; but if I were pressed for an answer I would probably say the one in a minor.' This gave Chopin much pleasure. 'I am glad you do,' he said; 'it is also my favorite.'" CHOE 158.

Work: Waltz in A-flat major, Op. 42 (1840)

Lenz wrote, "This waltz, springing form the eight-bar trill, should evoke a musical clock, according to Chopin himself. In his own performance it embodied his rubato style to the fullest; he would play it as a continued *stretto prestissimo* with the bass maintaining a steady beat. A garland of flowers winding amidst the dancing couples!" CHOE 87.

Work: Waltz in A-flat major, Op. 64, no. 1 (1847)

The famous story of the origin of this charming waltz was recounted in 1900 by James Huneker, who wrote, "The D flat Valse—'le valse du petit chien'—is George Sand's own prompting. One evening at her home in the Square d'Orléans, she was amused by her little pet dog, chasing its tail. She begged Chopin, her little pet pianist, to set the tail to music. He did so, and behold the world is richer for this piece. I do not dispute the story. It seems well grounded, but then it is so ineffably silly!" CHJH 247-248.

Work: Waltz in F minor, Op. 70, no. 3 (1829)

Constantia Gladkowska, the young Polish singer whom Chopin fell in love with in 1829 and who was the recipient of the dedication of the gorgeous f minor Concerto, is referred to again in connection with this Waltz. He composed this "little waltz" while dreaming of Constantia (Opus 70, no. 3). CHOM 35.

---

26 Frederick Niecks (1835-1924) was a German musical scholar and author, who was resident in Scotland for the bulk of his life. He is best remembered now for his biographies of Frederic Chopin and Robert Schumann.

Chapter 7
Debussy

General Observations:
"Make me forget the hammers," his publisher Durand quoted Debussy as saying; far from suggesting anything anaemic, it can be read as a call for imaginative boldness, effectively meaning, "Make me forget it's a piano," Roy Howat suggests. AFPM 215.

Work: Children's Corner (1906-1908)
Maurice Dumensil recorded his recollections of Debussy's comments on interpreting *Children's Corner*:

> *Dr. Gradus ad Parnassum: "Pas trop vite"* (not too fast), with a little humor aimed at good old Clementi. Faster and brilliant toward the end.
>
> *Jimbo's Lullaby: "jouez plus gauchement"* (more clumsily), for the first page. Emphasize the "wrong" accents.
>
> *Serenade for the Doll: "Délicate et gracieux"*, with nothing of the passion of a Spanish serenader.
>
> *The Snow is Dancing:* This is a mood picture as well as a tone picture. It must be "brumeux, triste, monotone" (misty, dreamy, monotonous), and not too fast—not fast at all.
>
> *The Little Shepherd:* Differentiate clearly between the improvisation of the shepherd on his flute and the dance motive.
>
> *Golliwog's Cakewalk:* The first and third sections *"très rythmé"* with a strong, sharp, rhythm. As a contrast the middle part must be very free. There is a suggestion of the trombone in the part marked *"avec une grand emotion"*. Don't be afraid to overdo it here. DEDU 10-13.

Work: Estampes (1903)

Pagodes (*Pagodas*)

Edward Lockspeiser[27] notes that this work is "said to have been inspired by the composer's conception, following the music he had heard played by Javanese and Cambodian musicians in Paris, of the pagodas of juggernaut and the Porcelain tower of Nanking." DEBU 147.

Soiree dans Grenade (*Evening in Granada*)

Oscar Thompson related that this work "has been described by Spain's foremost living composer, Manuel de Falla, as 'characteristically Spanish in every detail.' Said De Falla, 'This music… conjures up the effect of images mirrored by moonlight upon limpid waters of the large albercas [pools] adjoining the Alhambra.'" DEBM 257-258.

From Robert Schmitz[28] we read, "One evening in the middle twenties, Manual De Falla, my dear friend, was sitting with Mrs. Schmitz and me at the Fouquet on the Champs-Élysées in Paris, and I remember asking him which was the pianistic work he considered the most expressive of Spain. De Falla answered, without any hesitation, 'The Evening in Granada', which contains in a marvelously distilled way the most concentrated atmosphere of Andalusia." DEBS 85-86.

"Debussy…manages to conjure up impressions so genuine and so accurate that no less an authority than Manuel de Falla declared them to represent 'the images in the moonlit waters of the *albercas* adjoining the 'Alhambra.'" DEBU 148.

According to Marguerite Long, who heard him play this work, "When Debussy played it, this piece was all depth, allurement and an inexplicable magical charm. This grave, tender syncopation cradles our vague dreams in rhythms at once nonchalant and gracious." DEML 78.

Work: En Blanc et Noir for Two Pianos (In Black and White for Two Pianos) (1915)

From a letter to Robert Godet, Friday, February 4, 1916, Debussy writes, "Tres cher, Bring your brain to bear upon 'En Blanc et noir'…These pieces draw their color, their emotion, simply from the piano, like the 'greys' of Velázquez, if I may so suggest?" DELE 314.

The poems which accompany each movement of *En Blanc et Noir* follow:

---

27 Edward Lockspeiser (1905-1973) was an English musicologist, composer, art critic, and radio broadcaster on music who specialized in the works and life of French composer Debussy, and whose two-volume biography on that composer was the result of thirty years' research.

28 Elie Robert Schmitz (1889-1949) was a Franco-American pianist and composer.

He who stays in his stands aside
and doesn't dance
is quietly admitting some disgrace.
(J. Barbierr & M. Carre- «Romeo et Julliete»)

Prince, let him forth be borne by Eolus
To Glaucus in that forest far from us
Where hope nor peace may ever on him glance.
For he holds nought in him- but worthlessness
Who could wish ill unto the realm of France.
"Francios Villon Ballade contre les ennemis de France"
To Lieutenant Jacques Charlot killed by the enemy 3 March 1915

Winter, you're nothing but a villain

(Charles d'Orleans)
Translated by Phillip Bailey

DEBL

Work: Études (1915)
Debussy proclaimed in a letter to Durand on August 19, 1915, that "These Études hide a rigorous technique beneath the flowers of harmony." DEPR 304.

Pour les cinq doigts (For the five fingers)
Marguerite Long related Debussy's comments on this etude: "From the first A-flat the right hand must jest with the left in the swift raising of a finger, bent like a guitar player's: 'a quick pinch,' said Debussy, with an amused glint in his eye…. But finally, in the passage poco a poco accelerando, Debussy asked one to mark with an accent the last note of each group of semiquavers in the crescendo through to the repetition of the theme." DEML 43-44.

Pour les sixtes (For the sixths)
From a letter by Debussy on August 12, 1915 we read, "I have just finished the 8th Étude which will be called 'Pour les Agréments'-*but* not for the pleasure of pianists, the virtuosi will facetiously say. This Étude takes the form of a Barcarolle on an Italian sea…" DEML 41.

Debussy in a letter to Jacques Durand, Pourville, August 28, 1915, writes, "For a long time the continuous use of sixths reminded me of pretentious young ladies sitting in a salon, sulkily doing their tapestry work and envying the scandalous laughter of the naughty ninths…So I wrote this study in which my concern for sixths goes to the length of using no other intervals to build up the harmonies; not bad (Mea culpa….)!" DELE 300.

Work: Images, Book I (1905)

Of the first three melodic notes, Ab, F, and E Marguerite Long recalled, "'A little circle in water,' Debussy used to say, 'with a little pebble falling into it.' 'A little pebble', 'a circle': the real, inestimable water of the Debussyan diamond." DEML 25.

Hommage a Rameau

Oscar Thompson relates that it has been said of this piece that it may "spring from the depths of the soul of the race," and as the extreme of French opinion, Andre Saures has said that "with the 'Sunken Cathedral', 'Hommage a Rameau' is the most beautiful piece for the piano...written since the last three sonatas of Beethoven." Instead of stiffness he sees "grandeur and purity of architecture, gentle majesty of proportions, simplicity of effect, and extreme refinement." DEBM 260.

From Marguerite Long we have, "But this slow and grave dance, in my opinion, is not so much French as 'ancient'. Its rhythm, purely processional, is comparable to a Grecian frieze. 'Play it as if it were an offering,' the master (Debussy) insisted, 'and, as with the "Sarabande," use the metronome.'" DEML 26.

Work: Images, Book II (1907)

Cloches à travers les feuilles

According to Robert Schmitz, "Louis Laloy, who knew Debussy well, writes that he related to him the touching habit of some French villagers, of sounding the church bells (as a knell) unceasingly from All Saints Day until time of the Mass of the Dead on All Souls Day. The nostalgic vibrations of the bells permeating the forests from one village to another, from sunrise to evening, is, according to Louis Laloy's claim, the stimulus of the idea which suggested this composition." DEBS 110.

Et la lune descend sur le temple qui fût

Louis Laloy,[29] who was a Chinese scholar and an authority on Oriental art, was also probably responsible for the title "Et la lune descend sur le temple qui fût," which is a most delicate invocation of a Far Eastern landscape in which, to quote Laloy, "the music...is like a translucid previous stone, born of space and silence." MYER 97.

Poissons d'or

Schmitz notes, "Two sources agree that it [the stimulus for this piece] was a piece of Japanese lacquer owned by Debussy, showing one Goldfish and its reflection in the water...Before performing this work it is important to be

---

29 Louis Laloy (1874-1944) was a musicologist, writer and French sinologist.

convinced that the body of a goldfish is luminous and almost transparent, and that it displaces itself quite rapidly by dashes of rapid timing." DEBS 114-115.

The pianist Maurice Dumesnil, a student of Debussy, relates that Debussy was never satisfied with a performance of this work, always wanting more freedom. He said Debussy demanded "more grace" and "more elegance," yet at the same time wanted the piece played "more simply." Dumesnil recalls that the opening figuration was rarely light enough, that Debussy wanted it to be "almost immaterial, so one could hear 'two clarinets' above." DENI 160.

19th century Japanese painting said to have inspired 'Poissons d'or'

Work: L'isle joyeuse (1904)

Robert Schmitz writes, "It has been suggested that the initial stimulus to its composition might have come from the contemplation of Watteau's painting *The Embarkation for Cythere*: it is indeed imbued with the gaiety, animation, and sensual atmosphere of the Watteau painting... The play of rhythms is relentless, truly Bacchanalian. It is no longer the 'Embarkation for Cythere,' but rather 'The Revelry at Cythere' around the temple of Venus." DEBS 94.

Editor's note: In Greek mythology Cythera was the birthplace of Aphrodite, the goddess of love. It was a land famous for its sensual pleasures, and in the famous painting by Watteau, we view young lovers gathered around a statue of Aphrodite (Venus to the Romans) bedecked with roses for loveliness. The pastoral beauty of the hill leading to the water is complimented by an elegant shell-shaped barge and flying cupids, appearing like puffs of cloud in the sky.

L'Embarquement pour Cythère (1717)
Jean-Antoine Watteau

According to Marguerite Long, "At the beginning the cadenza, in the form of an introduction, was conceived, Debussy said, 'as a summons.'" DEML 31.

Marguerite Long says, "At bar 6, page 3, there is no *forte*. There is no *crescendo-only* a whisper, which is but an inflection. At the foot of the page, at the 3/8, Debussy wished for an extreme *pianissimo*. 'Tut,' he used to say, raising his hands; he never found the *piano* sufficient. Moreover, he himself played with the lid of the piano closed. The radiance of his sonority can only be communicated by talent and technique equal to Debussy's own." DEML 39.

Work: La plus que lente (1910)

Robert Schmitz recalls, "'Let us think of cabarets, let us think also of the numerous 'five o'clocks' where the beautiful feminine listeners of whom I thought meet,' wrote Debussy... It may be that the inspiration came from the New Carlton Hotel, where Debussy went with his wife, Emma, to be charmed by the gypsy fiddling of a violinist named Leoni, to whom the MSS was given by Debussy. A very popular tune in Paris at that time was 'La valse lente', hence the humorous title *La plus que lente* for the present work." DEBS 127.

Work: Masques (1904)

Marguerite Long wrote, "It is perhaps an obsession of mine that I hear the piece *Masques*—a tragedy for piano, one might call it—as a sort of transparency of Debussy's character. As I have said, he was torn with poignant feelings, which he preferred to mask with irony. The title Masque presents an ambiguity [which Debussy] protested with all his might [by saying]: 'It is not the Italian Comedy, but the tragic expression of existence.' After the composer's death his widow found a note in which he expounded this concept of the work. Mme. Debussy communicated its contents to me at once...1904 was, of course, a crucial year for Debussy: the year of *Masques;* of Debussy's captivation by Emma;[30] of Lily's[31] attempted suicide; of the completion of *La Mer.*" DEML 92-93.

Editor's note: Many pianists are unaware that *Masques* can be viewed as a "tragedy for piano." The title itself implies duality, that which is apparent and that which is covered or hidden. Here Debussy's artful deception is in keeping with the French aesthetic so well defined by Poulenc, who in a statement to Roland Gelatt in 1950 said, "You will find sobriety and dolor in French music as well as in German and Russian. But the French have a keener sense of proportion. We realize that sombreness and good humor are not mutually exclusive. Our composers, too, write profound music, but

---

30 Emma Bardac (1862-1934) was the second wife of Debussy, and the cause of the rupture with his first wife, Rosalie Texier. She was an educated and sophisti-cated woman, a brilliant conversationalist, and an accomplished singer. *Masques* was written the year he became captivated by Emma.

31 Marie-Rosalie Texier was a fashion model and the first wife of Debussy. After his affair began with Emma Bardac Texier attempted suicide, shooting herself in the chest with a revolver while standing in the Place de la Concorde. She sur-vived, although the bullet remained lodged in her vertebrae for the rest of her life. The ensuing scandal was to alienate Debussy from many of his friends, whilst Bardac was disowned by her family.

when they do, it is leavened with that lightness of spirit without which life would be unendurable."

Work: Pour Le Piano (1894-1901)
Sarabande
This work bears the following indication of expression at the head of it: "In a Sarabande movement—that is to say with slow serious elegance, rather like an old picture, or a memory of the Louvre, etc." COFP 10-11.

According to Marguerite Long, "Debussy... himself played it, as no one could ever have done, with those marvellous successions of chords sustained by his intense legato. 'To the metronome,' he said one day before I started playing. This shows how solicitous he was that his tempi should remain immutable for all time. It is not easy for us to achieve such precision." COFP 23.

Émile Vuillemoz[32] recalled how Debussy played the "Sarabande" of *Pour le Piano* "with the easy simplicity of a good dancer from the sixteenth century" in a way that "recaptured, bar by bar, the feel of a vanished civilization." AFPM 250.

Work: Preludes Book I (1909-1910)
From Alfred Casella[33] we read, "No words can give an idea of the way in which he played certain of his own *Préludes*. Not that he had actual virtuosity, but his sensibility of touch was incomparable; he made the impression of playing directly on the strings of the instrument with no intermediate mechanism; the effect was a miracle of poetry." DENI 96.

Danseuses de Delphes (Dancers of Delphi)
From Cortot: "They turn and pass, grave and silent, to the slow rhythm of harps, timbrels, and flutes. And in the mysterious shadow of the temple, heavy with the fragrant rising spirals of holy incense, there reposes, invisible but present, the unknown God, wrapped in a tranquil dream, meditating destinies." COFP 23-24.

Louisa Liebich wrote an interesting article in the *Musical Times* of 1918 recollecting her impressions of Debussy's pianism by writing, "On one occasion, after tea, Debussy played his first Prélude, *Les Danseuses de Delphes* to us... I have never heard more beautiful pianoforte playing. I have been

---

32 Émile Vuillemoz (1878-1960) was a French music, film, and drama critic and life-long friend of Ravel.

33 Alfred Casella (1883-1947) was a distinguished Italian, pianist, composer, and conductor.

told that he did not always play to advantage in a concert hall. He said that afternoon that many of the Préludes, especially *Les Danseuses* and *De pas sur la neige* should only be played *entre quatre-z-yeux*. But in the intimacy of his own room it was like hearing a poet recite some of his own delicate lyrics. He had a soft, deep touch which evoked full, rich, many shaded sonorities." DELL 250.

"Voiles" ("Sails")

From Cortot: "Boats lie to anchor in the luminous port. Their sails flutter gently, and on the breeze which stirs them, draw toward the horizon, bright with the setting sun, the flight of a white wing over the caressing sea." COFP 24.

From Marguerite Long we read, "Debussy criticized certain interpretations as being too colourful." DEML 63.

Loosely connecting Debussy's love for Degas with "Voiles," Robert Godet wrote, "The only painter who was constantly on his lips at the time was one whom, we can be sure, he never met: Degas, and even Degas the infrequent painter of pastel landscapes. He fascinated Debussy and at the same time gave an example of discipline to his imaginative promptings." DENI 36.

"Le vent dans la plaine" ("The wind across the plain")

From Cortot: "Furtive and rapid it glides over the cropped grass, stirs the bushes, and the hedges cower before it; now and then in the young glory of the morning, the growing corn bows in a long undulating wave before the onslaught of a fiercer gust." COFP 24.

Les sons et les parfums tournent dans l'air du soir… (The sounds and the perfumes revolving in the evening air…)

From Cortot: "This is the lingering sadness of the dying day, when perfumes wander in the air's caress, and the confused vibrations in the atmosphere are gathered up by the gently advancing night; and—to keep to the meaning of Baudelaire's epigraph—the languishing dizziness in which a heart faints without reason." COFP 24.

The title of this prelude is from the third line of the poem "Harmonie du soir" by Symbolist poet Charles Baudelaire:

Evening Harmony
Now for the hour when swaying on its stem
Each flower swings a censer to the night.
While sounds and perfumes turn in the evening air,
The melancholy waltz begins again.

Each flower swings a censer to the night;
A violin cries out as if in pain-
The melancholy waltz begins again!
The clouds all form an altar in their flight.

A violin cries out as if in pain.
Enough of death and darkness tender heart!
The clouds have formed an altar in their flight;
Drowned in a pool of blood the sun lies slain…

Enough of death and darkness. Tender heart,
Save every ray, of every setting sun
Drowned in a pool of blood the sun lies slain...
Your image shines in me, your acolyte!

DEBA 125.

Les collines d'Anacapri (The hills of Anacapri)
From Cortot: "Movement in the bright morning and a glimpse of the hills around Naples bathed in sunshine; the vivid rhythm of a tarantella unfolding to the caress of a popular refrain, the delicious age-old longing of an amorous melody, mingling intensely with the reflections of too blue a sky, jarring against the persistent and piercing note of a flute." COFP 24.

Des pas sur la neige (Footprints in the snow)
From Cortot: "Over the sad frozen background of a winter landscape which Debussy summons up in sound before us, footprints linger still when the absent friend has gone, each one sadly awaking the memory of joy no more." COFP 24.

The Editor cannot resist adding his own contribution from a never to be forgotten experience with Russian cinema and "de pas sur la niege." During my graduate studies at the Peabody Institute, I went to a Film Festival on the Johns Hopkins campus to watch a fairly recent Russian film one night. I remember neither the title of the film, or much of the plot, other than that the film was black and white, and that it took place in Moscow during WWII. There was one scene, however, which left a lasting and vivid impression. A messenger delivering a telegram knocked on the door of a poor and common apartment, and was answered by a care-worn middle-aged woman. The telegram communicated her young son's death on the German front. After reading it alone, the woman showed no expression on her face, but simply put on her boots, donned a headscarf and winter coat, and walked slowly down the stairs to the street in utter silence. The scene was abandoned and covered with snow. As she walked in silence through a park the camera followed her from behind so we were unable to know if she was staring numbly into space, weeping, or stoically walking forward. As the camera followed her from behind in the austere black and white Russian winter, the music of 'des pas sur la neige' subtly entered the soundtrack.

We followed her through the park from behind through the entire prelude. Heart breaking, without being able to cry…

Ce qu'a vu le vent d'ouest (*What the West Wind saw*)
From Cortot: "Through the livid gleam of the dawn, or in the night's terror, is hurled the vision of the tempest; and amidst the roar of the unchained sea, cries of agony are thrown back by the waves." COFP 25.

La fille aux cheveux de lin (*The girl with the flaxen hair*)
From Cortot: "A tender paraphrase of the Scottish song of Leconte de Lisle, singing the charm and sweetness of his distant love, 'sitting all among the flowering heather.'" COFP 25.

The original poem by Leconte de Lisle follows in translation by Siglind Bruhn:

> Sitting amidst the alfalfa in flower
> Who sings from the cool morning hour?
> It is the girl with the flaxen hair,
> The beauty with cherry lips so fair.
> Love, in the summer sun so bright,
> Sang with the lark for sheer delight.
>
> Your mouth has colors so divine,
> It tempts a kiss, o, were it mine!
> Come chat with me in the flow'ring grass,
> Girl with the long lashes, the silken tress.
> Love, in the summer sun so bright,
> Sang with the lark for sheer delight.
>
> Do not say no, o cruel girl!
> Do not say yes! Far better still
> To read your large eye's longing gaze,
> Your rosy lips which I so praise!
> Love, in the summer sun so bright,
> Sang with the lark for sheer delight.
>
> Farewell to deer, farewell to hare
> And to red partridges, I shall dare

A kiss of your crimson lips to steal,
Your flaxen locks to caress and feel!
Love, in the summer sun so bright,
Sang with the lark for sheer delight.

DESB 167.

La sérénade interrompue (*The interrupted serenade*)

From Cortot: "A mocking nocturnal fantasy in the manner of Goya, expressing the diffident passion of a 'Novio', his love songs under a closed window, his timid, peevish agitation at an unexpected sound, or at the passing of a noisy band of students in a street nearby; heard above a swaying sinewy strumming of guitars, in a rhythm that throbs already through the pages of Iberia." COFP 25.

Marguerite Long writes that of the serenade, "Poor fellow," said Debussy. "He keeps on being interrupted!" DEML 65.

La cathédrale engloutie (*The Sunken Cathedral*)

From Cortot: "An old Breton tale goes that once in a while in the clear morning light, when the sea is transparent, the cathedral of Ys, slumbering in its enchanted sleep under the waves, rises from the depths of the ocean and of antique time. The bells chime slowly, we hear the priests solemnly intoning, and the illusion sinks again below the rocking sea." COFP 25.

Le danse de Puck (*Puck's Dance*)

From Cortot: "In whimsical swiftness and airy mockery, this quicksilver spirit from Shakespeare flits about in play, vanishing and reappearing, amusing himself by teasing some country bumpkin, or tormenting a pair of lovers--then in a flash is gone." COFP 26.

Minstrels

From Cortot: "This is a witty and jocular picture of the atmosphere of the English music hall. Clowns appear and tumble on the stage in clumsy attitudes, and gusts of sensuous music suggest the idle pleasure of an evening's amusement." COFP 26.

Work: Preludes Book II (1912-1913)

Brouillards (*Mist*)

From Cortot: "A mist of tone hanging in confused tonalities, superimposed on the minor second, gives a supernatural phantom-like quality to the melodic line, which tries to disentangle itself from it. Luminous moments now and then gleam like lighthouse flashes at once swallowed up in the fog, vanishing to leave us wandering more and more uncertainly in the mist." COFP 26-27.

Feuilles mortes (*Dead leaves*)

From Cortot: "Dead leaves flutter and softly gyrate, dropping silently onto the ground; the sad splendor of an autumnal sunset seems to bear within it all the emotion of a long and wistful farewell." COFP 27.

La puerta del Vino

From Cortot: "Here is a brilliantly colored picture of a noisy quarter in a Spanish town; a low tavern where mule drivers loiter, shouting strident songs, and beating with their hands to goad on the sinewy writhings of a black haired dancing girl." COFP 27.

Actually we owe the inception of this astonishing piece to a postcard which Manual de Falla sent to Debussy of the famous gate at Granada known by that name. Debussy was so struck by the contrast of light and shade that he decided on the spot to describe it in music, with the remark: "I shall make something of that." COFP 27.

Les fées sont d'exquises danseuses (*Fairies are exquisite dancers*)

From Cortot: "Expressed is the exquisite flash of gossamer virtuosity. Ethereal forms flit by in the darting play of shadows, flames dance and smoke rises in billowing wreaths, dissolving under the caress of the air and the joy of light." COFP 27.

Paul Robert tells us, "The title is a...borrowing from an illustration by Arthur Rackham. Debussy was very fond of Rackham's work and no doubt *Ondine* and *Danse de Puck* were influenced by Rackham's illustrations of the same subjects." DEPR 228-229.

Bruyère (*Heather*)

From Cortot: "The intimate woodland romance of undergrowth where the penetrating perfume of the earth mingles with the flecks of sunlight through the purple heather." COFP 27.

Fairy's Tightrope
Arthur Rackham

'Général Lavine'--eccentric

From Cortot: "Here is all the incisive irony and verve of a Toulouse-Lautrec. It is the same old puppet that one has seen so often at the Folies-Bergere, with his coat several sizes too large and his mouth like a gaping scar, cleft by the set beatific smile. And above all the clumsiness of his gait, punctuated by the carefully stage-managed mishaps, and suddenly ended, like a released spring, by an amazing pirouette." COFP 27-28

Marguerite Long relates having a conversation with Debussy about *Images* when suddenly changing the subject he said: "Tomorrow we must work at General Lavine [Douze Preludes II, no. r6]. That 'wooden man' was a genius. He was musical." DEML 4.

Of this prelude Marguerite Long wrote, "We have already spoken of this portrait of the clown from Medrano's Circus, who entertained and was so much admired by Debussy. 'He was wooden,' the composer would repeat, to emphasize that mechanical rigidity he wanted, as much for the initial group of demi-semiquavers as for the chords in the middle section portraying the balancing act of the equilibrist." DEML 69.

La terresse des audiences du clair de lune (Translation)

From Cortot: "Under this slightly cryptic title, whose ceremonious charm is rather like the flowery grace of certain Chinese legends, we have one of the most deeply musical and exquisitely expressive works that Debussy ever wrote. The first two or three notes of the popular tune 'Au clair de la lune' are etherealized by a delicate harmony of sevenths, on which in a slow chromatic progression shafts of moonlight seem to fall, steeped in all the passionate unrest of the scented night and its sensuous delights." COFP 28.

From Robert Schmitz we read,

> The exact origin of the poetic, esoteric, and tortuous title… is variously ascribed to originating in Pierre Loti's *L'Inde Sous les Anglais*, in which he describes the terraces to hold counsel in moonlight… and to Rene Puaux…who in a letter written to a newspaper, while describing the ceremonies for the coronation of King George V, as Emperor of India, speaks of, 'the hall of victory, the hall of pleasure, the garden of the sultanesses, the terrace for moonlight audiences.'
>
> Both origins would suggest a Hindu scene… Is it not likely that this charming phrase captivated Debussy's sensitive imagination…? A daydream which has meandered far from its inception in reality invests the moonlit scene with innumerable sentiments: tenderness, cold loneliness, passionate unrest, delight and sensuous languor, but all permeated by an evanescence, a sense of unreality with which moonlight endows all that it touches. DEBS 175-176.

Leon Vallas tells us, "[T]he spur for this strange and beautiful creation was an article in the journal *Le temps* in December 1912, one of several dispatches from its correspondence in India entitled *Lettres des Indes*. The article descried, in highly moving and evocative language, the ceremony for the coronation of the English king, George V, as Emperor of India. Leon Vallas tells us that Debussy was struck by the phrase *la salle de la victoire, la salle du plaisir, le jardin des sultanes, la terrasse des audiences au clair de lune*- the hall of victory, the hall of pleasure, the garden of the sultans, the terrace for moonlight audiences." DEVA 209.

Ondine

From Cortot: "For those who know how to see her, she rises to the waist in shy nudity, from the calm sparkle of the waves that rock her. And for those who can remember how tender and alluring she is with her murmuring voice telling of the treasures and sea palaces beneath the waves and the sweetness of her love." COFP 28.

Hommage à S. Pickwick, Esq. P.P.M.D.C.

From Cortot: "It is quite impossible to conceive of a wittier musical expression than this, not only of Dickens's hero, but also of Dickens's own style. It is his own ironic good humor, his genial wit; every bar of this piece finds its mark, from the comic use of God Save the Queen to the snatches of whistling in the last page, passing through all the variations of absent-minded seriousness, diffidence and complacency that make up the humorous figure which is Samuel Pickwick, Esq." COFP 29.

One can visualize Pickwick's house, which according to Debussy had "here and there souvenirs of Zululand, views of Christiania, terrible rifles (which, happily, do not shoot anyone), family portraits, a peaceful garden." DEBE 182.

Canope

From Cortot: "The quiet thoughtful lines of this piece have the same nobility and restraint as the antique funerary urn they serve to symbolize. And this sad, tender chant, sung as if by a wailing flute, tells the inextinguishable love of the adolescent spirit whose secret torment sleeps here in these grey ashes, in a slumber that never forgets." COFP 29.

Les Tierces alternées (Alternate thirds)

From Cortot: "The technical manner, a legacy from the clavecinists, which is the germ of this fantasy, has been used by Debussy with charming ingenuity. In his hands it is not only the excuse for the play of musical style, but evokes a silky feline grace which in its turn forms the style. He plays with this round interval of a third as a cat plays with a ball, making it bounce and dashing after it into a corner, and then bringing it into play again with a swift little pat of his paw, after a moment of seeming indifference." COFP 29.

Feux d'artifice (Fireworks)

From Cortot: "This last Prelude is an enchantment with magical virtuosity. Curling smoke from Bengal lights shows an occasional splutter of sparks, rockets crackle and rise in a great parabola of stars, Catherine wheels spin and multi-colored bouquets of light burst into brilliance, and the night is full of sparkling color. All the enchantment of the scene is portrayed in the music, and with the painter's trick for giving his picture a touch of character, Debussy slips in a note or two of the Marseillaise in the last two or three bars, evoking the rowdy romance of the dusty evenings of the Fourteenth of July." COFP 28-29.

Work: Sonata for Cello and Piano (1915)

Leon Vallas tells us that "Debussy thought of calling his Sonata for Cello and Piano of 1915 *Pierrot fâché avec la lune*—Pierrot Raging at the Moon—perhaps manifesting a desire to give a bit of backbone to this wilting figure of Italian Comedy." DEPR 92.

Chapter 8
Fauré

Work: Ballade, Op. 19 (1879)

Joseph de Marliave,[34] in his remarkable Études Musicales, tells us this work was written "after an impression of the forest scene in *Siegfried*." COFP 117.

Editor's note: The Forest scene referred to above, and often called "Forest Murmurs," takes place in Act II of Wagner's *Siegfried*. The peaceful beauty of the forest enchants Siegfried. He listens to the song of a bird, who tells him of a beautiful woman named Brünnhilde, asleep on a mountain encircled by a ring of magic fire. Only one who has no fear can pass through the flames and awaken her from sleep. Siegfried immediately sets out to find her. The beauty of this scene left an enchanting impression on Fauré.

Marguerite Long writes, "Ravel said to me, after a rehearsal: 'Ah, its lovely, the *Ballade*, it is really delightful. I am unfair to Fauré's music in so far as I don't know it very well. When we get back, you'll have to play me lots of it.'" FAML 38.

Debussy likened Fauré's *Ballade* to "a pretty woman adjusting her shoulder strap." LIVE 83.

---

34 Joseph de Marliave (1873-1914) was a French musicologist, great friend and admirer of Fauré, and the husband of Marguerite Long, one of the foremost French pianists of the early twentieth century. He was a captain in the French army and killed in the first month, August 1914, of World War I. As one of the fallen victims of the war Ravel dedicated the 'Toccata' from Le Tombeau de Couperin to him.

Work: Barcarolle in F-sharp minor, Op. 66 (1894)

From Marguerite Long: "The glorious *Fifth Barcarolle*, alive and powerful, smells of salt, of sea-wind and breathes a vigorous and wholesome joy. One can hear the cries of sailors, and its melody has the pace of a fishing-boat riding on the waves which comes back to square and dashes off, its sails billowing. Here I feel, like Baudelaire: 'Music often takes hold of me like the sea.'" FAML 77.

Alfred Cortot wrote, "The *Fifth Barcarolle*, Op. 66 (1894) is to the other *Barcarolles* what the sixth *Nocturne* is to the other *Nocturnes;* it dominates the others by a similar emotional concentration. No longer is it the quiet vision of dreaming canals in a soft Venetian distance where a gondola glides silently by and emotion is slender and evanescent. This great wind swells the harmonies like flying sails on the open sea. The wild free passion of Anthony and Cleopatra is awakened by these powerful rhythms and it is the keep or their splendid bark that we glimpse against the distant luminous splendor of the West!" COFP 128.

Work: Dolly Suite (1893-96)

From Marguerite Long we read,

> Composed between 1893 and 1896, *Dolly* owes its title to the Christian name of the daughter of my friend Madame Bardac. Dolly, who now is Madame de Tinan, was then a little blonde girl of charming behavior and feminine precocity. The music which Fauré wrote for her is quite in her image. It is the only time that the composer used titles other than those of a musical genre. The album consists of six pieces: in the Berceuse one can perceive the musician's feelings in front of such childlike grace. Miau is not, as Emile Vuillermoz wrote, the name of the household cat that used to jump about mischievously, but the nickname that young Dolly gave to her brother Raoul Bardac, who was later himself a pupil of Fauré and Debussy. Le Jardin de Dolly is the garden in an enchanted dream, full of perfumed flowers, while Kitty-Valse illustrates the whirling leaps of a favourite dog. Tendresse makes clear its meaning in its delicate figurations. Finally the Pas Espagnol is the transposition in music of the bronze equestrian status of Frémiet, Fauré's father-in-law, which stood on a mantlepiece in Madame Bardac's house and which was much admired by young Dolly. FAML 96-97.

Work: Impromptu in A-flat major, Op. 34 (1883)

Marguerite Long has said, "It is built on two themes: the first, lively and supple, rests on a voluble bass line played with childlike dash. The more sensitive argument of the other theme is enlivened with tender and urgent

feelings entrusted to the left hand alone, 'like a memory', Fauré used to say."
FAML 92.

Work: Nocturne in E-flat major, Op. 33, no. 1 (1875)

From Marguerite Long we read, "Right from the beginning of the *First Nocturne* we enter a world of pure emotion, of quiet confidence and passionate ardour, of tenderness and poetry. Dark and profound, with rays of hope which are extinguished and outbursts of beauty, which fall back again. The piece ends with a heart-rending cry that calls to mind the Lament of the Sinner. On the second page Fauré indicated a change of speed to me for, given the agitated nature of the bass line, he wanted a more rapid tempo up to the return of the first subject. It also requires that care be given to the sound when the first subject is re-introduced in octaves (as Fauré said), 'like the silhouette of a shadow.'" FAML 81.

Work: Nocturne in B major, Op. 33, no. 2

From a letter by Camille Saint-Saëns to Faure, (Paris) Sunday, 23 January 1887: "And I'm grinding away at your pieces again; this time I'm getting somewhere. The more I look at them the more I love them. Especially the *Nocturne in B major*, which I find absolutely entrancing. I shall ask you for a lesson sometime." Commenting on this letter says, author J Barrie Jones commented, "The B major was to remain one of Saint-Saëns' favourite works of Fauré." FALE 103.

Work: Nocturne in D-flat major, Op. 63 (1894)

From Marguerite Long: "The *Sixth Nocturne*... is pervaded by an atmosphere of intimate meditation... It is one of Fauré's most beautiful inspirations. From it arises a 'song of great softness', hesitant and troubled at first, then more anguished. It rejoins the second part of the initial theme which brings back the delightful calm." FAML 85.

From Alfred Cortot we read, "From the first note of the fine exposition something in us grows warm and tender as we listen, as though this song, laden with contemplation and thought, were confiding to us a secret of a sadness never expressed before. Then, timid and hesitant, though full of latent passion, a second theme creeps in, grows bolder and finally breaks out in an outburst of grief." COFP 127-128.

Work: Piano Quartet No. 2, Op. 45 (1885-86)

From Marguerite Long,

> Fauré was too secretive about the sources of his inspiration for us to value his rare confidences as anything but priceless. (Says Faure) "It was not just in the Andante of the *Second Quartet* [composed in 1886]

that I remembered having translated (almost involuntarily) the distant memory of bells in the evening at Montgauzy—and this is some time ago—came to us from a village called Cadirac when the wind blew from the west. From this dull sound a vague dreaminess arose which, like all vague dreams, is literally untranslatable. Only, does it not happen often that some exterior fact numbs us so that our thoughts become so imprecise that in reality they are not thoughts, and yet are nevertheless something in which we can take pleasure? The desire for things which do not exist perhaps, and this is indeed where music holds sway." FAML 107.

Work: Thème et variations, Op. 73 (1895)

From Marguerite Long we read about the theme, "'It is like an Étude,' Fauré said, a little paradoxically. We can interpret that through a great simplicity in the exposition with a rigorous precision of the beat." FAML 97.

From Alfred Cortot, "The theme has five phrases, alternating regularly, of contrasting timbres, and creates a seriousness like a Greek frieze where weeping maidens, drawn by the rhythm of an inexorable fate, stand in sorrowful tears." COFP 129.

Elsewhere Cortot says of the same work, "[T]he theme of Fauré's *Variations* is charged with a sense of doom, which persists in the first variation, in which a shadow seems to brood over a graveyard." COMI 262.

Yvonne Lefébure recalled Fauré complaining that "for his taste the slower tempi [in his music] including the theme of the *Variations*—were always taken too slow." AFPM 271-272.

Work: Valse Caprices

Roy Howat writes, "Fauré's own tenderness for them [*Valse Caprices*] emerges from a letter he wrote in 1919, years after their composition, to one of his favourite pianists, Robert Lortat, 'May I ask you—how tedious composers are! —o take the opening theme of each of the *Valses-caprices* more slowly? The justification, as I see it, of the title *Valses-caprices*, is variety of tempo. They're always played too fast and too uniformly fast.'" AFPM 253.

Chapter 9
Granados

General Observations:

In his diary, Granados recounts an evening in Paris when he, Malats,[35] and Albéniz (in Paris on a concert tour) stayed up one night copying out a concerto by Bériot in order for Granados to take it back to Spain with him. They finally finished their labor, exhausted but exultant, at five in the morning. After a breakfast of ham, cheese, and wine, Granados began drifting off to sleep enchanted by the song of a nightingale. The bird assumed sentimental importance to him after that, and its song would "always resonate in my soul." GRVI 70.

Work: Cuentos de la juventad (Tales of Youth), Op. 1 (1906)

Walter Clark writes, "This work was inspired by a tune his son Eduardo used to sing and that Granados liked and used; it appears as a musical epigram at the top of the printed score. We do not know its date of composition or exactly when it was first published." GRAN 61.

Work: Escenas poéticas (Poetic Scenes) (1912)
Suenos del poeta (*Dream of the Poet*)

This piece is preceded by an unsigned poem, probably by Granados himself. For at the time he was composing his Poetic Scenes he was involved romantically with his student, Clotilde Godó, and the scene described in the poem strongly resembles the garden of her Tiana residence near Barcelona, luxuriant with cypresses and roses. Whom the "muse" represents is not difficult to gather if indeed this is the little verse's encrypted message:

---

35 Joaquím Malats (1872-1912) was a Catalan pianist and composer.

> In the garden of cypresses and roses
> Leaning against a pedestal of white marble
> And awaiting his hour,
> The poet slumbered...
> At his side, caressing his brow,
> The muse maintained her vigil.

GRAN 64.

Work: Goyescas o Los Majos enamorados, Op. 11 (1911) (Goyescas or the Gallants in Love)

Editor's note: *Goyescas* is Grandados' crowning pianistic achievement, and the characters and images in *Goyescas* may be better understood when compared with parallel scenes from the 1915 opera, *Goyescas*. The opera and the piano work are based on a series of paintings from Francisco Goya's early career, inspired by the stereotypical young men and women known as majos and majas, who were known for their bohemian and streetwise attitude and love of fine clothes and romance.

All pieces from the piano suite *Goyescas*, with the exception of *Epílogo: Serenata del spectro*, were included in the 1915 opera. The plot involves two couples, the aristocrats Rosario and Fernando, and the commoners Pepa and Pacquito. At a gathering Pacquito the bullfighter makes amorous advances toward Rosario which, while they are rejected, inflames her other suitor, the captain Fernando, with jealousy. During a clash at a dance party Fernando is challenged to a duel by Pacquito. Fernando is mortally wounded and dies in the arms of Rosario. Perhaps helpful interpretive imagery can be gleaned for the pieces in the piano suite by noting their place in the action of the 1915 opera.

Granados writes to Joaquím Malats in a letter of August 31, 1910, "This summer I have finished a collection of *Goyescas*, works of great flights of imagination and difficulty." GRAN 121.

Granados clarified his intentions in writing *Goyescas* when he wrote, "I should like to give a personal note in *Goyescas*, a mixture of bitterness and grace, and I desire that neither of these two phases should predominate over the other in an atmosphere of delicate poetry. Great melodic value and such a rhythm that it often completely absorbs the music. Rhythm, color, and life distinctly Spanish; the note of sentiment as suddenly amorous and passionate as it is dramatic and tragic, as it appears in all of Goya's work." GRAN 123.

In a letter to Malats on December 11, 1910, Granados wrote, "I have concentrated my entire personality in Goyescas. I fell in love with the psychology of Goya and his palette; with his lady-like Maja; his aristocratic Majo; with him and the Duchess of Alba, his quarrel, his loves and flatteries. That rosy whiteness of the cheeks contrasted with lace and black velvet with jet, those supple-waisted figures with mother-of-pearl and jasmine-like hands resting on black tissues have dazzled me." GRAN 123.

Los requiebros (*The Flirtations*)

Editor's note: This piece was inserted in the first tableau of the opera in which the *majos* and *majas* are flirting and dancing with each other, prior to the meeting of Rosario and Pacquito.

Walter Clark writes of this piece, "*Los requiebros* was inspired by the fifth of Goya's *Caprichos, Tal para cual* (Two of a Kind). Goya sketched this while visiting the Andalusian estate of the thirteenth Duchess of Alba, in Saluncár de Barrameda, sometime during 1796-97.

Granados attached so much importance to this sketch that it was used as the cover illustration for the first edition of *Goyescas*." GRAN 125.

Capricho Nº 5: *Tal para cual* (*Two of a kind*)
Francisco Goya

In *Los requiebros* Granados quotes a song, a tonadilla popular in the eighteenth century whose verses are as follows:

> With the trípili, trípili, trápala
> One sings and dances the Tirana.
> Go ahead, girl!
> I graciously conceded
> That you are stealing my spirit.

GRAN 125.

Coloquio en la reja (Dialogue at the Window)

This work appeared in the third tableau of the opera, in which Rosario and Fernando share a loving moment, Rosario pleading with her husband not to go off to duel with Pacquito. – *Editor*.

Walter Clark writes, "It would be difficult to understand this movement without making reference to Granados's own drawing of the subject in the *Apuntes*.[36] The conversation between the majo and his *maja* lover takes place through the screen, which barely separates them. This slight partition intensifies their passion (in the opera this scene is entitled "Duo de amor en la reja"). Significantly, however, the *majo's* back is facing us, the viewer. This conversation is very private, and we can only "hear" the murmurings and whisperings of endearment passing between the two. This explains the intimate and withdrawn character of the opening. As the movement develops, it becomes more passionate." GRAN 131.

El fandango de candil (The Fandango by Candlelight)

Editor's note: The second tableau of the opera opens and concludes with a magnificent ballroom scene for which this fandango is danced.

Salvador Miguel writes, "The common interpretation of this title is a fandango done by candlelight. The 'baile de candil' was a popular Spanish custom — a celebration held at someone's home in which dancing by candle light was accompanied by guitars and other string instruments. In an early sketch for the opera *Goyescas* Granados centers the second tableau around "El fandango de candil": 'Reunion of majos, chisperos, etc., in a small theater or room of classic styles,' as described by the eighteenth century neoclassical Spanish dramatist Ramón de la Cruz." GRSA 84.

---

36 The *Apuntes* to which Mr. Clark refers is a little book, now in the Pierpont Morgan Library, consisting of musical and artistic sketches penned by Granados during the early 1900's. These drawings and musical fragments became seminal ideas for *The Tonadillas, Los Ovillejos*, and *Goyescas*. GRAN 122

Quesjas o La Maja y el Ruiseñor (*Complaints or The Maiden and the Nightingale*)

Editor's note: This piece is used at the beginning of the third and final tableau of the opera. Rosario sits on a bench in the palace garden, listening to the sad song of a nightingale under the light of the moon. Her impassioned outpouring mirrors her worry about the impending doom of the duel. The text of the aria follows:

> Why does the nightingale pour out his ravishing song in the darkness?
> Does he have a grievance against the king, and try to revenge himself
> in this way? See how deeply he holds his pain within him, and hopes to
> find relief in the depths of the night, Sadly singing his love song!
> Somewhere perhaps there is a rose blushing with modesty at her
> thoughts of love, a slave, enchanted by his song! How mysterious is
> the melody which flows in the darkness of the night. Ah! Loves are
> like flowers at the mercy of the sea. Beloved! I cannot sing without
> love. Ah! - it is you who sings in praise of love, oh Nightingale!

Granados paid a surprise visit to Albeniz in 1909 during the last weeks of his life in Cambo-les-Bains. Granados entertained his dying friend, who was more like a father to him than a colleague, with renditions of his own compositions, including "La maja y el ruiseñor" and the lovely "Intermedio" from *Goyescas*. GRAN 265.

Alicia De Larrocha has said of this piece that it is "the most tender... and at the same time the most intensely passionate" music Granados ever wrote. GRRO 21-23.

Walter Clark writes that "The principal theme of this movement is a Valencian folk melody Granados evidently heard sung by a young girl in the countryside during one of his trips to that province... In the song's lyrics, a girl tells of hearing the sorrowful song of a little bird in her garden." GRAN 134.

Granados instructs us to play this piece "with the jealousy of a wife and not the sadness of a widow." Walter Clark comments, "His dedication of this work to Amparo [his wife] takes on significance in light of the affair he was carrying on with Clotilde Godó at the time he wrote this. No doubt Amaro would have complained bitterly about his infidelities." GRAN 135.

El amor y la muerte (*Love and Death*)

This work is used in the final tableau of the opera after Fernando has been mortally wounded in the duel and dies in Rosario's arms. – *Editor*.

Walter Clark writes, *"El amor y la muerte* was inspired by the tenth of Goya's *Caprichos*, of the same title. The etching depicts a young woman holding in her arms her dying lover, a look of terror and dismay on her face as he breathes his last." GRAN 135.

Epílogo: Serenata del espectro (Epilogue: Serenade of the Ghost)
Walter Clark writes, "In this concluding movement the spirit of the departing *majo* appears in a macabre vision, serenading his beloved with his ghostly guitar. This is the only movement of *Goyescas* which Granados did not include in his opera of the same name." GRAN 137.

Work: El pelele (Escena goyesca) The Straw Man (1913)
This work does not appear in the *Goyescas* piano suite but opens the first tableau of the opera. Alicia de Larocha has pointed out, "Inspired motivation, wide rolling phrases embroidered with arabesques and ornaments, the evident consequences of a dedicated reviewer and interpreter of the works of Scarlatti, enrich these pages, in which he describes the underworld of the *majas* and *chisperos* of Madrid." GRAN 23.

A *pelele* was a life-size straw man that young women enjoyed tossing up in the air, using a blanket that they held at the corners as a kind of trampoline. Goya portrayed the scene unforgettably in one of his tapestry cartoons, and this inspired Granados to capture the spirit of the game in his music. Granados opened his opera with this piece and it has been suggested that tossing the *pelele* into the air suggests that a man enamored of a woman (Fernando) is little more than a *pelele*. GRAN 139, 144.

Chapter 10
Liszt

Work: Années de pèlerinage Première année: Suisse (1848-1855)
Chapelle de Guillaume Tell (*William Tell's Chapel*)
In the *Chapelle de Guillaume Tell* the Swiss struggle for liberation is recalled and Schiller's motto "One for all – and all for one" heads the piece.

Au lac de Wallenstadt (*At Lake Wallenstadt*)
Liszt's caption is from Byron's *Childe Harold's Pilgrimage* (Canto 3 LXVIII - CV):

> "….Thy contrasted lake
> With the wild world I dwell in, is a thing
> Which warns me, with its stillness, to forsake
> Earth's troubled waters for a purer spring."

In her *Mémoires*, Liszt's mistress and traveling companion of the time, Marie d'Agoult, recalls their time by Lake Wallenstadt, writing, "Franz wrote for me there a melancholy harmony, imitative of the sigh of the waves and the cadence of oars, which I have never been able to hear without weeping." LISW 244.

Au Bord d'une source (*Beside a Spring*)
Au Bord d'une source is prefaced with a quotation from Schiller: "In murmuring coolness the play of young nature begins." LIS1 217.

Orage (*Storm*)
Liszt's caption is from Byron's *Childe Harold's Pilgrimage* (Canto 3 LXVIII – CV):

> "But where of ye, O tempests! is the goal?
> Are ye like those within the human breast?
> Or do ye find, at length, like eagles, some high nest?"

LISF 22.

Vallée d'Obermann (Obermann's Valley)

Inspired by Senancour's novel of the same title, set in Switzerland, with a hero overwhelmed and confused by nature, suffering from ennui and longing, finally concluding that only our feelings are true. The captions include one from Byron's *Childe Harold's Pilgrimage*:

> "Could I embody and unbosom now that which is most within me,
> could I wreak my thoughts upon expression, and thus throw
> soul--heart--mind--passions--feelings--strong or weak
> all that I would have sought, and all I seek, bear, know, feel
> and yet breathe into one word, and that one word were lightning,
> I would speak; But as it is, I live and die unheard,
> with a most voiceless thought, sheathing it as a sword."
> and two from Senancour's *Obermann*, which include the crucial questions,
> "What do I want? Who am I? What do I ask of nature?"

LISF 32.

Egloque (Eclogue)

Liszt's caption is from Byron's *Childe Harold's Pilgrimage* (Canto 3 LXVIII):

> "The morn is up again, the dewy morn,
> With breath all incense, and with cheek all bloom,
> Laughing the clouds away with playful scorn,
> And living as if earth contained no tomb!"

LISF 48.

Le mal du pays (Homesickness)

In this work Liszt introduces a "Ranz des Vaches" to depict unspoiled country scenes and hidden sanctuaries which, as Liszt remarks in a footnote, are the last refuge of a free and simple mind. LISF 53.

Editor's note: A "Ranz de vaches" is a simple melody traditionally played on the horn by the Swiss Alpine herdsmen as they drove their cattle to or from the pasture.

Les cloches de Genève: Nocturne (The Bells of Geneva: Nocturne)
Alan Walker writes, "Perhaps the most topical piece in the collection, an evocative testimonial to Liszt's stay in Geneva, is "Les cloches de Genève," which the composer dedicated to his daughter Blandine in commemoration of her birth in that city. It bears a quotation from Byron's *Childe Harold*:

> "I live not in myself, but I become
> Portion of that around me."

The opening page attempts to capture distant churchbells drifting across the Swiss valleys. At one point we hear a bell strike ten, perhaps in symbolic depiction of the hour of Blandine's birth." LIS1 218-219.

Work: Années de pèlerinage Deuxième année: Italie (1839-1849)
Sposalizio (Marriage of the Virgin, after the painting by Raphael)
Il Penseroso (The Thinker, a statue by Michelangelo)
Liszt requested that "Sposalizio" and "Il penseroso" both be illustrated with drawings by Kretschmer of the Raphael painting and Michelangelo sculpture on the inner title page, as if to emphasize their origins in these masterpieces of Italian art. LIS1 274.

Sposalizio
Raffaello Sanzio da Urbino

The story of the painting describes the Marriage of the Virgin Mary, as recounted in Jacobus de Voraigne's thirteenth-century *Legenda Aurea*: "Anon came a voice out of the oracle and said that, all they that were of the house of David that were convenable to be married and had no wife, that each of them should bring a rod to the altar, and his rod that flourished, and, after the saying of Isaiah, the Holy Ghost sit in the form of a dove on it, he should be the man that should be desponsate and married to the Virgin Mary... Joseph by the commandment of the bishop brought forth his rod, and anon it flowered, and a dove descended from heaven thereupon." (Translation by William Caxton.) LISV.

Il Penseroso
Michelangelo di Lodovico Buonarroti Simoni

These lines of Michaelangelo preface the score of "Il Penseroso":

"I am thankful to sleep, and even more that I am made of stone,
while injustice and shame still exist.
My great fortune is not to see, not to feel;
so do not wake me- speak softly."

LISW 245.

Canzonetta del Salvator Rosa
This robust and carefree marching song is based on a poem ascribed to
the seventeenth-century painter and adventurer Salvator Rosa, and is based
on a tune by Giovanni Bononcini (1760-1747). The text of the poem is:

Often I change my location
But I shall never change my desire.
The fire within me will always be the same
And I myself will also always be the same.

LISV

Petrarch Sonnets

Editor's note: *Petrarch Sonnets* are three of Liszt's most hauntingly beautiful creations. These love poems by Francesco Petrarca (1304-1374) expressed his love for a lady named Laura. Already a married woman when Petrarch first met her, she represented the unattainable ideal of womanhood.

Sonetto 47 del Petrarca 'Benedetto sia 'l giorno' (Blest be the Day)

Blest be the year, the month, the hour, and the day,
The season and the time, the point of space,
And blest the beauteous country and the place
Where first of two bright eyes I felt the sway:
Blest the sweet pain of which I was the prey,
When newly doomed Love's sovereign law to embrace,
And blest the bow and shaft to which I trace
The wound that to my inmost breast found way:
Blest be the ceaseless accents of my tongue,
Unwearied breathing my loved lady's name:
Blest my fond wishes, sighs, and teas, and pains:
Blest be the lays in which her praise I sung,
That on all sides acquired to her fair fame;
And blest my thoughts! For o'er them all she reigns.

(translation by Dacre)

Sonetto 104 del Petrarca 'Pace non trovo' (Peace not Found)

Warfare I cannot wage, yet know not peace;
I fear, I hope, I burn, I freeze again;
Mount to the skies, then bow to earth my face;
Grasp the whole world, yet nothing can obtain.
His prisoner Love nor frees, nor will detain;
He slays me not, not yet will he unchain;
No joy allows, nor lets my sorrow cease.
Sightless, I see my fair; though mute, I mourn;
I scorn existence, and yet court its stay:
Detest myself, and for another burn;
By grief I'm nurtured; and though tearful, gay;
Death I despise, and life alike I hate:
Such, lady, dost make my wayward state!

(translation by Nott)

Sonetto 123 del Petrarca 'I' vidi in terra' (I Beheld on Earth)
Yes, I beheld on earth angelic grace,
And charms divine which mortals rarely see,

Such as both glad and pain the memory;
Vain, light, unreal is all else I trace:
Tears I saw showered from those fine eyes apace,
Of which the sun oftimes might envious be;
Accents I heard sighed forth so movingly,
As to stay floods, or mountains to displace.
Love and good sense, firmness, with pity join'd
And wailful grief, a sweeter concert made
Than ever yet was poured on human ear:
And heaven unto the music so inclined
That not a leaf was seen to stir the shade,
Such melody had fraught the winds, the atmosphere.
(translation by Nott)

LIPT

Après une lecture de Dante: Fantasia Quasi Sonata (After Reading Dante:
Fantasia Quasi Sonata)

Alan Walker writes of the Dante Sonata that, "Inspired by Dante's
Divine Comedy, Liszt set out to encompass in music that world of' 'strange
tongues, horrible cries, words of pain, and tones of anger' which Dante
describes in his Inferno…. The introduction begins with a musical portrayal
of hell evoked by a descending series of tritones ('Abandon hope all ye who
enter'), that timeless symbol of the Devil which musicians still call diabolus
in musica." LIS2 275-276.

Editor's note: Liszt borrowed his title from the following poem by
Victor Hugo, which may have contributed to his personal inspiration when
composing the *Dante Sonata*.

Après une lecture de Dante
After A Reading of *Dante*, August 1836

When the poet paints hell, he paints his own life. His life, a fleeing
shadow pursued by spectres; A mysterious forest where his terrified feet
Wander, stumbling astray from the well-worn paths; A dark journey,
obstructed by strange encounters; A spiral with vague boundaries and
enormous depths, whose hideous circles go forever onward into a gloom
where there moves the vague and living hell! This stair is lost in the
obscure mist; At the base of each step a wretched figure sits, and one
sees pass by with a slight sound white teeth grinding in the dark night.
One sees visions, dreams, illusions there; The eyes that sorrow turns to
bitter tears; Love, as a couple embracing, sad and still ardent, who pass
in a whirlwind with a wound in their sides; In one corner, the impious

sisters, Vengeance and Hunger, crouch side by side over a skull they have gnawed; Then pale Want, with her impoverished smile; Ambition, Pride nourished upon itself, And shameless Lust, and infamous Avarice, All the leaden cloaks with which the soul can be weighed down, Farther on, Cowardice, Fear, and Treason Offering keys for sale and tasting poison; And then, lower still in the very depths of the gulf, The grimacing mask of suffering Hatred! Yes, that is Life, O inspired poet! And its murky way beset with barriers. And, so that nothing may be lacking in this narrow path, You show us forever standing to your right The genius with the calm brow and radiant eyes, Virgil unperturbed saying: "Let us go on."

Translation by James Johnson.

LIHU 13-15.

The Editor takes the liberty of adding a letter written in 2004 from a personal friend, Dr. Helen Hughes, Professor Emeritus at Hendrix College, on Dante's *Divine Comedy*. On my first occasion to teach the Dante Sonata I asked for her insights into Dante's literary work. While Liszt never gave a program for the Dante Sonata, her response to my query is not without value in elucidating the philosophical content of this work. The letter was written in her 85th year:

Dear Neil,

You wanted to know if Dante's motivation in writing the Divine Comedy was to glorify Beatrice. I imagine that was part of his complex motivation. When I taught DC, I thought a major part of the work- two thirds- was to THINK (reason, and of course writing certainly enhances thinking) his way out of the Dark Wood he and humanity, he believed, were in. I said THINK his way out because Virgil (REASON) was his guide through Hell and Purgatory. But of course it was Beatrice (DIVINE REVELATION) who sent Virgil to Dante and then led him to Heaven. The physical journey certainly corresponds to a spiritual journey of profound inner development.

Dante wrote a patron that the literal subject of DC is "the state of souls after death" but the description of this state is not the ultimate purpose. Rather, he said, "the end of the entire work.... Is to remove those living in this life from a state of misery and to lead them to a state of happiness". This goal, then, surely was a stronger motivation.

Divine Comedy, Inferno, Canto 28-
The Severed Head of Bertrand de Born speaks
Gustave Doré

Moreover, I think writing this poem led him out of a personal Dark Wood of deep despair because he had been exiled from his beloved Florence he had served as a soldier and one of the 6 chief magistrates, on penalty of being buried alive if he returned. He wandered around Italy, dependent upon patrons for the rest of his life. He denounced the political corruption he saw, as well as the self-seeking men in holy orders, and he must have brooded on his political enemies (some are in Hell in DC). In addition, (the real) Beatrice had died young (in her twenties), and her death obviously made him grieve profoundly....

He wrote that when he first saw Beatrice and she seemed "in her perfect beauty the image of divinity on earth." So he begins to make her a symbol of heavenly or spiritual love as he does in DC. I like what John Gardiner, one of my favorite 20th century novelists, wrote in *On Moral Fiction* "Dante believed in God....but it was the memory of Beatrice, not the thought of God directly, that stirred his emotions and enabled him to realize that something was still vital in him, that he might somehow find his way back to the road that he had lost. Maybe Liszt felt the same?"

Divine Comedy, Purgatorio, Canto 30,
Beatrice appears among Angels
Gustave Doré

Thank you for making me think again about Dante, for I have been in a Dark Wood of despair lately at age 85 and I have seen so much evil in world news- kidnapping and killing innocent children, retaliation after retaliation in the Middle East, 9/11, terrorism all over the world, and now the DC sniper. This seems to bring evil somewhat closer to my home in 3 Cherokee Circle. Dante, though, has helped me immensely to adjust to the fact that, while evil has always been here since my young womanhood in WWII, the world today is no longer the wonderful world I had known. Thank you again my good friend,

Affectionately,
Helen

P.S...I hope all of this will be helpful in teaching and interpreting Liszt's Dante Sonata.

(Letter in possession of Editor.)

Work: Années de pèlerinage Troisième année (1867-1877)
Angélus! Prière aux anges gardiens (Angelus! Prayer to the Guardian angels)
   In a letter of October 14, 1877, Liszt indicated that he had just written "Angelus!: In early October there was the feast day of the Holy Angels. I wrote a hundred or so measures for them… and wish I could better express my intimate devotion to the divine messengers." LISM 294-295.
   The English cleric Hugh Reginald Haweis recalls a conversation with Liszt,

> As we were talking of bells," he said, "I should like to show you an 'Angelus' which I have just written"; and, opening the piano, he sat down. This was the moment which I had so often and so vainly longed for… "You know," said Liszt, turning to me, "They ring the Angelus in Italy carelessly; the bells swing irregularly, and leave off, and the cadences are often broken up thus": and he began a little swaying passage in the treble- like bells tossing high up in the evening air:

Angelus, mm. 1-6. Henle Edition.

> It ceased, but so softly that the half bar of cadence made itself felt, and the listening ear still carried the broken rhythm through the pause. The Abbate himself seemed to fall into a dream; his fingers fell again lightly on the keys, and the bells went on, leaving off in the middle of a phrase. Then rose from the bass the song of the Angelus, or rather, it seemed like the vague emotion of one who, as he passes, hears in the ruins of some wayside cloister the ghosts of old monks humming their drowsy melodies, as the sun goes down rapidly. And the purple shadows of Italy steal over the land, out of the orange west!

Angelus, mm. 21-27. Henle Edition.

We sat motionless—the disciple (Pohlig) on one side, I on the other. Liszt was almost as motionless: his fingers seemed quite independent, chance ministers of his soul. The dream was broken by a pause; then came back the little swaying passage of bells, tossing high up in the evening air, the half bar of silence, the broken rhythm- and the Angelus was rung. LIS3 395.

Les jeux d'eaux à la Villa d'Este (The Fountains of the Villa d'Este)
Alan Walker writes, "Liszt transcended simple visual imagery and turned these streaming fountains into mystical symbols, associating them with the well known verse the Gospel of John (4:14) which is written in Latin in the score 'Sed aqua quam ego dabo ei, fiet in eo fons aquae salientis in vitam aeterman' (But whosoever drinketh of the water that I give him shall never thirst, but the water that I shall give him shall be in him a well of water springing up into everlasting life)." LIS3 372.

Aux Cyprès de la Villa d'Este nos. 1 and 2
Liszt's spiritual involvement with the Villa's famous Cypresses is indicated in a letter to Princess Caroline, 15 June 1877, "These three days I have spent entirely under the cypresses! It was an obsession, impossible to think of anything else, even church. Their old trunks were haunting me, and I hear their branches singing and weeping, bearing the burden of their unchanging foliage! At last they are brought to bed on music paper... May the good angels make the most beautiful inner music for you [Princess Caroline]- the music we shall hear fully, in its boundlessness, there above!" LISL 818.

In a letter to Countess Olga von Meyendorff on October 14, 1877 Liszt wrote, "I shall call them *Threnodies*,[37] as the word élégie strikes me as too tender, and almost wordly." LISM 293.

Cypress I
In a letter to Olga von Meyendorff of 13 September 1877, Liszt wrote of this work as "a fairly gloomy and disconsolate elegy...illumined toward the end by a beam of patient resignation." LISM 292.

Sunt lacrimae rerum, en mode hongrois ('Tears of things,' in Hungarian style)
Alan Walker writes, "The title of this work is taken from Virgil's *Aeneid* (Book I, lines 461-2), as Aeneas considers the fate of Troy: 'Here are tears for misfortune, and here men's hearts are touched by human plight.'" BUWA 178.

---

37 A threnody is a song, hymn or poem of mourning composed or performed as a memorial to a dead person.

Work: Ballade in B minor (1853)

When Edwin Klahre[38] turned up in Weimar for his first lesson on May 2, 1884, he played Liszt's *Ballade in B minor*. He recalls that he had formed the habit of, "moving my body from side to side, my nose close to the keys. He [Liszt] stopped me, one hand under my chin, the other on top of my head, and said to sit still and hold my head erect.

His first remark was at the opening period of the *Ballade*, [that] it be played broad and majestic and [that one] should sit accordingly. He put me aside and sat down and played from the beginning. It was a revelation to me. Every note of the melody of the right hand he played with a very marked and large tone, his hand at least a foot high, remarking that one should not play for the people who sit in the front row and usually have free tickets, but play for those in the gallery that pay ten pfennigs for a ticket. They should not only hear but see.'" LIS3 248.

Work: Two Concert Etudes (1862-1863)
Waldesrauschen

The splendid characterization of this Etude by distinguished British music critic Sacheverell Sitwell deserves a place here: "The wind in a pine wood; one of those German or Bohemian woods where the lines of straight stems are like an army of lances, and the boughs droop down, not so much as leaves but as tassels, which the wind sways and dashes to and fro." LISC 247.

Work: Deux Légendes (1862-1863)
St. François d'Assise La prédication aux oiseaux (*St. Francis Preaching to the Birds*) (1866)

Liszt had in mind the charming story of St. Francis of Assisi extracted from the 13th-century work, *The Little Flowers of St. Francis*:

> And he [St. Francis] went into the field toward the birds that were on the ground. And as soon as he began to preach, all the birds that were on the trees came down toward him. And all of them stayed motionless with the others in the field, even though he went among them, touching many of them with his habit. But not a single one of them made the slightest move, and later they did not leave until he had given them his blessing...Now at [the sermon of] St. Francis, all those birds began to open their beaks, stretch out their necks, spread their wings and reverently bow their heads to the ground, who sang by their movements and their songs that the words which St. Francis was saying gave them great pleasure...

38 Edwin Klahre was an American student of Liszt who later taught at the New England Conservatory.

Then all the birds rose up into the air simultaneously, and in the air sang a wonderful song. . . And each group rose high in the air and flew off in a different direction: one toward the east, another toward the west, the third toward the south, and the fourth toward the north. And each group sang marvelously as it flew away. STFR 76-77.

Recalling her work with the legendary French pianist, Francis Planté, Marguerite Long wrote, "He was indefatigable...He played Liszt's 'Legende de Saint Francois d'Assise' an octave higher than the original text, for according to him this brought it much nearer to the tessitura of the birds. And Liszt, on hearing it, had apparently said nothing." DEML 31-32.

St. François de Paule marchant sur les flots (St. Francis walking on the water)
The life of St. Francis written by Guiseppe Miscimarra contains the story on which this lovely piece is based. Miscimarra writes,

Having arrived at last in site of the lighthouse of Messina, and then at that part of the shore of Cattona, he found a barque there, which shipped staves for casks to Sicily. He presented himself with his two companions to the master of the vessel, one Pietro Colono, saying: "For the sake of Christian charity, my brother, take us across to the island in your barque." And he, being ignorant of the holiness of him who had just begged, demanded the price of passage from him. And when he answered that he did not possess it, the master of the vessel replied, that he had no barque to take them in.

The people of Arena, who had accompanied the saint, and were present at the refusal of his request, begged the master of the vessel to embark these poor Brothers, saying that he might rest assured that one of them is a Saint. "If he is a Saint," answered he with the greatest incivility, "let him walk on the water, and work miracles"; and sailing off he left them on the shore.

Not disturbed in anyway by the rude behavior of the jeering mariner, and cheered by the divine spirit which always supported him, the Saint separated himself a little from his companions, and in prayer, invoked divine aid in his difficulty. On returning to his companions, he said unto them, "Be of good cheer, my sons by the grace of God, ...the Lord has provided us with another good and safer ship, with this my cloak," which he now spread over the water... "we have a better ship in which we can cross over"...and then lifting up a part of his cloak like a little sail, and supporting it with his staff as a mast, he with his companions stepped onto the marvelous vessel, and sailed away, to the amazement of those of Arena, who watched from the other shore, crying out after him in terror and tears, and beating their hand, as did also their sailors on the barque, and their unfriendly master, who implored pardon of him for the refusal of his request, and begged him to come into his ship. But God who for the glory of his holy name, desired to manifest that he had put not only Earth and Fire in subjection to our Saint, but also the waters, caused him to refuse this offer, and to arrive in port before the barque. LIMI 82.

Alan Walker writes, "The moral of the Legend, wrote Liszt, was to show that the laws of faith govern the laws of nature. St. Francis of Paola, incidentally was Liszt's patron saint, which may have been one reason why he retained a particular affection for this piece until the end of his days." LIS3 58-59.

Work: Études d'exécution transcendante (1852)
Paysage
Ferrucio Busoni's image of this etudes is "A calm renunciation of everything wordly—taking breath during the contemplation of nature, a self-contemplation but not quite without passion; this was only achieved completely by the later Liszt." LIBU 162.

Feux Follets (Will-o-the-wisp)
In English *Feux Follets* translates to *Will-o-the-wisp*, which is the most common name given to the mysterious lights that were said to lead travelers from the well-trodden paths into treacherous marshes. It is according to the *New Encyclopaedia Britannica*, "a ghostly light seen by travelers at night, especially over bogs, swamps or marshes. It resembles a flickering lamp and is said to recede if approached, drawing travelers from the safe paths. In popular legend it is considered ominous and is often purported to be the soul of one who has been rejected by hell carrying its own hell coal on its wanderings. The phenomenon is generally believed to be the spontaneous ignition of marsh gases, which consists mainly of methane." LIEN 454.

Vision
Discussing *Vision* Busoni wrote, "We may think—so we learn from the superscription—of the funeral of the first Napoleon, advancing with solemn and imperial pomp." LIBU 162.

Mazeppa
Editor's note: The quotation placed at the conclusion of this triumphant work—"Il tombe enfin...et re relève Roi!" (He falls at last...and rises as a king!)—comes from the Romantic narrative poem by Lord Byron of 1819 based on the gory and magnificent legend of Mazeppa.

According to the *New Encyclopaedia Britannica*,

> The poem of Byron and later Victor Hugo, recounts the young Mazeppa, while serving as a page at the Court of King John II Casimir Vasa, having a love affair with a Countess named Theresa, who was married to a much older man. The Count, on discovering the affair, punishes Mazeppa by tying him naked to a wild horse and setting the horse loose. The bulk of the poem describes the traumatic journey of the hero strapped to the horse which carried him to Ukraine. There, he was released by the Cossack, who later made him King. There is historical accuracy in the poem as Ivan Mazeppa (1644-1709) did serve as a page in the court of John II and rose to become the leader of the Ukrainians. There is no documentary record, however, of either his love affair or the wild ride on the horse, which is the exciting stuff of legend and poetry. LZEN 981-982.

Mazeppa and the Wolves
Horace Vernet (1789-1863)

Ricordanza

Ferrucio Busoni poetically referred to this work of delicate nostalgia as "a bundle of faded love letters from a somewhat old-fashioned world of sentiment." LIBU 162.

Busoni's phrase has also been translated as "a bundle of yellowed love letters." – *Editor.*

Harmonies du soir (Harmonies of the evening)
Once, when Arthur Friedheim was playing "Harmonies du soir" late one afternoon, Liszt stopped the performances, pointed towards the beautiful sunset that had mellowed the landscape outside, and said: "Play that, *there* are your evening harmonies." LIS3 247.

Chasse-niege
Busoni writes of this etude, "The noblest example, perhaps, amongst all music of a poetising nature—a sublime and steady fall of snow which gradually buries landscape and people." LIBU 162.

Work: Harmonies poétiques et religieuses (1845-1852)
This work was named after a volume of poetry by Alphonse de Lamartine. Both the cycle as a whole as well as three of the individual pieces—Invocation, Bénédiction de Dieu dans la solitude, and no. 9—are prefaced with poems of great spiritual depth from Lamartine's work.

No. 1 Invocation

Rise up, voice of my soul,
With the dawn, with the night!
Leap up like the flame,
Spread abroad like the noise!
Float on the wing of the clouds,
Mingle with the winds, with storms,
With thunder, and the tumult of the waves.
Rise up in the silence
At the hour when, in the shade of evening,
The lamp of night sways,
When the priest puts out the censer;
Rise up by the waves
In these deep solitary places
Where God reveals himself to faith!

LIHA

No. 3 Bénédiction de Dieu dans la solitude (The Blessing of God in Solitude)
Whence comes, my God, this peace that floods me?
Whence comes to me this faith, with which my heart overflows?
To me, who but lately, uncertain, restless,
And tossed to the four winds on waves of doubt,
Sought good, and truth, in the dreams of the wise,

And peace at the turbulent heart of storms.
Though scarce a few days have passed before my face,
It seems to me that a century, and a world, have gone by;
And that, separated from them by a mighty abyss,
A new man revives within me, and begins again.

LIHA

No. 4 Pensée des morts (In Memory of the Dead)

Lina Ramann, in her biography of Liszt, said that the composer directed the performer to play this work, "Avec un profound sentiment d'ennui" (with a profound feeling of ennui)." LIPM 212.

Editor's note: To nineteenth century romantics *ennui* was a mixture of cosmic suffering, spleen, chagrin, and despair.

No. 7 Funérailles (*Funerals*) "October 1849"

Editor's note: "Funérailles" is an elegy written in October 1849 in emotional and patriotic response to the merciless and violent crushing of the Hungarian Revolution of 1848 by the Hapsburgs. Not only were thousands of lives lost on the battlefields, but on the first anniversary of the uprising thirteen Hungarian generals were executed in Vienna, and the former Prime Minister of Hungary was taken to a courtyard in Budapest, stood against a wall, and shot.

Alan Walker writes, "Inspired by the memory of Hungarians who had died in the revolution, this work is not simply the expression of a personal sorrow but a symbol of that universal suffering felt by mankind when great ideals perish and the heroes who espouse them (whatever nationality) are no more. The opening of the work evokes funeral bells, which rise in volume to a deafening roar...

Funérailles, mm. 1-3. Breitkopf and Hartel Edition.

which eventually collapses into a march for the dead, one of Liszt's noblest utterances."

Funérailles, mm. 24-25. Breitkopf and Hartel Edition.

LIS2 71-72.

That Chopin is suggested in the martial triplets that lead to the work's climax is verified by a statement made by Liszt himself to his students. "That is essentially an imitation of Chopin's famous polonaise [op. 53]; but here I have done it somewhat differently," LISG 61.

No. 9 Andante lagrimoso

> Fall, silent tears,
> Upon an earth without pity;
> No more between pious hands,
> Nor on the bosom of friendship!
> Fall like an arid rain,
> Which splashes on the rock,
> That no ray from the sky can wipe away,
> That no breath can come to dry.

LIHA

Work: Liebesträume (Love Dreams) (1850)

The three Nocturnes in this famous group are written to poems by Johann Ludwig Uhland and Ferdinand Freiligrath.

Notturno I 'Holy Love' by Johann Ludwig Uhland

> Within Love's arms to bliss invited
> To ye life's sweet enjoyments call:
> On me one glance alone has lighted,
> Yet I am rich beyond you all.
> I yield Earth's joys without resistance
> And, as a martyr, gaze on high,
> For over me in golden distance
> There opens a celestial sky.

Notturno II 'Blissful Death' by Johann Ludwig Uhland

> I was as dead
> In love's fond blisses,
> And in her arms
> Lay buried quiet:
> I was awakened by her kisses,
> And in her eyes
> Saw heav'n's own light.

Notturno III 'Oh Love' by Ferdinand Freiligrath

> O love! O love, so long as e'er thou canst, or dost on love believe;
> The time shall come, when thou by graves shall stand and grieve;
> And see that still they heart doth glow, doth hear and foster love divine,
> So long as e'er another heart shall beat in warm response to thine.
> And, whoso bears his heart to thee, O, show him love where in thy power
> And make his every hour a joy, nor wound his heart at any hour.
> And keep a guard upon thy tongue- an unkind word is quickly said:
> Ah me!- no ill was meant- and yet
> The other goes and weeps thereat.

LILB

Work: Mephisto Waltz no. 1 Episode: Der Tanz in der Dorfschenke aus Lenau's "Faust" (Mephisto Waltz no. 1 Episode: The Dance at the Village Inn after Lenau's poem "Faust") (1863)

The following programmatic note, which Liszt took from Lenau's poem, appears in the printed score, "There is a wedding feast in progress in the village inn, with music, dancing, carousing. Mephistopheles and Faust pass by, and Mephistopheles induces Faust to enter and take part in the festivities. Mephistopheles snatches the fiddle from the hands of a lethargic fiddler and draws from it indescribably seductive and intoxicating strains. The amorous Faust whirls about with a full-blooded village beauty in a wild dance; they waltz in mad abandon out of the room, into the open, away into the woods. The sounds of the fiddle grow softer and softer, and the nightingale warbles his love-laden song." EWEN 519-520.

Work: Grandes études de Paganini (1851)
La Campanella

Of this work Liszt remarked mischievously, "The difficult octave accompaniment in the left hand on the last page may be simplified...When I wrote that I did not teach as much as I do now." LISA 33

Work: Sonata in B minor (1852-1853)

Editor's note: No other work of Liszt has had so much attention from its admirers who feel constrained to find in it programs and hidden meanings. While there were many poetic ideas and programs current during Liszt's lifetime, he did not sanction any of them and offered no indication of its program or poetic representation while he lived.

I cite Alfred Cortot's intelligent observations which are along the same lines. His summarizing concept is wise: "Imagine one for your own use."

Cortot writes,

> From the expressive point of view I see in its unfolding an illustration of Goethe's *Faust*, which, with the *Divine Comedy*, always haunted Liszt's thoughts. It seems to me to envisage a sort of first sketch for a *Faust Symphony*—the expression of restless tormented genius, who seeks in action, in love, in religion, a certainty, a consolation, that suddenly eludes him, and who ends by taking refuge in a philosophic concept. Liszt has summed up all the feelings of Faust in this Sonata—despair, ardour, enthusiasm, reverie, tenderness, irony.
>
> I have devised a story about it for myself, a story that I shall not tell you, as I am not certain that it is the same as Liszt's. Imagine one yourselves for your own use; let it support your interpretation, and contribute unity to it. Liszt has not confided his story to us, but it is obvious that the inventor of the *poeme symphonique* did not write the most gigantic of his piano compositions without enclosing in it, if not situations, at least *certain ideas*. COMI 152.

Work: Todtentanz (1859)

Cortot says,

> At Pisa is found one of the most arresting conceptions of the Triumph of Death, in the form of a frescoe attributed to Orcagna, a frescoe embellishing the wall of the Campo Santo of that city. Here, in 1839, Liszt sketched his *Todtentanz*....
>
> Liszt was too faithful a believer not to have been struck, not merely as an artist, but as a man, in the inmost recesses of his soul by the fantastic, ironical lesson set forth by the old Christian theme. And he shows us the hand of death seizing, one after the other, Pope, Emperor, King, Bishop, *seigneur,* as in the numerous and well known engravings, where no one, be he soldier, monk, or labourer, is spared, and even children are seized by Death....
>
> The work is as violent, as arresting, as tormented and glorious, as that of Campo Santo at Pisa...By this feature the variation in this case escapes

being purely musical in character. The person represented changes with each variation, which then takes on a very special character. Thus in the slow variation, so tender and so unexpected, it is the young virgin martyr who is being led to her death. In studying pieces of this kind free scope should be given to the imagination, to permit the association of images capable of setting up the necessary intellectual fermentation. COMI 264-265.

Work: Variations on 'Weinen, Klagen, Sorgen' (Weeping, groaning, fearing) (1859)

Alfred Cortot wrote, "These three painful words—'To weep, to groan, to fear'—not only serve Liszt from the point of view of musical coloring but permit him to establish a division and a progression. The chorale *Was Gott tut das ist wohlgetan* intervening at a most tragic moment, as if to deliver us from a harsh and terrible ordeal and to show us the light, is a Protestant theme employed by Bach in the same cantata from which Liszt drew the first theme. What a feeling of solace and splendor this theme brings after the bewildered suspense, the terror, the sensation of fatality and menace, by which we have been weighted down. When Liszt resumed the work [on this piece] he had just taken holy orders." COMI 254.

Chapter 11
Mendelssohn

Work: Caprice in F-sharp minor, Op. 5 (1835-1836)

Ferdinand Hiller recalls the following conversation with Mendelssohn after the latter played the f sharp minor Caprice for Rossini:

> Mendelssohn soon began to rebel a little. "If your Rossini", said he to me one morning when we met at our bath in the main, "goes on muttering such things as he did yesterday, I won't play him anything more."
>
> "What did he mutter? I did not hear anything."
>
> "But I did: when I was playing my F sharp minor Caprice, he muttered between his teeth, ' Ca sent la sonate de Scarlatti.'"
>
> "We'll, that's nothing so very dreadful."
>
> "Ah—bah!"

FHFM 576-558.

Editor's note: Perhaps Rossini was correct in his estimation of this piece, and was paying Mendelssohn a compliment.

Schumann wrote of this work, "I regard Mendelssohn's Capriccio in F-sharp minor as a masterwork." SCMM 120.

Work: Three Caprices for Piano, Op. 16 (1829)

Mendelssohn wrote to his sisters in Berlin from London an explanation of the genesis of his *Three Fantasias or Caprices* (opus 16): "I shall always remember my stay with the three Taylor girls... I shall never forget the meadows, the wild flowers and the murmur of the gravelly brook." For the eldest girl he composed an *Andante con moto* meant to depict pink carnations and red roses:

Caprice, Op 16, no. 1, mm. 1-4. Breitkopf and Hartel Edition.

for the youngest, he set to music the yellow trumpet blossoms in her hair. But to the middle one, "I gave the brook which so pleased us once when we were out riding that we dismounted and sat down beside it. This last piece is, I think, the best; it flows so slowly and gently and is a bit tediously simple, so that I played it for myself every day and waxed quite sentimental over it." MEND 153.

Work: Three Caprices for Piano, Op. 33, no. 2 (1843-1835)

Writing of the second Caprice, Robert Schumann commented in the *Neue Zeitschrift Für Musick*, "The initials F. M. B. stand on every page of the second one; it is a geni that has secretly stolen earthwards. Yet no spectre hides in it, no fairy beckons from it; it storms not, it excites not, in it we tread the firm flowery German earth; it is Walt's "Summer Journey through the Country" (by Jean Paul). I am almost convinced that no one can play this piece with such inimitable grace as its composer, for few could wholly render its transparently shining veins, its glowing colour, its changing expression of face; and I think Eusebius is right when he says the composer might make the most constant of maidens inconstant with it for a few moments!" SCRE 386.

Work: Prelude and Fugue in E minor, Op. 35, no. 1 (1837)

Cortot emphasizes the ardent, emotional, and pathetic character of Mendelssohn's prelude from the *Prelude and Fugue in e Minor* when he wrote, "The arpeggios...are leggiero, like flames lighting up the entire horizon. Mendelssohn wrote it in 1837, soon after his marriage to a Protestant and his own conversion to Protestantism. It is not a *Song without Words* but a page of exaltation. The tone will not be full enough unless the notes of the melody are always played with the thumb, the latter being in contact with the keyboard right up to the first joint, and reinforced each time by a light pressure of the hand." COMI 33-34.

Alfred Cortot writes elsewhere, "Mendelssohn, that fine, pure artist, played an ergetic and conspicuous part…in the struggle against music mongers who were degrading the music of his age; the …motive which impelled him to compose the noble E minor Fugue at the bedside of a dying friend, can be taken as the index of an aesthetic and moral quality." COFP 56-57.

Stephen Samuel Stratton relates a similar event in his 1910 book *Mendelssohn* in which he says, "Moreover this spring he had been deeply affected by the death of a dear young friend, August Hanstein, by whose bedside he composed the Fugue in e minor, Op. 35, no. 1, in which Schubring says he marked the progress of the disease as it gradually destroyed the sufferer, until he made it culminate in the Choral of Release in E major." MESS 43.

In Schubring's original account of 1866 of this deathbed scene he recalled, "[H]ow he [Mendelssohn] devoted the time, as he watched through the night by the bed of his dying friend, Hanstein, to marking in the first fugue, composed here, of the six he afterwards published—E major—the progress of the disease as it gradually destroyed the sufferer until he made it culminate with the chorale release in E major." MESC 227.

Work: Sonata in E major, Op. 6 (1825)

Writing of this sonata in the *Neue Zeitschrift Für Musick* Robert Schumann comments, "If, indeed, much in this sonata is reminiscent, for example in the first movement of the sadly reflective movement in Beethoven's last A major sonatas; if the last movement generally recalls Weber—it is not because of weak dependence but because of spiritual affinity. On the other hand, how it grows, burgeons, and bursts forth! How green and matinal is everything, as in a vernal landscape! It is not the foreign, the novel, which speaks and attracts us here, but the beloved and the familiar. Nothing seeks to impose on us or astonish us; the right words are merely imparted to our feelings in such a way that we seem to have found them ourselves." SCMM 210.

Work: Songs without Words

Mendelssohn hardly ever attempted to explain his art to others. But he did make some important statements about the *Songs without Words*. In a remarkable letter to Marc Andre Souchay, a relative of his wife who was then in Lubeck, he wrote from Berlin on 15th October 1842,

> If you ask me what I thought [in connection with one or another of the *Song without Words*,] I must say: the song itself as it stands. If, with one or the other of them, I had a specific word in mind, I should not

like to give them these titles, because words do not mean the same to one person as they mean to another; only the song says the same thing, arouse the same feeling, in one person as in another-a feeling that, however, cannot be expressed in the same words.

Resignation, melancholy, praise of God, a foxhunt-these are words which everyone interprets differently. What is resignation to one person is melancholy to another; a third thinks of both as lifeless. For a man who loves hunting, the foxhunt and praise of God might well be equivalents; he would feel that the winding of horns was really and truly the right way to praise God. To us a foxhunt is merely a foxhunt, and no matter how much we discussed the matter, we would get nowhere. The word remains ambiguous; but in music we would understand on another rightly. MEND 185-186.

Songs without Words, Op. 30 (1833-1834)

In a review of Mendelssohn's Op. 30 Schumann wrote,

But to our songs! Clear as sunshine they meet us... Florestan says [of the first], "This, I think, is the song I like best; he who has sung such a one may hope to live long, before and after death." The second reminds me of Goethe's "Hunter's Evening Song,"
"The fields I wander, silent, wild,
My ready gun," etc.
And its tender, airy build equals that of the poet... I think the fourth very charming...self-concentrated and melancholy, yet whispering, from the distance, of hope and home... The last, a Venetian barcarolle, softly and tenderly closes the whole. SCRE 455-456.

Song without Words, Op. 38 (1836-1837)

In a review Robert Schumann wrote of these songs, "They are all equally the children of a blooming imagination; ... And so I fancy the composer preferred first the second song, then the duet at the close, and then the fifth, which contains more passion, if I may so term the rarer throbs of a noble heart... In the 'Duet' I feel dissatisfied that this rich, thoroughly German conversation is not in words, which would more freely enable it to express itself—but these are really lovers who converse so trustfully, softly, securely." SCRE 471-472.

Chapter 12
Poulenc

General Observations:

Some of the best advice on how to approach the piano music of Poulenc comes from the composer himself in a series of interviews from 1954. Poulenc said,

> "The great technical errors which deface my piano music, to the point of rending it unrecognizable, are: tempo rubato, stinginess in the use of pedal, and too much articulation in certain arpeggiated phrases which should, on the other hand, be rather smooth and blurred.

> Let me explain: I hate rubato…once a tempo is adopted, under no circumstance should it be altered unless I so indicate. Never stretch or shorten a beat. That drives me crazy. As for the use of pedals, that is the great secret behind my piano music (and often its true drama!) *One can never use enough pedal, do you hear me! never enough! never enough!*

> In a fast movement I often rely on the pedal for the realization of a harmonic passage that could not be rendered completely in writing. [Finally], the arpeggios and accompanimental chords should be in the background most of the time so that the melody can be heard." POEN 32-33.

Nadia Boulanger, French conductor, composer, and teacher, wrote the following profile of Poulenc, recollecting, "I can't remember without laughing one dinner with friends where Poulenc told us an absolutely uninteresting story. He had arrived at the Vienna railway station to board his sleeper; the sleeper was already occupied by somebody he had to turn out. A banal story. He told it to us until we laughed until we cried…This was not at all amusing in itself and yet it was irresistible; so was his way of playing his own work at the piano.

You've never heard Poulenc play *Les Mamelles de Tiresias?* It was dazzling, fireworks. He played with too much pedal, it was drowned, but it rang out in an unforgettable way." NABO 103.

Here is the French musical aesthetic so well defined by Poulenc, who in a statement to Roland Gelatt in 1950 said, "You will find sobriety and dolor in French music as well as in German and Russian. But the French have a keener sense of proportion. We realize that sombreness and good humor are not mutually exclusive. Our composers, too, write profound music, but when they do, it is leavened with that lightness of spirit without which life would be unendurable." ESCA 606.

Poulenc's self-deprecation in evaluating his own keyboard music is refreshing. Keeping in character with his lighthearted humor he is quoted from a 1954 radio interview with Claude Rostand, "I can tolerate the *Mouvement perpétuels*, my old *Suite in ut*, and *Trois pièces* (the former Pastorales). I am very fond of my two books of *Improvisations*, an *Intermezzo in A flat* and certain of the *Nocturnes*. I condemn outright *Napoli* and the *Soiree de Nazelles*. As for the rest, I don't care one way or the other." POCO 343.

Work: Concerto pour deux pianos (1932)
Poulenc describes the mood and style of the second movement, "In the Larghetto of this concerto, I allowed myself, for the first time, to return to Mozart for I cherish the melodic line and I prefer Mozart to all other musicians. If the movement begins *alla* Mozart, it quickly veers, at the entrance of the second piano, toward a style that was standard for me at that time." POUL 149.

Work: Concerto pour piano (1949)
Responding to criticism that this movement is too lighthearted, to the point of vulgarity, Poulenc explains, "As opposed to the famous concertos of the past, which called for great virtuosos, I decided to write a light concerto, a sort of souvenir of Paris for pianist-composer. I had no fear that such a project would be poorly received, so I interjected into the *rondeau à la française*, the rhythm of the mixixe [a type of Brazilian tango] and a Negro spiritual derived from an old song sung by La Fayette's sailors; I myself was amused and pleased with this handshake with a country, that at present, contains my greatest and most loyal audience." POUL 154.

Work: Elégie for Two Pianos (1959)

In a letter to Arthur Gold and Robert Fitzdale[39] of September 28, 1959, Poulenc writes, "The Elégie is finished...It is an odd piece, rather 'sweet' in style...The Elégie consists solely of alternating chords. I hope the balance is good... Anyway, it is very easy—too easy perhaps for serious critics, but that's too bad. To hell with them." POCO 268.

The score of the Elégie is preceded by the following instructions by Poulenc in French, English, German, and Spanish: "This Elegy should be played as if you were improvising, a cigar in your mouth and a glass of cognac on the piano. The syncopated notes (a sort of vibration of the preceding chord) should hardly be touched. On the whole you can never use too much pedal." POEL Foreword.

Work: L'Embarquement pour Cythère (The Embarkation for Cythera) (1951)

This piece is an evocation of Poulenc's carefree childhood summers at his family's country home in Nogent-sur-Marne (also the home village of Watteau, painter of *L'Embarquement pour Cyth*ère, and thus perhaps the title). It is a kind of gay and tuneful café-concert entertainment. Poulenc says, "It is a question here of evoking the Isle of Love and the Isle of Beauty, where one could find Nogent *guinguettes* [rustic outdoor nightclubs], with their sentimental and waggish accordions." POUL 189.

Work: Histoire de Babar, le petit éléphant (The story of Babar, the little Elephant) (1945)

From Winifred Radford we read, "The story of the origin of *Babar* is quite amusing. While staying with Martha Bosredon in Brive-la-Galiarde after his demobilization in 1940, Poulenc received a visit from some of his cousins. The little daughter of one of these cousins, hearing him improvise, went up to him saying: "Oh, Uncle Francis, what you are playing is so boring! Why don't you play this?" And she placed in front of him her copy of Jean de Brunhoff's book *Histoire de Babar, le petit elephant*. Poulenc began to improvise for her, noting down the ideas that appealed to her. It was not until five years later, however, prompted by the same cousin who asked "Et *Babar?*" that Poulenc took up the work again and finally completed it. His music illustrates and elaborates upon Jean de Brunhoff's text, spoken by a narrator." POWR 373.

---

39 Arthur Gold (1917-1990) and Robert Fizdale (1920-1995) were an American two-piano ensemble; they were also authors and television cooking show hosts.

Work: Huit Nocturnes (1929-1938)
Nocturne no.2 (1933)
Graceful and animated, this work is subtitled "bal de juenes filles" (Dance of the young girls). PONC.

Nocturne no. 3 (1934)
Based on a melodic ostinato, this piece is subtitled "Cloches des Malines" (Bells of Malines). PONC.

Nocturne no. 4 (1934)
This nostalgic mazurka is subtitled "Bel fantôme" (Handsome Phantom). Accompanying it is an atmospheric quote by Julian Greene:

Not a single note of the waltzes and scottishes was lost in the whole house,
so that the invalid also shared in the party
and was able to dream on his death bed of the good years of his youth.
Translated by Phillip Bailey.

PONC.

Work: Les Soirées de Nazelles (1930-1936)
Poulenc describes the genesis of *Le soirées* in its preface, "The variations which form the body of this work were improvised during long country evenings at Nazelles, when the author played musical 'portraits' with a group of friends gathered around the piano. One hopes that these variations, presented here between a Préamble and a Final will be able to evoke this game in its proper Touraine setting, a window of the salon opening to the evening." PONZ Foreword.

Variation seven
Keith Daniel informs us, "The only person who can be identified by her portrait is 'Tante' Liénard, to whom the entire suite is dedicated. This marvelous woman, depicted in variation 7, 'L'Alerte vieillesse,' was one of Poulenc's closest 'country' friends, a woman who in her seventies appreciated Stravinsky, modern art, and a good glass of wine; it was at her house in Nazelles that the variations were sketched out, in 1930. Poulenc does clarify one other portrait: He says, '[T]his suite contains… a 'Final,' which is a sort of self-portrait.'" POUL 186.

Work: Sonate pour deux pianos (1952-1953)
Referring to the Andante of this work Poulenc wrote, "[T]his *Andante* is, for me, the true center of the work. It is no longer as in the Andante of the *Concerto pour 2 pianos*, a question of a poetic homage to Mozart… but rather a lyric, profound outpouring. Taking inspiration, moreover, from my

choral music, I attempted in several places a great purity of line…I would venture to say that the *Concerto pour 2 pianos* is bright and many-coloured, while the *Sonate* has the gravity of a string quartet." POUL 192.

Work: Thème varié (1951)

In a letter to Henri Suaget of August 15, 1951 Poulenc wrote, "I have just finished my *Thème varié* for piano, a serious work but I hope not boring. The coda of the last variation is strictly the theme backwards. You see, Mr. Leibowitz,[40] that we too…" POCO 191.

Work: Trois mouvements perpétuels (1919)

Poulenc was fond of calling these pieces "three little spots of color." POUL 172.

Work: Trois Pièces (completed 1928)
Toccata

When Sergei Rachmaninoff was interviewed for *La Nation Belge* and asked why he rarely played modern music he answered, "A single work has found favor alongside my undiminished passion for the classics: this is Poulenc's *Toccata*. This is distinguished by spontaneous inspiration, and it is written for a musician of temperament." RALM 297.

---

40 In a footnote to this letter Sidney Buckland writes, "The coda of the final variation presents the theme in reverse and is Poulenc's mocking allusion to the twelve-tone system" espoused by Rene Leibowitz (1913-1972). Leibowitz was a French composer who taught serial technique to Boulez and others in the 1940's.

Chapter 13
Prokofiev

Work: Concerto no. 2 in G minor, Op. 16 (1912-1913 lost, rewritten 1923)

In his autobiography Prokofiev wrote of this work that "The charges of showy brilliance and certain 'acrobatic' tendencies in the *First Concerto* induced me to strive for greater depth in the Second." PRAU 144.

From an entry in Prokofiev's diary of December 30, 1912, we read, "When composing the Second Concerto I paid a great deal of attention to the challenges of the solo part, but even so there are times when the composer-musician in me prevails over the composer-pianist, and I have not been able to avoid dull or, so to say routine, passages for the soloist." PROD 281.

Work: Four Pieces for Piano Op. 4, no. 4 (1908, revised 1910–1912)
Suggestions Diabolique

This work's Russian title, "Navazhdeniia,"which means an incantation or seductive dance by supernatural power intended to lure the innocent into evil, was provided by Nouvel.[41] Immediately upon hearing it, he jumped up and exclaimed, "But that's some sort of incantation!" The best French translation that could be found for this very Russian word was *Suggestions diabolique*. PRRH 60-61.

Prokofiev wrote,

> I went to Karatygin's,[42] and there, along with all the "Modernists," was a tall thin fellow in a rumpled suit with stubble on his cheeks. It was

---

41 Walter Nouvel (1871-1949) was a longtime friend of Prokofiev and Diaghilev and wrote an early history of the Ballets Russes.

42 Viacheslav Gavrilovich Karatygin (1875-1925) was a Soviet music critic and composer.

Iovanovich, who proved to be of Scriabin origin. He said he had not yet thoroughly worked up my pieces but had only looked them over. "Play them anyway," I replied. "It will be a pleasure to hear them." After awhile he sat down at the piano.

"Now you'll hear," Nurok said in an undertone.

And Nouvell added, "He also sings a beautiful falsetto, although that has nothing to do with your pieces."

Iovanovich played Fairy Tale, and Suggestions diabolique, and something else. The playing was by no means on the concert level but rather mere sight reading. In particular, Suggestions diabolique did not sound impetuous and was not played with the rather dry vigorous touch that I had imagined and with which, apparently, I played it myself.

He finished, and I remained silent. He said, "I haven't yet learned these pieces."

"In that case, allow me to show you in what direction you should work."

Somewhat jarred by this he yielded me his place at the piano, and I started playing excerpts—chiefly from 'Suggestions diabolique'—while explaining what he had done wrong and what he should strive for. PROK 297.

Work: Sarcasms, Five Pieces for Piano, Op. 17 (1912-1914)

The influential Russian music critic and friend of Prokofiev, Boris Asafyev, was often amazed at the way Prokofiev got away with such audacity in his music, and in his memoirs wrote, "Prokofiev's Sarcasms are more taunting, more trenchant than the verses of the early Mayakovsky,[43] and the horror of them is electrifying." PRSM 94-95.

Work: Sonata no. 2 in D minor, Op. 14 (1912)

From an entry in Prokofiev's diary of February 24, 1913, we read,

He [his friend, Yurasovsky] heard me play my Sonata No.2 and said that while of course it was very interesting and inventive, it had not a scrap of real melody in it, just a series of "tigerish leaps." This annoyed me, and when he said that the movement he liked best was the Scherzo, I retorted, "Well, I take just the opposite view, that's my least favourite movement ..."

"Why?"

"Because the other movements are all more subtle; the Scherzo is targeted at a less discriminating taste." PROD 324.

---

43 Vladimir Vladimirovich Mayakovsky (1893-1930) was a Russian iconoclastic and controversial poet and writer and was the foremost representative of Russian Futurism.

Work: Sonata no. 5 in C major, Op. 38 (1923)

Reflecting on this work in a letter of July 15, 1924, to Mayakovsky, Prokofiev ascribed the slower tempos of this Sonata to "my poor state of health…when I was planning out the sonata; my heart was in poor condition as a result of the scarlet fever I contracted four years ago." PROF 194.

Work: Sonatas no. 6-8 (1939-1944)

While Russian musicology does not use this term, in the West these three Sonatas are referred to as the "War Sonatas." Author Boris Berman suggests, "While the Sixth Sonata reflects the nervous anticipation of World War II and the Eighth looks back to those terrible events retrospectively, the Seventh Sonata projects the anguish and the struggle of the war years as they were experienced in real time." PRBB 151.

It was Prokofiev who wanted the percussive passages of these sonatas, marked "con pugno", with the fist, in the score, to be played "so as to startle grandmother." PRTS 117.

Work: Sonata no. 7 in B-flat major, Op. 83, (1939-1942)

Pianist Sviatoslav Richter was one of the foremost interpreters of this work, having been introduced to it by Prokofiev himself. It moved him to the following eloquent description,

"With this work we are brutally plunged into the anxiously threatening atmosphere of a world that has lost its balance. Chaos and uncertainty reign. We see murderous forces ahead. But this does not mean that what we lived by before thereby ceases to exist. We continue to feel and love. Now the full range of human emotion bursts forth. Together with our fellow men and women, we raise a voice in protest and share the common grief. We sweep everything before us, borne along by the will for victory. In the tremendous struggle that this involves, we find the strength to affirm the irrepressible life-force." PRBM 80.

Richter continues with his and the Moscow audience's first reaction to this work: "Early in 1943 I received the score of the Seventh Sonata, which I found fascinating and which I learned in just four days…The work was a huge success. The audience clearly grasped the spirit of the work, which reflected their innermost feelings and concerns." PRBM 78-80.

Work: Sonata no. 8 in B-flat major, Op. 84 (1939-1944)

Boris Berman suggests, "By the time this Sonata was written the outcome of World War II had become clear in favor of a Russian victory over Germany and Japan. This may explain both the victorious coda of the finale and the general reflective mood of the first movement." PRBM 169.

Work: Sonata no. 9 in C major, Op. 104, (1947)

Richter recalled Prokofiev showing him the score of this work in 1947, "[W]hereupon he [Prokofiev] produced the sketches of the Ninth Sonata. 'This will be your sonata. But do not think it's intended to create an effect. It's not the sort of work to raise the roof of the Grand Hall.' At first glance it did indeed look a little simplistic. I was even a tiny bit disappointed... In 1951 he [Prokofiev] turned sixty. On his birthday Prokofiev was once again ill. On the eve of his birthday a concert was held at the Composers' Union and he listened to it over the phone. It was on this occasion that I played the Ninth Sonata for the first time, a radiant, simple and even intimate work. In some ways it is a *Sonata domestica*. The more one hears it, the more one comes to love it and feel its magnetism. And the more perfect it seems. I love it very much." PRBM 83-84, 87.

Mira Mendelson-Prokofieva, Prokofiev's second wife and the dedicatee of this work, recorded her impression of the Ninth Sonata in her diary on September 29, 1947: "This sonata is very different from the three preceding ones. It is calm and deep. When I told [Prokofiev] that my first impression was of it being both Russian and Beethoven-like, he answered that he himself found both of these qualities in it." PRBM 194.

Work: Visions Fugitive, Twenty Pieces for Piano, Op. 22 (1915-1917)

Visions Fugitive is a French translation for the Russian title *Mimoletnosti*, meaning fleeting and transient impressions or ideas; the root of the Russian word is "fly." The title comes from a poem, "I Do Not Know Wisdom," by Balmont, whom Prokofiev met around this time:

> In every fugitive vision
> I see whole worlds:
> They change endlessly,
> Flashing in playful rainbow colors.

PRRH 129.

No. 19, Presto agitatissimo e molto accentuate

In his autobiography Prokofiev said he wrote the nineteenth vision at least in part as a musical response to the February Revolution (March 1917). Prokofiev found it necessary to apologize for such a small and indirect response, saying, "It was more a reflection of the crowd's excitement than of the inner essence of the Revolution." PRRH 128-129.

Chapter 14
Rachmaninoff

General Observations:

Two recurring elements in Rachmaninoff's music are the liturgical and the gypsy. Rachmaninoff's friend and fellow musician Alexander Goedicke recalled how even in Rachmaninoff's daily life these two elements co-existed naturally, "He loved Church singing very much and quite often, even in the winter, would get up at seven o'clock in the morning and hail a cab in darkness, mostly to drive to the Taganka, to the Andronyev monastery, where he stood in the half-darkness of the enormous church through the whole liturgy, listening to the austere ancient chants from the *Oktoekhos*,[44] sung by the monks in parallel fifths... It commonly happened that on the same evening he would go to a symphony concert... and then, more often than not, go to have supper at the restaurant Yar or the Strelna, where he would stay late into the night, listening with great enthusiasm to the singing of the gypsies." RABM 30.

In a 1934 interview with Norman Cameron, Rachmaninoff said the following on imagination,

> "To my mind, there are two vitally important qualities innate in the creative artist which are not found, to the same degree, in the man who is solely an interpreter. The first is imagination. I do not suggest that the interpretive artist has no imagination; but it is safe to assume that the composer possess the greater imaginative gift, because he must first

---

44 Oktoekhos is the name of the eight mode system used for the composition of religious chant in the Eastern Orthodox Churches.

imagine before he can create… It follows that when a composer comes to interpret his own work, his own picture will be foremost in his mind, whereas every musician performing the work of another must imagine an entirely new picture for himself. Upon the vividness and extent of the performer's imagination the success and vitality of his interpretation largely depend." RAMM 201.

Work: Concerto no. 2 in C minor, Op. 18 (1900-1901)
First Movement
Russian composer Nikolai Medtner wrote of the profoundly Russian quality of the opening of the concerto, "The theme of Rachmaninoff's inspired Second Concerto is not only the theme of his life but always conveys the impression of being one of the most strikingly Russian of themes, and only because the soul of this theme is Russian; there is no ethnographic trimming here, no dressing up, no decking out in national dress, no folksong intonation, and yet every time, from the first bell stroke, you feel the figure of Russia rising up to her full height." RABM 127.

Work: Concerto no. 3 in D minor, Op. 30 (1909)
First Movement
When questioned by the American musicologist Josef Yasser in a 1935 conversation about the possible ecclesiastical origin of the first theme of the opening movement, Rachmaninoff responded that the theme was "borrowed neither from folk songs nor from church sources. It simply wrote itself… If I had any plan in composing this theme, I was thinking only of sound. I wanted 'to sing' the melody on the piano as a singer would sing it, and to find a suitable orchestral accompaniment or one that would not 'muffle' the singing." RABM 211.

Work: Etudes-Tableaux in G minor, Op. 33 (1911)
Etude no. 8 in G minor
Oskar von Riesemann, the author of *Rachmaninoff's Recollections*, has written, "[T]he G minor Etude-Tableau was prompted by a painting (or the painting 'Morning') by Arnold Böcklin (1827-1901), a Swiss Symbolist painter, whose pictures portray mythological, fantastical figures along with classical architecture constructions (often revealing an obsession with death) creating a strange, fantasy world."[45] RABM 178.

Work: Etudes-Tableaux, Op. 39 (1916-1917)
Most of Rachmaninoff's biographers suggest that Op. 39 was written at a time when the composer suffered from depression, exhaustion, and despair.

---

45 After extensive consulation with scholars of Symbolist painting, I have found that no work entitled "Morning" by Bocklin seems to exist.

The death of Scriabin had profoundly affected him and on November 5, 1915, Rachmaninoff had written to his friend Marietta Shaginyan asking if he might see her the next day to discuss something on his mind. She recalled, 'He asked me in a very anxious and hesitant tone, "What is your attitude toward death, dear Re? Are you afraid of death?'...The occurrence of two deaths—of Scriabin and Taneyev—had affected him deeply and he had come across a fashionable novel about death and had immediately become ill from terror of it....What scared him was the uncertainty, the impossibility of knowing... 'I have never wanted immortality personally. A man wears out, grows old... But if there is something beyond, then it is terrifying.' He immediately became rather pale and his face began to tremble." RABM 271.

Editor's note: Rachmaninoff uses an obsessive recurrence of the *Dies Irae* throughout Op. 39. Translated from the Latin as "Day of Wrath," this is a thirteenth-century Latin hymn tune referring in liturgical thought to the retribution meted out to the wicked at the Day of Judgement. Rachmaninff used the *Dies Irae* motif probably more than any other composer, almost as a sort of leitmotif for fate and death. The 1915 death of Scriabin, his wife's illness from pneumonia, followed by the death of his father, and his own treatment in the spa town of Essentuki in 1916, all may have contributed to a more morose attitude, and his use of the *Dies Irae* in Op. 39 is likely to have come from something other than his usual fascination with the chant.

When in 1930 Ottorino Respighi suggested orchestrating some of the *Etudes* Rachmaninoff gave him the following explanations in a letter of January 2, 1930, "Will you permit me, Maître, to give you the secret explanations of their composer? These will certainly make the character of these pieces more comprehensible and help you to find the necessary colors for their orchestration. Here are the programs of these Etudes:

> The first Etude in A minor represents the Sea and Seagulls.
> The second Etude in A minor was inspired by the tale of Little Red Riding Hood and the Wolf.
> The third Etude in E-flat major is a scene at a Fair.
> The fourth Etude in D major has a similar character, resembling an oriental march.
> The seventh Etude in C minor is a funeral march. Let me dwell on this a moment longer.

I am sure you will not mock a composer's caprices. The initial theme is a march. The other theme represents the singing of a choir. Commencing with the movement of 16th notes in C minor and a little farther on in E-flat minor a fine rain is suggested, incessant and hopeless. This movement develops—culminating in C minor—the chimes of a church. The finale returns to the first theme, a march." RALM 262-63.

Etude no. 1 in C minor
Riesemann recalls this work was inspired by Böcklin's painting, *Waves* [presumably *The Play of the Waves*]. RAOS 237.

Im Spiel der Wellen (The Play of the Waves)
Arnold Bocklin

Etude no. 6 in A minor
Publicity attached to the Ampico piano roll the composer made of this work in 1922 refers to the "suggestion" that it depicts the story of Little Red Riding Hood and the Wolf. Rachmaninoff confirmed this story privately in a letter of January 2, 1930, to the composer Ottorino Respighi. RABM 274.

Editor's note: Rachmaninoff's daughters were aged four and eight in 1922. Author Barrie Martyn suggests that, as it is known that Rachmaninoff would go into see them every night before they went to bed, it is possible that he read this story to them, putting it in his mind to set it to music. Mr. Martyn gives a very lively and convincing outline of the Red Riding Hood story in this Etude on p. 274 of his book *Rachmaninoff, Composer, Pianist, Conductor*.

Etude no. 7 in C minor

Rachmaninoff describes this etude as a Funeral March, representing the singing of the choir, the "incessant and hopeless rain," ringing of church bells, and the resumption of the march. Barrie Martyn suggests that, "Although Rachmaninoff had presumably recently been present at his father's funeral, it is likely that what is depicted here is his impression of Scriabin's funeral in Moscow, on 16 April, 1915, which he also attended; for not only did that event take place on a bleak and rainy day, but Rachmaninoff himself recalled to Oskar von Riesemann in his *Recollections* the great effect the funeral had on him." RABM 275.

Work: Six Moments Musicaux, Op. 16 (1896)

Moments Musicaux no. 3 in B minor

Author Barrie Martyn writes that of this lovely piece, "Rachmaninoff himself admitted was a picture of a funeral, and the punctuated asymmetrical phrases are like mourners' spoken utterances of grief." RABM 112.

Work: Morceaux de fantaisie, Op. 3 (1892)

Prelude in C-sharp minor, Op. 3, no. 2

Rachmaninoff wrote,

> Absolute music (to which this Prelude belongs) can suggest or induce a mood in the listener; but its primal function is to give intellectual pleasure by the beauty and variety of its form. This was the end sought by Bach in his wonderful series of Preludes, which are a source of unending delight to the educated musical listener. Their salient beauty will be missed if we try to discover in them the mood of the composer. If we must have the psychology of the Prelude, let it be understood that its function is not to express a mood, but to induce it....
>
> The first technical caution is to strike just the right pace in the proclamation of the opening theme and then maintain that pace strictly throughout the first section. One common mistake is to play this opening theme too loudly... the climax does not come at the outset. I have marked these three notes ff. You will find several fff marks later on....
>
> In the agitated section the melody in the right is carried by the first note in each group. But for this I might have marked the passage allegro con fuoco. The player must accommodate his pace to his technical ability. He must not hurry the passage beyond his capacity to make the melody stand out. The repetition of the first movement in doubled octaves calls for all the force the player is capable of. The pupil must be cautioned against mistaking fury for breadth and majesty... RACH 51-53.

Editor's note: The original source for these words of Rachmaninoff is an article in the *Delineator* of 1910 giving his advice on how to play and interpret the Prelude, a portion of which is quoted here. This article in its entirety is recommended for anyone wishing to know Rachmaninoff's views on the interpretation of this work.

Work: Preludes, Op. 23 (1903)
Prelude no. 6 in E-flat major
Elena Gnesina (1874-1967), the Russian composer, once told Rachmaninoff after a concert performance that this prelude seemed to her so radiant and joyous that it must have been composed on a very special day, to which Rachmaninoff replied, "Yes, you are right: it really came to me all at once on the day my daughter was born," that is on May 14, 1903. RABM 151.

Work: Preludes, Op. 32 (1910)
Prelude no. 10 in B minor
Having performed this prelude for many years, the great pianist Benno Moiseiwitsch, a friend of the composer, came to the idea that it had been prompted by Arnold Böcklin's painting *The Return*. This shows a man looking towards a cottage to which he is returning, presumably after a long absence. Moiseiwitsch was able to get Rachmaninoff to admit that this painting had been the source of his inspiration, and also that this was his favorite among the preludes. RAMH 172.

Here is the same story with a slightly different angle. When Moiseiwitsch made his American debut in 1919 he had included this prelude on the program. Rachmaninoff congratulated him on his success and asked him why he had played this particular work, upon which Moiseiwitsch said that it was his favorite among the preludes. Rachmaninoff happily agreed that it was his favorite too. In London, in the spring of 1933, they met again and Moiseiwitsch recalls,

> I was with him after luncheon one day when he smilingly showed me a postcard from a lady admirer asking him if the C-sharp minor Prelude meant to describe the agonies of a man having been nailed down in a coffin while still alive. When I asked him what reply he was going to give, he said, "If the Prelude conjures up a certain picture in her mind, then I would not disillusion her." This gave me courage to ask him something that had been on my mind for very many years. It concerned his Prelude in B minor, for which I had so visualized a certain picture that I could almost translate every bar into words.

They were both amazed to learn that Moiseiwitsch's mental picture and Rachmaninoff's actual source were the same painting, *The Return* by Böcklin. RALM 296-7.

Die Heimkehr (The Homecoming)
Arnold Bocklin

In a filmed interview Moiseiwitsch further elucidated Rachmaninoff's words about the relationship between Bocklin's painting and this Prelude by recalling the composer's words, "That's what it is, it's the *Return*. It was an exile." RAMS

Work: Rhapsody on a Theme of Paganini, Op. 43 (1934)

How surprising it is to find Rachmaninoff suggesting a program for the *Paganini Variations*! But in 1937, when Russian-born dancer and choreographer Mikhail Fokine suggested mounting it as a ballet, Rachmaninoff came up with the following scenario as suggested to Fokine in a letter from August 29, 1937,

> Should one not revive the legend of Paganini selling his soul to the devil in return for perfection in his music-making and also for women? All the variants on the *Dies Irae* theme are the devil and the whole of the middle section (variation 11 to 18) contain love stories. Paganini appears in the theme himself (his first appearance) and for the last time

when vanquished, in the first 12 bars of variations 23. There follows till the end the exultation of the conqueror. The devil first appears in variation 7 and the passage at figure 19 could be a dialogue with Paganini, as his theme blends here with the *Dies Irae*. Variations 8 to 10 show the development of the devil. Variation 11 is the transition into the realm of love; from variation 12 (the minuet) to variation 18 the woman appears for the first time. In variation 13 we see Paganini's first encounter with women; variation 19 is the celebration of Paganini's art—his diabolical pizzicato. It would be useful to see Paganini with a violin—not a real one of course, but something dreamt up, fantastical. What's more, it occurs to me that at the end of the piece a few of the representatives of evil in the struggle for women and art should bear a caricatured, absolutely ludicrous resemblance to Paganini himself. They too should have violins here, but even more fantastically grotesque ones. You are not going to laugh at me, are you? RAKH 108.

Editor's note: While these phrases were re-creative imagery in reverse, it reinforces Rachmaninoff's oft-spoken belief that imagination must be ever present in the creative artist, even in relation to music originally conceived as absolute and non-programmatic.

Work: Sonata in D minor, Op. 28 (1908)

Konstantin Igumnov, the pianist who was to give the premiere of this work, recalled Rachmaninoff telling him, "I heard from him [Rachmaninoff] that he had Goethe's *Faust* in mind when he was composing it: the first movement represents Faust, the second Marguerite and the third the flight to Brocken and Mephistopheles." RAKH 54.

Work: First Suite for Two Pianos, Op. 5 (1893)

On June 5, 1893, Rachmaninoff wrote to Natalya Skalon, a family friend in Moscow, "At present I am working on a fantasy for two pianos, consisting of musical pictures. This was the work now known as the *First Suite for Two Pianos*, Op. 5. The movements are musical representations of epigraphs printed in the score:"

Barcarolle	'At dusk half-heard the dull wave leaps beneath The gondola's slow oar...' (Lermontov)
O Night, O Love	'It is the hour when from the boughs the nightingales' High note if heard...' (Byron, in Russian translation)
Tears	'Tear, human tears, that pour forth beyond telling Early and late, in the dark, out of sight...' (Tyutchev)
Easter Festival	'Across the earth a mighty peel is sweeping Till all the booming air rocks like a sea...' (Khomyakov)

RABM 75.

Chapter 15
Ravel

Work: Concerto in G major and Concerto for the Left Hand

Describing his composing of the two concerti for piano, Ravel told a correspondent of the *Daily Telegraph,*

> It was an interesting experience to conceive and realize the two Concertos at the same time. The first, which I propose to play myself, is a concerto in the strict sense, written in the spirit of Mozart and Saint-Saens. I believe that a concerto can be both gay and brilliant without necessarily being profound or aiming at dramatic effects. It has been said that the concertos of some great classical composers, far from being written for the piano, have been written against it. And I think that this criticism is quite justified.
>
> At the beginning, I meant to call my work a 'divertissement,' but afterwards considered that this was unnecessary, as the name Concerto adequately describes the kind of music it contains. In some ways my Concerto is not unlike my Violin Sonata; it uses certain effects borrowed from jazz, but only in moderation.
>
> The Concerto for the left hand alone is quite different, and has only one movement with many jazz effects; the writing is not so simple. In a work of this sort, it is essential to avoid the impression of insufficient weight in the sound texture, as opposed to a solo part for two hands. So I have used a style which is much more in keeping with the consciously imposing style of the traditional concerto. After an introductory section pervaded by this feeling, there comes an episode like an improvisation which is followed by a jazz section. Only afterwards is one aware that the jazz episode is actually built up from the themes of the first section. RAVE 101-102.

M. Roland-Manuel writes, "The *adagio* [from the Concerto in G major] is really a *lied* whose calm contemplation brings it unusually close to Fauré's musings. The composer confessed to Mme. Long [Marguerite Long], when she praised the free development of the leisurely melody, which she felt came so naturally, that he had written it 'two bars at a time, with frequent recourse to Mozart's Clarinet Quintet.'" RAVE 102.

Work: Gaspard de la Nuit (1908)

The name "Gaspard" is derived from its original Persian form, denoting "the man in charge of the royal treasures": "Gaspard of the Night" or the treasurer of the night thus creates allusions to someone in charge of all that is jewel-like, dark, mysterious, perhaps even morose. DESB 28.

The eerie poems of Aloysius Bertrand, on which Ravel based each movement of *Gaspard*, follow:

Ondine

.... I thought I heard
A vague harmony enchanting my slumber and,
near me, spreading, a murmur like the interrupted songs
of a sad, tender voice.
G. Brugnot—The Two Genii

Listen! - Listen! - It is I, it is Ondine brushing with these drops of water the resonant diamond-panes of your window illuminated by the dull moonbeams; and here in a dress of moire, is the lady of the castle on her balcony gazing at the beautiful starry night and the beautiful slumbering lake.

Each wave is a water sprite swimming in the current, each current is a path winding towards my palace, and my palace is of fluid construction, at the bottom of the lake, within the triangle formed by fire, earth, and air.

Listen! - Listen! - My father is beating the croaking water with a branch of green alder, and my sisters are caressing the cool islands of grasses, water lilies and of gladiolas with their arms of foam, or are laughing at the tottering, bearded willow that is angling.

After murmuring her song, she besought me to accept her ring on my finger, to be the husband of an Undine, and to visit her palace with her, to be the king of the lakes.

And when I replied that I was in love with a mortal woman, she was sulky and vexed; she wept a few tears, burst out laughing and vanished in showers that formed white trickles down my blue window panes.

Le Gibet

What do I see stirring around that gibbet?
—from Faust
Ah! Could what I hear be the cold night yelping, or the hanged man uttering a sigh on the gallows fork?
Could it be some cricket singing from its hiding place in the moss and sterile ivy with which the forest covers its floor out of pity?
Could it be some fly hunting for prey and blowing its horn all around those ears deaf to the fanfare of the gallows?
Could it be some cockchafer plucking a bloody hair from his bald scalp in its uneven flight?
Or could it be some spider embroidering a half-ell of muslin as a tie for the strangled neck?
It is the bell ringing by the walls of a city below the horizon, and the carcass of a hanged man reddened by the setting sun.

Scarbo

He looked under the bed, in the fireplace, in the chest; nobody. He could not understand where he had entered or where he had escaped.
Hoffmann—Nachtstücke
Oh! how often have I heard and seen Scarbo, when at midnight the moon shines in the sky like a silver shield on an azure banner strewn with golden bees!
How often have I heard his laughter booming in the shadow of my alcove, and his nails grating on the silk of my bed curtains!
How often have I seen him come down from the ceiling, pirouette on one foot and roll around the room like the spindle that has fallen from a witch's distaff!
Did I at such times think he had vanished? Then the dwarf would grow bigger between the moon and me like the bell tower of a Gothic cathedral, a round golden bell shaking on his pointed cap!
But soon his body would become blue, diaphanous as the wax of a taper; his face would become pale as the wax of a candle end—and suddenly he would be extinguished.

RAPM 89.

In a letter to Ida Godebska on July 7, 1908, Ravel wrote, "At the moment inspiration seems to have quickened. After all too many months of pregnancy, *Gaspard de la Nuit* will perceive the light of day…As for *Gaspard*, the devil has had a hand in it. No wonder, for the devil himself is indeed the author of these poems." RAVL 111.

Ondine
Stuckenschmidt wrote, "We know from Vlado Perlemuter[46] that Ravel did not wish his *Ondine* to be played too slowly." RAVL 112.

---

46 Vlado Perlemuter (1904-2002) was a distinguished Lithuanian-born French pianist and teacher.

Ravel is reported as saying that in the opening of his "Ondine" he was more interested in a sense of rippling water than hearing every note. AFPM 221.

Scarbo

According to Stuckenschmidt, "when the pianist Perlemuter studied the *Gaspard de la Nuit* cycle with him, Ravel told him he planned the "Scarbo" as a caricature of romanticism but that (and here his voice sank to a whisper) perhaps he had let himself be captivated by it. The vehement, driving seventh, under which Ravel wrote the words *quelle horreur*, is closer to true romantic feeling than to any caricature of it." RAVL 114.

Editor's note: While Stuckenschmidt does not indicate where Ravel's annotation '*quelle horreur*' was placed, based on the "driving seventh" clue there are two likely spots. One is at ms. 32 and the other at ms. 121. Either place would justly reflect the mood "what horror."

Work: Jeux d'eau (1901)

Ravel, realizing that *Jeux d'eau* was the starting point for every pianistic innovation in his work, wrote, "This piece, inspired by the sound of water and the music of fountains, waterfalls, and streams, is built up on two themes like the first movement of a sonata, without being entirely subjected to the classical scheme of tonality." RAVE 31.

In a letter to Jacques Durand from Chalet Habas Saint Jean-de-Luz, 27 September, 1917, Debussy wrote some comments on the pianist Francis Plante: "Mon cher Jacques, ...may I be allowed to tell you about Francis Plante?... He played- very well- the 'Toccata' (from *Pour le piano* by C Debussy) and was marvelous too in Liszt's *Feux Follets*. Much less good in Ravel's *Jeux d'eau*. This piece's butterfly wings can't support a virtuoso's weight (or his pedaling, whichever you will)." DELE 331.

Work: Miroirs (Reflections) (1904-1905)

Ravel wrote, "The title, *Miroirs*, five piano pieces composed in 1905, has authorized my critics to consider this collection as being among those works which belong to the Impressionistic movement. I do not contradict this at all, if one understands the term by analogy. A rather fleeting analogy, what's more, since Impressionism does not seem to have any precise meaning outside the domain of painting. In any case, the term 'mirror' should not lead one to assume that I want to affirm a subjective theory of art. A sentence by Shakespeare helped me to formulate a completely opposite position...'the eye sees not itself but by reflection, by some other things'" (*Julius Caesar*, Act 1 Scene 2.). RAVV 17.

Of *Miroirs*, Ravel's friend and biographer Roland-Manuel writes, "Ravel was harking back to a secular tradition of French music which, unlike Beethoven, preferred to 'paint' rather than to 'express emotion.' He sought not so much to express and give life to states of mind as to represent the faces and scenes which give rise to them." RAVE 42.

Noctuelles (Nocturnal Moths)

This first piece is dedicated to the poet Léon–Paul Fargue and was inspired by his lines, "The nocturnal moths in their barns launch themselves clumsily into the air, going from one perch to another." RAVV 6.

Perlemutter, who studied Ravel's work with him, said the composer wanted the sudden crescendos (especially at bars 23, 26, 106, and 107) brought out in contrast with the surrounding texture. RAVV 6.

With regard to the central section the French pianist Henriette Faure recalled, "[W]hen I played him [Ravel] this passage with its frequently *expressif* markings, he said to me in anxious and slightly irritated tones, 'Keep going, keep going, and don't be lachrymose.'" RAVV 6.

Oiseaux Tristes (Sad Birds)

"The *Miroirs*," said Ravel, "are a collection of piano pieces that mark a change in my harmonic development that is so profound that they have put many musicians out of countenance who up to that point have been familiar with my style.

Chronologically the first of these pieces—and the most typical of them all—is, I think, the second of the group: *Oiseaux Tristes...* In it I evoke birds lost in the torpor of a somber forest during the most torrid hours of summertime." RAVE 41.

Émile Vuillermoz, French music and drama critic and intimate of Ravel, recalls that the idea for the piece came to him in the forest of Fontainebleau: "He was staying with friends and one morning he heard a blackbird whistling a tune, and was enchanted by its elegant, melancholy arabesque. He had merely to transcribe this tune accurately, without changing a note, to produce the limpid, poetic piece which spiritualises the nostalgic call of the French brother of the Forest Bird in *Siegfried*." RAVV 6.

To Henriette Faure Ravel emphasized the importance of distinguishing two levels in the texture: "the bird calls on a high, rather strident level, with rapid arabesques, and by contrast, the somber, stifling atmosphere of the forest on a lower level, rather heavy and muted, with a lot of pedal but not much movement." [And discussing the last page, he said] "*ad libitum* does not, as some pianists think, mean all over the place—and to keep them on the straight and narrow, I've written *presque ad libitum...*" RAVV 6.

Ravel's friend Roland-Manuel wrote,

> One evening after he had been giving his interpretation of *Un cahier d'esquisse* to the famous composer (Debussy) of this little known work, Vines arrived at the Rue de Crivy still enraptured by what he had just heard: Debussy had told him that he hoped to compose music with a form so free as to seem like an improvisation; and to write works which gave the impression of being taken straight out of a sketch book.

> Ravel was there that evening. Contrary to expectation, he approved the idea. He admitted that the work he had on hand was concerned with a similar problem: "I should like to do something to help me shake off *Jeux d'eau.*" Shortly afterwards Ravel played "Oiseaux Tristes" to his friends. RAVE 41.

Une barque sur l'océan (A Boat upon the Ocean)

Of this work Ravel asked Vlado Perlemuter to make sure the opening was not hustled or too fast—he did not want the piece to become an exercise in virtuosity. RAVV 7.

Ravel told Henriette Faure that *Une barque* should not "sink into formulaic uniformity as I've heard it do with some pianists, making it boring for the listener. You must diversify it." RAVV 6.

Alborado del gracioso

From a letter of 14 September, 1907, Ravel wrote to Ferdinand Sinzig of Steinway and Sons in New York, "I understand your bafflement over how to translate the title "Alborado del gracioso". That is precisely why I decided not to translate it. The fact is that the *gracioso* of Spanish comedy is a rather special character and one which, as far as I know, is not found in any other theatrical tradition. We do have an equivalent in the French theatre: Beaumarchais's Figaro. But he's more philosophical, less well-meaning than his Spanish ancestor. The simplest thing, I think, is to follow the title with the rough translation "Morning Song of the Clown" ("Aubade du bouffon"). That will be enough to explain the humoristic title of this piece." RAVV 7.

Henriette Faure stated that Ravel regarded the execution of the repeated notes as less important than that of the glissandi, "which by interrupting the repeated notes reduce them to a secondary role. The tempo, however, must be implacable." RAVV 7.

Ravel suggested to Perlemutter that the arpeggiated chords must be "very taut, like plucked notes on a guitar." RAVV 7.

La vallée des cloches

Of this work French pianist Robert Casadeus said Ravel told him it was inspired by the sound of the bells at midday in Paris. RAVV 7.

Henriette Faure recorded that,

> Ravel was merciless about my playing of this piece, which he condemned as being heavy and unvaried in timbre. At the opening, he tried to get me to play the carillon of double notes in semiquavers in the right hand, and the more settled sounds of the high octave bells which punctuate them in the left, on two very distinct levels. And the whole thing had to remain within a *pianissimo* which he could, some mysterious way, produce without it sounding feeble.

> The insinuating character of the high left hand octaves means that one must not use the wrist, which would only over-ink the sketch. The great calm, lyrical outpouring [of the central section], on the other hand, requires a profound sonority and a *legato* which comes from a hand closely wedded to the keys, and from a weight of arm that one gets ideally from sitting rather low at the keyboard. RAVV 7.

Work: Tombeau de Couperin (1914-1917)

Ravel at first planned to write a suite of French dances for piano, as an homage to 18th-century French composers, especially Francios Couperin. After the First World War began in 1914 people with whom he was intimately acquainted were killed in combat. Ravel dedicated a movement of the Suite to each of his fallen comrades. The suite now had a dual purpose.

Prelude-	dedicated to Lieutenant Jacques Charlot, who transcribed Ravel's four-hand piece *Ma mère l'oye for solo piano*, killed in battle, 1915.
Fugue-	dedicated to Second Lieutenant Jean Cruppi, killed in battle in unknown year.
Forlane-	dedicated to Lieutenant Gabriel Deluc, a Basque painter from Saint Jean de Luz, killed at the battle of Souain, 1916.
Rigaudon-	dedicated to Pierre and Pascal Gaudin, brothers killed by the same shell on the first day of their arrival at the front, 1914.
Menuet-	dedicated to the memory of Jean Dreyfuss, killed in battle in 1916 or 1917.
Toccata-	dedicated to Joseph de Marliave, French musicologist and husband of noted pianist Marguerite Long. He was killed in the first month of the war, August 1914.

RAFP

Of this work Alfred Cortot has said, "*Le Tombeau de Couperin* of Ravel, conceived in the beginning as a tribute to the old French master, has become little by little a tribute to the memory of friends who were killed in the Great War, and thence a glorification of French genius in general." COMI 85.

Stuckenschmidt writes, "There is a deep, painful, even tragic emotion concealed beneath the bright, playful movement of these dances and their artful imitation of harpsichord speech.   Each of the six movements is dedicated to a man who lost his life in the World War." RAVL 173.

Forlane
This movement was dedicated to the memory of Lieutenant Gabriel Deluc, a Basque painter from Saint-Jean-de-Luz.

Because of its bizarre character, the *forlane* has often been the subject of conjecture about its programmatic associations. Stuckenschmidt compiles the following images: "Hélène Jourdan-Morhange sees in the piece only a solemn obeisance on bended knees, while an English essayist (Norman Demuth) claims it has been said that, 'it suggests the taste of pineapple.' Vlado Perlemuter, who studied the *Tombeau* with Ravel, calls the "Forlane" the piece that most faithfully affirms its allegiance to the past through the sound of its cadences, influenced by antiquity; he speaks of its ending, without the slightest retard, as a music box effect." RAVL 177.

Work: Valses Nobles et Sentimetales (1911)
Roland-Manuel has said, "Conditioned by this invocation of gratuitous enjoyment, the *Valses Nobles et Sentimentales* by their title acknowledge the patronage of Schubert, who, in his *Valses Nobles* and his *Valses Sentimentales*, intended to offer the fair Viennese the homage of a smile." RAVE 60.

At the beginning of the score is the seductively languorous phrase, "delicious and ageless pleasure of a useless occupation." This aphorism is borrowed from Henri de Regneirs: preface to *Recontres de Monsieur de Breot*[47] (1904). RAVE 60.

Stuckenschmidt writes, "Along with the dedication the manuscript carries as motto a quotation from Henri de Regnier that is typical of Ravel:

'the delightful and always new pleasure of a useless occupation.'

---

47 Henri-François-Joseph de Regnier (1864-1936) was a French Symbolist poet and novelist.

This coy recognition of uselessness, or 'art for art's sake,' typifies the attitude of many artists just before World War I.

It is a part of the musical and intellectual dandyism that Ravel embodies so distinctly." RAVL 144-145.

Ravel wrote, "The title *Valses Nobles et Sentimentales* sufficiently indicates my intention of writing a cycle of waltzes after the example of Schubert. Following on the virtuosity that is the basis for *Gaspard de la Nuit* I use here a distinctly clearer style of writing. This makes the harmony more concrete and ceases the profile of the music to stand out. The *Valses Nobles et Sentimentales* was given its premiere at one of the concerts of the S.M.I., where the composers are not named, in the midst of protest and catcalls. The audience voted the authorship of each piece. By a small majority the paternity of the waltzes was ascribed to me. The seventh strikes me as most characteristic." RAVL 142.

Work: La Valse, transcription (1919-1920)

Editor's note: *La Valse* was originally scored for orchestra as a *poème chorégraphique* and was meant to be staged as a ballet during the 1920-21 season. Owing to a personal rift with Sergei Diaghilev it was performed as an orchestral work until it was finally staged in 1928. From the beginning, however, it came replete with stage directives and imagery. It was arranged by Ravel for solo piano and two pianos in 1921.

La Valse bears a sort of scenic directive at the beginning of the score, "Through whirling clouds, waltzing couples may be faintly distinguished. The clouds gradually scatter: one sees at letter A an immense hall peopled with a whirling crowd. The scene is gradually illuminated. The light of the chandeliers bursts forth at the fortissimo letter B. Set in an imperial court, about 1855." RAVL 189.

Stuckenschmidt writes, "And yet the work eventually named *La Valse* is essentially tragic. Ravel's own commentary permits no doubt of it. He is said to have appraised it as a 'fantastic and fatefully inescapable whirlpool,' though this idea was merged into his original concept of a kind of apotheosis of the Viennese waltz." RAVL 187.

Th. Lindenlaub classed *La Valse* as an occasional piece, a picture of post-war Vienna, animated by "the contrast between the light and careless dances of bygone days and the distressed and unhappy people who either dance from habit or to dull their sadness and hunger in dead delights. And this rising and mournful frenzy, the struggle between the life loving Johann Strauss and the will to destruction, takes on the phases of a *danse macabre*." RAVE 86.

In a letter to Maurice Emmanuel of October 14, 1922 Ravel stated, "While some discover an attempt at parody, indeed caricature, others categorically see a tragic allusion in it—the end of the Second Empire, the situation in Vienna after the war, etc.... This dance may seem tragic, like any other emotion... pushed to the extreme. But one should only see in it what the music expresses: an ascending progression of sonority, to which the stage comes along to add light and movement." RAOR 229.

Chapter 16

Schumann

Work: Album fur die Jugend, Op. 68 (1848)

Editor's note: In 1920 the only surviving daughter of Robert and Clara Schumann, Eugenie Schumann, wrote her memoirs. Her charming recollections of lessons with her mother on several pieces from the *Album for the Young* follow.

Armes Waisenkind (Poor Orphan)

The first piece I learned was 'Armes Waisenkind,' and my mother explained it to me like this, "This is a theme of eight bars divided into twice four. The second four are a repetition of the first, all but the ending, which leads back to the tonic, while the first four end on the dominant. In a case like that you must vary the dynamics of the second four bars from those of the first, either shade them more strongly or more softly, but end them as strongly as you began the piece. Where the entire eight bars are repeated play them exactly like the first time. If they are again repeated in the source of the piece, shade them differently the third time. In this "Armes Waisenkind" I should play the last repetition softly, graduating to a pianissimo. She taught me to play this piece with the greatest patience, and according to this rule, which helped me understand and interpret other pieces where it applied." SCEU 99.

Jägerliedchen (Little Hunting Song)

"Of the 'Jägerleidchen,' no. 7, she said, 'I can see the whole hunt before me, horns blowing, horses prancing, the hunters arriving from all sides.' Where the middle part is marked piano she said, 'The startled deer are flying into the bushes.' Four bars from the end, where the F unexpectedly becomes a G, she said, 'A bugler's note has cracked; you will have heard the horns in the orchestra do that sometimes.'" SCEU 99.

Wilder Reiter (Wild Rider)
"I remember the sforzati, which I played meaninglessly and, as my mother said 'anaemically,' in '*Wilder Reiter*,' no. 8. 'When a breakneck rider gallops about the room, he knocks his hobby horse against chairs and tables.' Suddenly not only could I play these sforzati, but the idea of sforzati altogether, the suddenness with which it appears between the two less powerful notes, became once and for all clear to me and easy to execute." SCEU 99.

Frölicher Landmann (Happy Farmer)
"Of the 'Frölicher Landmann' she said that 'the father was at first singing alone; his little son joins him in the middle part. Neither this not the 'Schnitterlied' should be played too fast: Look at peasants doing their work; you will find that they never hurry themselves, not even in their dances.'" SCEU 100.

Knecht Ruprecht
"In 'Knect Ruprecht' Santa Claus could be heard stumbling upstairs knocking his staff on each step. In the middle part the trembling children hide, the old saint speaks encouragingly to them, empties his sack, and stumps downstairs again." SCEU 100.

Lustig and Mai, lieber Mai (Folk Song and May, sweet May)
"With no. 9 'Lustig,' and no. 13, 'Mai, lieber Mai,' my mother took untold trouble. It was long before I played every tie, every portamento, every bit of phrasing as it was meant. She gave me no rest, and I am grateful to her to this day, for these pieces are truly enjoyable only when the minutest detail is observed." SCEU 100.

Kleiner Morgenwanderer and Reiterstuck (Little Morning Wanderer and The Horseman)
"In the "Kleiner Morgenwanderer" she taught me to play the chords as though I were lifting my feet in marching, not quite legato, and I felt at once that this gave the right character to the piece. She thought that the little wanderer was rather depressed in the beginning of the second part, at the thought of leaving home, but soon relieved his feelings with a yodel and walked on bravely, until the village was lost to his sight and he only heard the church bells ringing. I had to practice the slow diminuendo of these, as also the diminuendo of the hoofs in "Reiterstuck," no. 23, for a long time before Mama was satisfied. In the latter piece it was all the more difficult as the diminuendo already starts piano." SCEU 100.

Landliches Lied (Rustic Song)
"In 'Landliches Lied,' no. 20, clearly only a few girls were singing at first; then a mixed chorus of boys and girls joins in. At the beginning of the second part one girl is singing a solo, and at the return of the first theme 'one of the boys accompanies her on a reed pipe which he has just cut for himself.'" SCEU 101.

Erinnerung (Remembrance)
"This work, so lovingly written in the style of a Song without Words, has the subtitle, 4 November 1847. 'Todestag Mendelssohns (Mendelssohn's death date).'" SCJC 119.

Mignon
"'*Mignon*' was one of her favorites, and she taught it me with such love that it became my favorite too. I was always looking forward to the fourth and third bars from the end, where careful shading will quite naturally give the intended significance to the dissonance." SCEU 100.

Matronslied (Sailor's Song)
"Last of all I studied the '*Matronslied*' no. 37. I do not remember if I saw in it at the time all that my mother did; but when I play it now I see before me, as in a picture, the infinite loneliness and melancholy of the seas, the watch's call, the heavy tread of sailors, their ponderous dance. Explanations of this kind were very helpful to me." SCEU 100.

Eugenie Schumann continues about Clara's view of images by writing, "But it must not be thought that my mother was at all lavish with picturesque illustrations of this kind. She only gave them where she thought that they would help with the interpretation, and sometimes with no intention to instruct, simply because these images were a pleasure to herself. Later in life I once asked her whether all music conveyed pictures to her, and she said, 'Yes; and the older I grow, the more.'" SCEU 100.

In a letter to Adolf Schubring from Lichtenthal bei Baden-Baden, 25 June, 1865, Brahms writes, "The three stars in one place of the *Album fur die Jugend* denote the day of Mendelssohn's death, I thought that the date is given there." BRAL 235.

Work: Carnaval, Op. 9 (1834-1835)
Editor's note: Schumann's *Carnaval* is a pianistic representation of an elaborate and luxurious masked ball during Carnival season. Traditionally Carnival in Roman Catholic countries was a time of excessive festivity generally observed in February in anticipation of Lent, a six-week period of prayer, penance, repentance, and self-denial. In light of the impending Lent,

Schumann's *Carnaval* should not only be played with impeccable artistry, taste, and pianism, but with enthusiastic colors and, at times, luxurious abandon.

The pieces are named after characters at this ball, personalities either imaginary, legendary, or from Schumann's own acquaintances. In a letter of August 23, 1837, Schumann actually referred to the pieces as "masked dances." For those not familiar with the imagery of some of the movements a brief description follows.

Pierrot

A character from the Italian *Commedia dell'arte*, usually a simpleminded and honest servant. He was usually portrayed as an unsuccessful lover and the victim of pranks of his fellow comedians. Unlike most of the other stock characters, he played without a mask, his face whitened with powder. It is in this guise that he is probably meant to appear in *Carnaval*. PEEN 236.

Arlequin

A depiction of Harlequin, a faithful valet and servant from the *Commedia dell'arte*. Always in search of food and female companionship, he had the wit and cunning of a mischievous child. His black half mask had tiny eyeholes and quizzically arched eyebrows that were accentuated by a wrinkled forehead. HAEN 708.

Eusebius

Eusebius is one of the alter egos of the composer and a member of the *Davidsbünd* (League of David). He is calm, intimate and sensitive.

Florestan

Florestan is another alter ego of Schumann in attendance at the ball and also a member of the *Davidsbünd*. He represents the composer's fiery, impetuous side.

Coquette and *Réplique*

Coquette is the depiction of a flirtatious young lady at the ball and could *Réplique* be the sarcastic masculine response to the flirtation? Niecks says it "is no doubt a mocking reply to *Coquette*." SCNI 176.

Sphinxes

Sphinxes were mythological animals with the body of a lion, the wings of a bird, and the face of a woman who asked difficult, unanswerable riddles. Schumann's Sphinxes consist of three sections of one bar each, with no key, tempo or dynamic indications. The notes use the configurations S-C-H-A, A-S-C-H and A-S-C-H, providing a thematic basis for the masked personages of *Carnaval*. ROSE 221-222.

Editor's note: The Sphinxes are often omitted in performance though Rachmaninoff, Horowitz, Cortot, and Uchida have included them in their recordings.

Chiarina

Niecks writes, "Chiarina is Clara (Clärchen)." SCNI 176-177.

Chopin

Here is an evocation of the Polish composer, who is also in attendance at the ball.

Estrella

While Frederick Niecks writes that *"Estrella* is Ernestine von Fricken," with whom Schumann was romantically involved when *Carnaval* was composed, Niecks also shares an 1837 letter by Schumann to Moscheles in which he called *Estrella* "a name such as is placed under portraits to fix the picture better in one's memory." SCNI 177.

Reconnaissance

Schumann described this movement in the same letter to Moscheles as a "scene of recognition." SCNI 176.

Editor's note: Could this be Schumann and Ernestine (Estrella) recognizing each other at the ball, or more tantalizing, Ernestine and Clara's (Chiarina's) mutual recognition?

Pantalon et Colombine

These were both stock characters from the *Commedia dell'arte*. Pantalon was an older avaricious man always desirous of romantic entanglements with younger women. Columbine was usually a saucy and adroit servant girl, often the object of Pantalon's pursuit. PAEN 475.

Intermezzo: Paganini

Here is a musical depiction of the stunning virtuosity of the celebrated violinist Niccolo Paganini, who is also in attendance at the ball.

Aveu

According to Schumann this is "a confession of love." SCNI 176.

Promenade

Schumann described Promenade as "a walk such as one takes at a German ball with one's partner." SCNI 176

Marche des "Davidsbündler" contre les Philistins

The final movement is a March of Triumph. The title "David against the Philistines," alluding to the Biblical story from the seventeenth chapter of the First book of Samuel, serves only as a backdrop for more pressing issues to Schumann.[48] The *Grossvater Tanz*, identified by Schumann in the score as a "Theme from the 17th Century" represents the Philistines of his day, or those holding to old-fashioned, outdated and inartistic ideals. SCWD 151.

Work: Davidsbündlertänze, Op. 6 (1837)
The inscription at the beginning of the score reads:

> 'Along the way we go are mingled weal and woe:
> in weal though glad, be grave, though sad, be brave.'

SCHN 48.

In a letter to Clara on January 5, 1838, Robert wrote, "There are many marriage motifs in the dances; they were written in the 'finest frenzy' in my experience. Someday I will explain them to you." SCSL 179.

In a letter from February 6, 1838, Robert wrote to Clara, "Didn't you receive the *Davids Tänze*...? I sent them to you a week ago Saturday...My Clara will find out what's in the *Tänze*; they are dedicated to her more than anything else of mine—the story is a bachelor's party,[49] and you can imagine the beginning and the end. If ever I was happy at the piano, it was when I composed them." SCLL 94-95.

At the end of a letter to Clara from February 12, 1838, Robert wrote, "I have just discovered that it strikes twelve at the end of the *Davids Tänze*

I wonder if that means anything." SCEL 263.

In a letter to Clara of March 17, 1838, Robert made an interesting comparison between *Davidsbündler Tänze* and *Carnaval* with the following

---

48 The Davidsbünd (League of David) was a group of characters which existed in Schumann's imagination, and were written about frequently in his early essays in the *Neue Zeitschrift für Musik*. They stood for the highest ideals in music and were united against the Philistines, who were reactionary, uncultivated enemies, representing the current vogue of empty virtuosity and inartistic values. The allusion to David and the Philistines originates with the Biblical account from 1 Samuel 17.

49 The German word used here is 'Polterabend', which is a party held on the eve of a wedding day.

remarks: "You haven't looked deeply enough into my *Davidsbündler Tänze*; I think they are quite different from *Carnaval* and are to the latter as faces are to masks…One thing I know: they were conceived in joy while the other one was often difficult and painful." SCLL 130.

Schumann wrote touchingly at the top of the 18ᵗʰ piece, "Superfluously, Eusebius added the following, and his eyes filled with tears of happiness." ROSE 233.

Schumann wrote over the ninth piece, and end of first book, "Here Florestan stopped and his lips quivered in pain." ROSE 235.

Work: Etudes after Paganini Caprices, Op. 3 (1832)

The only work of his own which Schumann reviewed in the *Neue Zeitschrift Für Musick* was the Paganini Variations, of which he remarked,

> Among other observations, I would like to have noticed: In No. 2, I selected a different accompaniment, as I thought the tremolo of the original would too greatly fatigue player and hearers. I consider this number especially tender and lovely and sufficient in itself to assure Paganini's position as one of the first among modern Italian composers. Florestan says: "Here he is an Italian river which reaches the sea across Germany."

> The effectiveness of No. 3 does not appear to be in proportion to its difficulty; but he who has vanquished this has conquered many things along with it.

> In the working out of No. 4 the Funeral March from Beethoven's *Eroica* Symphony floated before me. Perhaps others will guess as much. This entire number is filled with romanticism.

> In No. 5 I intentionally omitted the expression marks, leaving students to seek out for themselves its heights and depths. This will afford a good opportunity for testing the pupils' perceptive faculty.

> I doubt that No. 6 will immediately be recognized by anyone who has played the violin caprices. Played faultlessly as a pianoforte piece, it is charming in the flow of its harmonies. I may mention that the left hand, crossing the right (excepting the twenty-fourth bar) has but one key to strike—that of the highest upward-pointing note. The chords sound fullest when the crossing finger of the left hand sharply meets the fifth of the right hand. The following Allegro was difficult to harmonize. The hard and somewhat flat return to E major (pages 20 to 21) could scarcely be softened; one would have to write a new composition. SCMM 257.

Work: Fantasiestücke, Op. 12 (1837)

In Der Nacht (In the night)

From a letter to Clara, April 21, 1838, Robert wrote, "After I finished it I found, to my delight, that it contained the story of Hero and Leander.

Hero and Leander
Jean Joseph Taillasson

Of course you know it: How Leander swam every night through the sea to his love who awaited him with a beacon and showed him the way with a lighted torch. It is a beautiful, romantic old story. When I am playing "In der Nacht," I cannot get rid of the idea; first he throws himself into the sea; she calls him; he answers; he battles with the waves and reaches land in safety; then the Cantilena, when they are clasped in each other's arms, until they have to part again, and he cannot tear himself away until night wraps everything in darkness once more. Do tell me if the music suggests the same thing to you." SCEL 274-274.

Ende vom Lied (End of the Song)

In a letter of March 13, 1838, Robert wrote to Clara describing his feelings about *Ende vom Lied*, "I thought, now I had reached the end, everything would resolve itself in a merry wedding. But when I thought of you, sorrow came over me, and the result was a chime of wedding bells mingled with a death knell." SCHI 4.

Work: Fantasy in C major, Op. 17 (1836, revised 1839)

Friedrich Schlegel's[50] motto, which appears at the beginning of the Fantasy, was not connected with this work until the *Stichvorlage* of 1838:

Through all the tones
in earth's many colored dreams,
a quiet tone sounds through all others
for those who quietly listen

Many pianists take the motto to refer only to the first movement of the *Fantasy*, but as Marston writes, "In the *Stichvorlage*, where the motto first appears, Schumann directed that it was to be printed on the verso of the title page in the first edition. Placed there, it would clearly seem to be a motto for the *Fantasie* as a whole. But Schumann's instructions were not followed, and in the first edition the motto stands at the head of the first movement, which is otherwise untitled. Later editions have all tended to follow suit..." SCHU 61.

In the formative stages of the Fantasy Schumann bestowed an imaginative title on each movement. In a letter to Clara on April 13, 1838, Robert wrote, "The next things to be printed are some Fantasies, but to distinguish them from the Phantasie-Stücke I have called them *Ruine, Siegesbogen und Sternbild,* and *Dichtungen* [Ruins, Triumphal Arch and Star-Pictures, and Poems]. It was a long time before I could think of that last word. It strikes me as being a very refined and characteristic title for a piece of music." SCEL 268.

First Movement

Schumann wrote in a letter to Clara on March 17, 1838, "The first movement is probably the most passionate thing I've ever done—a profound lament for you..." SCLL 129.

A year later on April 22, 1839, Robert wrote to Clara, "You can understand the *Fantasy* only if you remember the unfortunate summer of 1836 when I gave you up. I don't have any reason to compose in such an unhappy and melancholy manner now..." SCLL 166.

On June 9, 1839, Robert wrote to Clara, "Tell me what you think of the first movement of the Phantasie. Does it also conjure up many images in your mind? I like this melody best—

---

50 Karl Wilhelm Friedrich Schlegel (1771-1829) was a German poet, author, critic, scholar, and leading figure in German Romanticism.

I suppose you are the *Ton* in the motto [the Schlegel motto referred to above]? I almost think you must be." 291-292.

According to Anton Strelezki, Liszt observed in a lesson after hearing Strelezki play the Fantasy that "everyone plays this opening movement in too vigorous a style, it is preeminently dreamy, *träumerisch*, as he (Liszt) expressed it in German, and altogether the reverse of 'noisy and heavy.' I do not mean though that it should be played at all *apathetically*, for, of course, here and there are phrases which demand vigorous execution; but the whole outline of the movement should preserve more of the *dreamy* character, than is usual to depict in it." SCHU 93-94.

Second Movement

On May 23, 1839, Clara wrote to Schumann on receiving the score of the *Fantasy* for the first time, "Yesterday I received your wonderful *Fantasy*—today I am still half ill with rapture, as I played through it I was involuntarily drawn towards the window, and there I felt like leaping out to the beautiful spring flowers and embracing them. I dreamed a beautiful dream during your *Fantasy*. The 'March' is enchanting, and bars 8-16 on page 15 (that is, bars 8-16 of the second movement) make me quite beside myself. Just tell me what you were thinking of in them? I have never had such a feeling, I heard a full orchestra, I can't tell you how I felt. It hurt me much and made me unhappy to think how long it is since I heard a single note of yours—and yet your notes are still so vivid in my memory." SCHU. 9-10.

On May 28, 1839, Clara wrote to Robert, "I have already learned the 'March' from the *Fantasy* and revel in it! If only I could hear it played by a large orchestra! I'm always going hot and then again cold in it. Do tell me what kind of inspiration is in you." SCHU 10.

On 16 June, 1839, Clara wrote to Robert about her own 'programme' of the 2nd movement: "The 'March' strikes me as a victory march of warriors returning from battle, and in the A flat section I think of the young girls of the village, all dressed in white, each with a garland in her hand crowning the warriors kneeling before them." SCHU 85.

Third Movement

From Charles Rosen we read of this movement, "Schumann wrote to his distant beloved, Clara Wieck, from whom he was still separated by order of her father, 'For hours I have been playing over and over again a melody from the last movement of my Phantasie...Are you not the secret tone that runs through the work?' The melody from the last movement about which he writes to Clara must be this one [which is repeated continually], marked 'etwas bewegter'":

Fantasy, mm. 31-37.

ROSE 101-103.

Work: Humoresque, Op. 20 (1839)

From the reminiscences of Eugenie Schumann we read the recollection of a conversation with her mother, Clara, who said, "Whatever your father did, saw, read, would at once shape itself into music. When he read poetry resting on the sofa after dinner, in turned into songs. When he saw you children at play, little pieces of music grew out of your games. While he was writing down the Humoresque, some acrobats came along and performed in front of our house; imperceptibly the music he made stole into the composition. He was quite unconscious of these inspirations. It would be foolish to think that he used them intentionally as an incentive." SCEU 98.

Work: Intermezzo, Op. 4 (1832)

Of the second of the set in E minor Joan Chisell suggests it "is of the greatest artistic value." The mood of the opening is one of disturbed agitation, and in the contrasting middle section Schumann reveals the inner meaning of the music by writing Gretchen's words 'Meine Ruh' ist hin' in the score. SCJC 104.

Work: Kinderscenen, Op. 15 (1838)

In a letter to Clara on March 17, 1838, Robert wrote of the origin of *Kinderscenen*, "But before I forget it let me tell you what else I have composed. Whether it was an echo of what you said to me once 'That sometimes I seemed to you like a child,' anyhow, I suddenly got an inspiration, and knocked off about thirty quaint little things, from which I have selected twelve and called them "Kinderscenen." They will amuse you but of course you must forget that you are a performer. They have such titles as "Füurchtenmachen" "Am Kamin" "Haschemann" "Bittendes Kind" "Ritter vom Steckenpferd" "Von fremden Ländern" "Curiose Geschicte" etc., and I don't know what besides. Well, they all explain themselves, and what's more they are as easy as possible." SCEL 264-265.

Editor's note: fear many of us have lost Schumann's original conception— that these works "are as easy as possible" and "that one must forget that he is a performer."

Work: Kreisleriana, Op. 16 (1838)

Editor's note: Kreisleriana refers to Kappelmeister Johannes Kreisler, the intense, wild musician invented by the poet, musician, and novelist E.T.A. Hoffmann. Along with a literary tom-cat, he is the hero of Hoffmann's novel *The Life and Opinions of Kater Murr*, as well as two collections of short stories known as *Kreisleriana*, which also form the literary and imaginative basis for Schumann's set of piano pieces.

In a letter to Simonin de Sire on March 15, 1839, Schumann wrote, "I like *Kreisleriana* the best of all these things. The title can only be understood by Germans.   Kreisler is an eccentric, wild, and gifted *Capellmeister*, a character created by E. T. A. Hoffmann; you will like him in many respects…" SCMM 259.

Hoffmann's portrait of Kapellmeister Johannes Kreisler

Illustration of Kater Murr
E.T.A. Hoffmann

From the tale by E. T. A. Hoffmann[51] we find the following words from Kreisler himself, epitomizing his vivid and surreal imagination: "Less in actual dreams than in those dreamlike moments before the onset of sleep, and particularly after I have been listening for a long time to music, I find correspondences of colours, scents and sounds. I have the sensation that they have all been produced in the same mysterious manner by a ray of light and must ultimately unite in glorious concert. The scent of crimson carnations has a strange mystic power over me; unconsciously I sink into reveries as the deep notes of the basset-horn rise from afar in a gradual crescendo and then die away." ETAH 59.

Charles Rosen suggests, "The title Kreisleriana comes from E.T.A. Hoffmann; the work is based, I think, less on the collection of stories and essays called Kreisleriana than on the novel *Kater Murr* (*Cat Growl*), which has Johannes Kreisler as its hero. In this unfinished novel, the manuscript account of the stormy and passionate life of the young musician is found by his cat, Murr, who proceeds to write his own biography on the back of each sheet of paper. The manuscript is sent in this state to his publisher, who prints it as he finds it, alternating pages of Kreisler and Murr." ROSE 673.

---

51 Ernst Theodor Amadeus Hoffmann (1776-1822) was a German Romantic author of fantasy and horror, a jurist, composer, and music critic.

Robert Schumann wrote in a letter to Clara on August 4, 1838, "Play my *Kreisleriana* very often. A positively wild love is in some of the movements, and your life, and mine, and the way you look." SCLL 250.

Work: Novelletten, Op. 21 (1838)
Joan Chisell writes, "The *Novellettes* were described by Schumann as, 'a series of longish tales of adventure... intimately connected and written with passionate joy—cheerful and flighty...but somewhere I also hit rock bottom.' They are underplayed works, perhaps because their structure is more influenced by the literary structure of stories he read as a boy or adult, like Hoffmann and Bonaventura. He knew such literary devices and used them instead of strict musical form." SCJC 86.

No. 3
The Intermezzo of the *D major Novellette* originally had the words of Shakespeare's witches in Macbeth, "When shall we three meet again?" inscribed above it, which explains what in later editions is hidden in the indication "Rasch und wild." SCJC 84-85.

In a letter to Clara of March 20, 1840, describing a concert in which Franz Liszt had performed his *Novelletten* in Leipzig, Robert wrote, "The second *Novelletten* in D gave me peculiar pleasure. You can hardly believe the effect it makes. Liszt is going to play it at his third concert here." SCSL 225.

No. 5
According to Schumann this work depicts "the wind through the leaves." SCSL 24.

Work: Papillions, Op. 2 (1829-1831)
On April 17, 1832, Robert wrote to his mother explaining *Papillions*: "Then tell them all to read the last scene of Jean Paul's 'Flegeljahre' as soon as possible, because the 'Papillions' are intended as a musical representation of that masquerade: and then ask them if they can find anything there reflecting Wina's angelic love, Walt's poetic nature, or Vult's sparkling intellect. SCEL 160.

Editor's note: *Flegeljahre* or *The Awkward Age* is an unfinished novel written by Jean Paul in 1804-05 about youth inheriting a large fortune. *Papillons* is meant to depict the last scene of *Flegeljahre*—a ball at which the twin brothers Walt and Vult confront each other over the love of Vina. Walt is the poetic sentimentalist, a Romantic type, and Vult is a forceful realist, the intent of the respective sections of the music being in effect to portray these different personalities.

In a letter of 19 April, 1832, to the critic Rellstab, Robert wrote,

> Not so much for the sake of the Editor of the "Iris", as because I consider you a poet and a kindred spirit with Jean Paul, I am now going to add a few words about the origin of the "Papillions," as the thread which connects them is a very slender one indeed. You may remember the last scenes in the "Flegeljahre" with the "Larventanz" "Walt" "Vult" "Makes" "Vina" "Vult's Dances" "The Exchange of Masks" "Confessions" "Angers" "Discoveries" the hurrying away, the concluding scene, and the departing brother. I often turned to the last page, for the end seemed like a fresh beginning, and almost unconsciously I found myself at the piano, and thus one "Papillions" after another came into existence. I trust you may consider their origin an apology for the whole composition, as the separate numbers often require explaining.

> Hoping that the "Iris" may never lose that pithiness and freshness which runs through every page. SCEL 161.

Joan Chisell writes, "The finale is a direct musical account of the masked ball described at the end of *Flegeljahre*, complete with a striking clock to denote the end of the festivities. The finale makes use of the *Grossvatertanz*, a tune which obviously had some tongue-in-cheek significance for Schumann, since he used it humorously in the finale of *Carnaval*". SCJC 103.

Work: Sonata in F-sharp minor, Op. 11 (1835)
Wolfgang Helbig, a student of Liszt's, remembered his words about the opening of this Sonata in one of his lessons: "Of the heavy bass he said: 'Think how strong the arches must be that are to support this magnificent melody.'" LIS3 163.

Work: Sonata in F minor, Op. 14 (1835)
Sergei Prokofiev recorded a very strong reaction to this Sonata in a December 20, 1913, entry in his diary, "Why is it that so few people know Schumann's F minor Sonata? It is a marvellous work, especially the first two movements. If I ever have to give recitals not of my own works, I shall definitely play it. The cerebrally conceived B double flat in the coda of the first movement (a passing note added to another passing note) is particularly enjoyable. This double flat is some thing that could never have been conceived at the piano, only in the head." PROD 572.

Work: Toccata, Op. 7 (1832)
On one occasion Lachmund was playing Schumann's Toccata in C major to Liszt. "Ah," remarked Liszt, "this is a difficult piece." He then turned to Katharina Ranouchewitsch, a pupil of Henselt, who was attending the class

that day, held up the music and said: "That is something you should work at; it is solid and one must learn to bite it while still young—when one is old the bite is gone!" LIS3 237.

The great pedagogue, Cecile Genhart, who taught at the Eastman School of Music from 1929 until 1981, suggested her students consider the Biblical story from Numbers 20:11 at the opening of the Toccata, "Then Moses raised his arm and struck the rock twice with his staff. Water gushed out, and the community and their livestock drank with joy (New International Version)." Mrs. Genhart suggested the sharp chords in the two opening measures represent Moses striking the rock twice, and the babble of notes which follow (and horrify most pianists) are nothing more than the spring of living waters gushing out. She gave credit for this image to one of her early teachers in Munich, Josef Pembauer (1875-1950). GENH 56.

Work: Variations for Two Pianos, Op. 46 (1843)
In a letter to Clara Schumann of December 23, 1892, Brahms compared Schumann's Variations for Two Pianos with "a lovely, mild day of spring… When one never tires of enjoying the quiet air, which is neither cold nor warm…" WOLF 275.

In a letter to Johannes Verhulst[52] on June 19, 1843, Robert wrote of the variations, "I must have been in a melancholy mood when I wrote them, for they leave a mournful impression." SCSL 244-245.

Work: Waldszenen, Op. 82 (1848-1849)
This exquisite set of nine pieces abandons Schumann's beloved youthful eccentricities and feverish passions. Instead *Waldszenen* seems a loving tribute to Mendelssohnian nobility and charm. It was inspired by *Jagdbrevier* (*Hunting Guide* of 1841) by Heinrich Laube, a volume of hunting poems and a glossary of hunting terms. SCJC 85.

Waldszenen was conceived as a personal journey away from the reality of this world and commences with an "Entry" into the poetic atmosphere of the forest, and concludes with a nostalgic "Farewell" from that world. Schumann originally meant for poems to accompany each pieces. Schumann's regard for *Waldszenen* is documented in a letter to his publisher Senff in which he refers to the piece as one which "I have greatly cherished for a long time." SCWD 69.

---

52 Johannes Verhulst (1816-1891) was a Dutch composer. As a composer mainly of songs and as administrator of Dutch musical life, his influence during his lifetime was considerable.

Haunted Spot
The ghoulish poem that accompanies this work follows:

The flowers, which grow so tall
Are as pale as death;
Just one in the middle
Stands there in dark red.
She does not have that from the sun:
Never did she meet the suns glow:
She has it from the earth,
And it drank human blood.

SCHL 97.

Vogel als Prophet
From the insightful Wolf-Dieter Seiffert we read,

There is only one bird that is believed, from ancient times, to possess a prophetic gift to foretell the future or bring good luck. It is the shy cuckoo that cries only in the springtime! Its cry, usually a short downward minor third, is very well hidden in Schumann's composition "The Prophet Bird", hidden so well that nobody noticed it until now! For example, the cuckoo cries throughout the main motif, across both hands (c# – bflat; etc.) or, markedly accentuated by *fp*, … a – f#. In the same main motif the nervous agility of the bird seems to be imitated in 32nd notes, the way it flits up and down branches, "always alert", ever "lively and spirited" (so written by Schumann into his holograph, with Joseph von Eichendorff's words, and originally intended as a motto for the "The Prophet Bird")….

And then, unexpectedly…in the middle section Schumann quotes, and certainly not as a coincidence, a part from his "Scenes from Goethe's Faust…" Suddenly, effortlessly the listener, intent on hearing the forest and bird sounds, "understands" everything for one single moment. The forest opens to him like a dome…filled with the sound of a "chorale" in G major. In the sense of a "prophesy" God himself speaks to the enrapt one, he speaks through nature, through the bird and forest sounds. In the famous E flat major passage … this moment that compares to an epiphany, fades, and we stand again with the listener amidst the unintelligible chirping of the birds. SCPB.

Chapter 17
Scriabin

Editor's note: After about 1903 with the commencement of the *Misterium*,[53] Scriabin's philosophic imagination gravitated toward extreme mysticism, theosophy, and Friedrich Nietsche's Übermensch theory. Music, mystical literature, colors, and moving toward divine knowledge and illumination all coalesced in his mind, propelling him to seek for the ultimate artistic creation, which he felt was his sacred *Misterium*. The interpreter of Scriabin's later piano works must indeed act as a medium, whose fine-tuned extrasensory perception can transmit these thoughts, spiritual impressions, and moods to any listener.

---

53 *Mysterium* is an unfinished musical work by Scriabin. He started working on the composition in 1903, but it was incomplete at the time of his death in 1915. Scriabin planned that the work would be synesthetic, exploiting the senses of smell and touch as well as hearing. He wrote that "There will not be a single spectator. All will be participants. The work requires special people, special artists and a completely new culture. The cast of performers includes an orchestra, a large mixed choir, an instrument with visual effects, dancers, a procession, incense, and rhythmic textural articulation. The cathedral in which it will take place will not be of one single type of stone but will continually change with the atmosphere and motion of the *Mysterium*. This will be done with the aid of mists and lights, which will modify the architectural contours." Scriabin intended that the performance of this work, to be given in the foothills of the Himalayas in India, would last seven days and would be followed by the end of the world, with the human race replaced by "nobler beings".

Work: Concerto in F-sharp minor, Op. 20 (1896)

Leonid Sabaneyev, Scriabin's friend and Russian musicologist, recorded a vital discussion with the mature Scriabin on his composing principles in which the composer said, "I create my themes mainly by principle, so they will have concordant proportion.

Take for example, my Concerto. The bedrock of its design is the descending sequence of notes. Against this background the whole theme grows and unfurls."

Sabaneyev concluded, "He played me the theme of the Concerto and accented these descending steps richly, and the melody took on quite a different meaning and sense." SCR1 240.

Work: Twelve Etudes, Op. 8 (1894)

Etude no. 8 in A-flat major

Faubion Bowers[54] relates the following about this work,

> Scriabin wrote this etude for Natalya Sekerina, the composer's first love. She was seventeen in 1894 and Natalya's mother did not approve of the relationship. After finding one of Scriabin's letters to Natalya in 1892 her mother sent for Scriabin, intending to explain to him that "feelings" may not be addressed to a girl of fifteen. From then on the relationship was clandestine. Scriabin asked Igmunov, piano professor at the Moscow Conservatory, to teach this etude to Natalya... Full of wandering tonalities, hovering constantly between major and minor key, the piece breathes Russianism and romance. It proved to be one of his most popular pieces, and second to the D# minor etude, he played it more frequently than any other etude. He gave this music to Natalya on manuscript paper bordered with hand-drawn flower wreaths and exquisitely wrapped in colored paper... He explained to her sister Olga that Natalya 'creates my mood, and I create the music.' He apologized for not sending white roses, his favorite flower, for fear of interception [presumably by Natalya's mother]. SCR1 184.

Work: Poème Satanique, Op. 36 (1903)

Referring to Scriabin's tendency to represent malevolence in music the composer's biographer Sabaneyev recalled, "I could hardly be mistaken... Scriabin was peculiarly attracted to moods of sin, corruption, and perversity...Any artist is both sorcerer and saint. Scriabin himself mixed

---

54 Faubion Bowers (1917-1999) was a noted academic and writer in the area of Asian Studies, especially Japanese theatre. He also wrote the first full-length biography of Scriabin. During the Allied Occupation of Japan, he was General Douglas MacArthur's personal Japanese language interpreter and aide-de-camp.

the satanic and the saintly, black and white magic. He was a holy man and a wicked wizard. He justified himself on the grounds of artistic contrast... Scriabin spoke thus, 'My *Poeme Satanique* isn't true evil. It is an *apotheosis of insincerity*. Everything in it is hypocritical and false...Satan is not really himself there. He's just a little devil. Not in earnest. In fact, there's a lot of the parlor about him. He's genteel, and rather sweet... say, a guest in the home.'" SCR1 338.

Work: Twenty Four Preludes, Op. 11, (1896)
Prelude no. 14 in E-flat major
Faubion Bowers writes that "At Bastei he [Scriabin] watched a rushing mountain stream pounding against rocky boulders, and promptly composed the powerful *Prelude Op. 11 no. 14 in E flat minor*." SCR1 203.

Work: Four Preludes, Op. 22 (1897)
Prelude no. 1 in G-sharp minor
Scriabin's wife Vera recalled the genesis of this piece by writing, "I was not mistaken about the birth of something new. That evening when he came home he sat at the piano and played very softly, forgetting his promise to his fiancée to go to bed early. I dropped off to sleep at four, and he was still playing and continued all night. After it was daylight he was practicing his *Concerto*, and then he played something else with such a radiant and blissful face. I asked him if something new hadn't been born, and he assured me that good was resulting. I could see by his face that he was in a truly blessed state of grace." SCR1 231.

Work: Five Preludes, Op. 74 (1914)
In June [1914] the proofs of Op. 74 reached Scriabin, but he could not bother. They lay unopened in their package. Schloezer had to persuade him to play them. When he did, he talked. "Listen to their simplicity, and yet, how complicated they are psychologically..." With Op. 74 Scriabin said he created music which could be played to mean different concepts. "It is like a crystal, the same crystal can reflect many different lights and colors." SCR2 265.

Prelude no. 2, très lent, contemplatif
Scriabin saw this prelude, marked only "slow and contemplative," as a desert: "An astral desert, mind you, and here is fatigue, exhaustion (the descending chromatic line). See how this short prelude sounds as if it lasts an entire century? Actually it is all eternity, millions of years..." Once he played the Prelude Op. 74, no. 2 twice for his biographer Sabaneyev and asked the difference. Sabaneyev could not answer, but he knew that the piece the second time had lost "every trace of caressing *eros* which once shadowed it...the warmth was gone." "Yes," Scriabin whispered. "It is *death*

now. It is death like the appearance of the Eternally Feminine which leads to the Final Unity. Death and love…I call death 'Sister' in my Prefatory Action,[55] because there must be no trace of fear about it. It is the highest reconciliation, a white radiance…" SCR2 265.

Work: Sonata no. 2 in G-sharp minor, Op.19 (completed 1897)
Scriabin appended brief program notes and regarded it [Sonata no. 2] as a vision of the sea remembered. "The influence of the sea," he wrote, "and the first section represents the quiet of a southern night on the seashore; the development is the dark agitations of the deep, deep sea. The E major middle section shows caressing moonlight coming after the first darkness of the night. The second movement, presto, represents the vast expanse of ocean stormily agitated." SCR1 226.

Work: Sonata no. 3 in F-sharp minor, Op. 23 (1897-1898)
Scriabin subtitled the third sonata, *Etats d'Ame*, or "Soul-States" with the following epigraphs for each movement:

I

The free, untamed Soul plunges passionately into an abyss
of suffering and strife.

II

The Soul, weary of suffering, finds illusory and transient respite.
It forgets itself in song, in flowers…
But this vitiated and uneasy Soul invariably penetrates the
false veil of fragrant harmonies and light rhythms.

III

The Soul floats on a tender and melancholy sea of feeling. Love, sorrow,
secret desires, inexpressible thoughts are wraithlike charms.

IV

Now the elements unleash themselves. The Soul struggles within their vortex
of fury. Suddenly, the voice of the Man-God rises up
from within the Soul's depths.
The song of victory resounds triumphantly.
But it is weak, still…
When all is within its grasp, it sinks back, broken,
falling into a new abyss of…nothingness.

SCR1 254-255.

---

55 At the time of his death, Scriabin left 72 pages of sketches for a prelude to the *Mysterium* entitled *Prefatory Action*.

Third Movement

Faubion Bowers quotes Scriabin as saying to a student of this movement, "Here the stars sing." Bowers comments that Scriabin's thought has now evolved into "starlight"—Scriabin's second reference to light in music. SCR1 255.

Work: Sonata no. 4 in F-sharp major, Op. 30 (1903)

Scriabin composed a poem in free verse to accompany this Sonata.

In a light mist, transparent vapor
Lost afar and yet distinct
A star gleams softly.

How beautiful! The bluish mystery

Of her glow
Beckons me, cradles me.

O bring me to thee, far distant star!
Bathe me in trembling rays
Sweet light!

Sharp desire, voluptuous and crazed yet sweet
Endlessly with no other goal than longing
I would desire.

But no! I vault in joyous leap
Freely I take wing

Mad dance, godlike play!
Intoxicating, shining one!

It is toward thee, adored star
My flight guides me

Toward thee, created freely for me
To serve the end
My flight of liberation!

In this play
Sheer caprice
In moments I forget thee
In the maelstrom that carries me
I veer from thy glimmering rays
In the insanity of desire
Thou fadest
O distant goal

But ever thou shinest
As I forever desire thee!
Thou expandest, Star!
Now thou art a Sun
Flamboyant Sun! Sun of Triumph!
Approaching thee by my desire of thee
I lave myself in thy changing waves
O joyous god
I imbibe thee
Sea of light
My self-of-light
I engulf Thee!

SCR1 332-333.

In connection with this first "Poem Sonata" Faubion Bowers defines Scriabin's intentions in applying poetry to music: "Scriabin, however, used the designation [poetry] in his piano music to mean something more fleeting—a spell of enchantment, a passing and inexplicable mood, even a tender fragrance rendered in sound. Very rarely do his piano poems (unlike his huge symphonic poems to come) tell a psychical or philosophic story. Usually, they merely weave a texture of languor, sweetness, aimless wandering, a floating in air or on flames. Most always they are ethereal and elusive." SCR1 334.

Work: Sonata no. 5, Op. 53 (1907)

Scriabin included the following epigraph, extracted from his essay *Le Poème de l'Extase*, as a heading for the exuberant *Fifth Sonata*:

You have heard my secret call, hidden powers of life, and you begin to stir.
The billow of my being, light as a vision of dreams, embraces the world. To
Life! Burgeon!

I awaken you to life with kisses and the secret pleasures of my promises.
I summon you to life, hidden longings, lost in the chaos of sensations. Rise
up from the secret depths of the creative soul.

SCR2 59-60.

Work: Sonata no. 6, Op. 62 (1911)

This period in Scriabin's life was unique in reconciling simultaneously two such pieces of music. The *Seventh Sonata* descends from the heavens; the *Sixth Sonata* rises like subterranean demons. Faubion Bowers suggests, "The total traffic of the Sixth is satanic." SCR2 230.

Scriabin himself feared this *Sixth Sonata*, and never played it. Bekman Shcherbina gave its premiere in Moscow, 6 March, 1912. Writing in October 1912, he asks Siloti to choose any sonata he should play "except the 6th." SCR2 230.

Work: Sonata no. 7, Op. 64 (1911-1912)

Scriabin considered this sonata holy and subtitled it "The White Mass," to dramatize its sacerdotal character, and to purge himself of the malevolence of the *Sixth Sonata*. To Scriabin its performance was ritual. Sounding the tocsin of Theosophy, he spoke of its "purest mysticism...total absence of human feeling...complete lack of emotional lyricism." Faubion Bowers suggests, "At last Scriabin felt he had reached his sainthood and manifest dematerialization." SCR2 231.

According to Sabayenev the composer would occasionally,

> Talk when playing for intimates. He began the *Seventh Sonata* once for Sabayenev saying, "Perfumes, like clouds, are here...already this music approximates the Mysterium...listen to this quiet joy...it's so much better than Prometheus." When he reached the second theme he said: "All is born here...the waves lift...the face of the sun dispels the clouds... Listen to how it burns, how it grows and grows, more and more..." (Pianist Richter feels the first pages are "hot and stifling...suffocating in their heat..."). Then explaining that the "clouds" were "mystic clouds," not tangible ones, he [Scriabin] unexpectedly skipped ahead to point out passages of "flight." "Here melody flutters overhead...wings...here is maximum flight in music...How it lifts and soars in heaven itself ..." The "glimmering theme" or "fountain of fire" leads into the "last dance and dissolution." Trumpets of archangels herald it...Everything here is mixed, blended,... This is real *vertigo!*" He whispered his emphasis as he played, "This is truly holy. Here is the last dance before the act itself, before the instant of dematerialization. BY MEANS OF THIS DANCE ALL IS ACCOMPLISHED..." SCR2 231-232.

Work: Sonata no. 8, Op. 66 (1912-1913)

Bowers writes,

> Scriabin proudly played the *Eighth Sonata's* majestic, gorgeously blooming harmonies derived from five fragmentary melodies... These supposedly represent the elements of earth, air, fire, water and the mystic ether. Woven together they form a cobweb of gossamer filigree. "And you say I have no counterpoint after hearing this?" he would say defiantly to friends. "Note well how all the notes of the counterpoint are harmony. They are not at war with each other as in Bach. Here

they are reconciled." Regarding the center of the melody in the third measure, he said, "See how I break mood within the one phrase." And playing the figure rising to a "B" and emphasizing the end of the rise and following it with "B" and the descending figure he would add, "Listen to the tragedy born out of such a dissolution…in two notes I alter hope into despair." And that same half-step descent appears in *Prometheus's* opening theme. There Scriabin called it, inflatedly, "the most tragic episode of my creative work." He also felt the behemoth harmonies in the Eighth were "drawn from Nature, as if they had existed before, like the bells in the Seventh Sonata bridges between harmony and geometry, life visible and life unseen." SCR2 244.

Work: Sonata no. 9, Op 68 (1912-1913)
Robert Rimm writes, "Given the title 'Black Mass' by his close friend it is demonic and satanic. Scriabin said he was 'practicing sorcery' while playing it." SCRR 113.

From Bowers we read, "Scriabin especially loved its second theme (p. 4). In conversation he called it 'dormant or dreaming saintliness…' Its ritual is perverse. The rite is a spitting at all that is holy or sacred. If the Seventh Sonata exorcises demons, the Ninth resummons them." SCR2 244-245.

Work: Sonata no. 10, Op. 70 (1913)
Bowers writes, "Scriabin used to amuse his guests by playing the first three measures of the *Tenth Sonata*, following it with the scale of G major. 'You hear,' he would say, 'my music lies between the tones.' And certainly the scale sounds as wide and gaping as teeth in a pumpkin." SCR2 244.

Work: Trois Morceaux, Op. 52 (1907)
Enigma
The title of this work originated in a conversation Scriabin had with his second wife, Tatyana. Scriabin had just composed it on the little piano in Servette when Tatyana walked in. She asked what the piece was he was playing. "What do you think it should be called," was his reply. "I don't know. It's a puzzle." So it was titled zagadka, "puzzle," or as translated in French by the composer himself, *Enigma*. SCR2 113.

Chapter 18
Miscellaneous Composers

Albéniz

Work: Chants d'Espagne, Op. 232 (1892-1898)
Cordoba

Albéniz wrote the following programmatic notes at the beginning of this work: "In the silence of the night, interrupted by the whispering of the jasmine scented breezes, guzlas [a musical instrument with a single string] are heard accompanying and radiating into the air ardent melodies and notes so sweet, like the wavering of the palms high in the heavens." ALBE 101.

Work: Iberia (1905-09)

Artur Rubinstein threw some intriguing light on the subject of Albéniz's own execution of *Iberia*. The Polish pianist described a visit to Albéniz's widow and daughter during which they requested he play selections from *Iberia*. At first Rubinstein demurred, stating, "It might shock you to hear me leave out many notes in order to project the essence of the music." But they insisted. When he finished "Triana," the composer's widow turned to Laura and expressed her amazement that Rubinstein played it "exactly as your father used to play it." Laura concurred, approving of his omission of the "nonessential accompaniment." ALBE 224.

Fête-Dieu à Séville

Walter Clark writes, "This work is programmatic and describes the Corpus Christi Day procession in the city of Seville, during which the statue of the Virgin is carried through the streets accompanied by marching bands, singers, and penitential flagellants. The opening 'rataplan' conveys the sound of the drum rolls as the procession nears. For dramatic effect, Albéniz would rest his hands on his ample abdomen during the rests in between these strokes." ALCO 160.

Lavapiés

Lavapiés is a district in Madrid named for the local church where a foot-washing ritual was performed on Holy Thursday. This locale was known in Albéniz's time for its working-class denizens called *chulos*. There was a great deal of noisy street life, and its accidental sounds are represented by the surface dissonance in this piece. ALBE 241.

Work: La Vega (1899)

In a letter to Albéniz of December 10, 1899, the pianist José Tragó said of *La Vega,* which translates as 'the fertile plain' and depicts the view over the plain of Granada, as seen from the Arabian palace, the Alhambra, "One sometimes hears distant sounds produced by Arab instruments; there is something of...nostalgia and the flavor of our precious Andalusian songs." ALBE 204.

Chabrier

General Observations:

Alfred Cortot, in speaking about the *Bouree Fantastique*, writes the following about Chabrier's performance preferences, "I am able to quote Chabrier's own views on the playing of his music, he adhered, apparently, to meticulous detail of tempo; Paul Dukas and Ravel, in our generation, have the same legitimate strictness. He insisted on the full value of a sforzando, he would not allow a forte to become a fortissimo, not a diminuendo meant to establish a piano to vanish in a pianissimo. In the same way he maintained the fine difference between a ritenuto and rallentando, and would not allow one to be taken for the other. He was rigidly insistent on the simultaneous attack by both hands, and all tempo and expression indications provided him with an endless stream of suggestions." COFP 166-167.

Work: Pieces pittoresques (1880)

Francis Poulenc said, "I have no hesitation in declaring that [Chabrier's] Pieces pittoresques are as important for French music as Debussy's Preludes." AFPM 92.

On hearing the premiere of some of Chabrier's *Pieces pittoresques* Cesar Franck's reaction was, "We have just heard something extraordinary. This music links our era to that of Couperin and Rameau." AFPM 145.

Work: Valses romantiques (1880-83)

Vincent D'Indy gives an account of rehearsing the two piano *Valses romantiques* with Chabrier in January 1887 (exactly a year after Debussy and Paul Vidal played the same pieces to Liszt), "So I practiced the three waltzes *con amore*, making a point of carefully observing all the markings—of which there are plenty! At the rehearsal...Chabrier cut me short halfway through the first waltz, and, with a look both astonished and facetious, erupted, 'But, *mon p'tit*, it's nothing like that at all!' When, a bit taken aback, I asked him to explain, he riposted, 'You're playing it as if it were by a member of the *Institut!*'—Then followed a wonderful lesson in playing *alla Chabrier*, contrary accents, pianissimos to nothing, sudden detonations in the middle of the most exquisite tenderness, and also obbligato miming, lending the whole body to the musical interpretation." AFPM 319-20.

Couperin

The following images come from the writings of French pianist, Alfred Cortot.

Work: 6th Ordre de clavecin in B-flat major (1717)

Les Baricades mystérieuses (The Mysterious Barricades)

"*Les Baricades mystérieuses* are bits of lace, furbelows [ruffles of flounce on a garment]. Play this with the tone colours of shimmering stuffs." COMI 73.

Les bergeries (Sheep Pens)

"In *Bergeries* contrast the affected character of the Versailles shepherds with the rustic and simple mein of true shepherds." COMI 71.

La commère (The Gossip)

"*La Commère*: there are two of them, one in the right hand, and the other in the left. Our opera-comíque had its origins in this type of piece; it requires vivacity and freedom." COMI 71.

Le moucheron (The Gnat)

"In *Le Moucheron* let there be a real buzzing to and fro: the insistent hum of the insect must be carefully *imitated*." COMI 71.

"Couperin himself says, besides, that many of his pieces are portraits. Such are Auguste, Majestuese, etc. It cannot be stated more explicitly that he wanted something different from the cold and academic execution that we are all too frequently offered." COMI 70.

Work: 17th Ordre de clavecin in E minor (1722)
Petits Moulins a vent (The Little Windmills)

Alfred Cortot writes, "Some compositions which seem to aim at mere imitation may carry at the same time a veiled and malicious intention. Such is the case of 'Petits Moulins a vent.' Behind the imitation proper, there is in this piece, especially, a suggestion of the whirl of Court life and of witless young lords." COMI 73.

Franck

Work: Prelude, Fugue, and Variation (1868) (Bauer transcription)

Cortot says, "Christian feeling and religious conviction, the basis of the beautiful in Bach's art, are found with equal intensity in Franck. The *Prelude, Fugue, and Variation* will convince us of this still more." COMI 35.

Work: Prelude, Chorale, and Fugue (1884)

Cortot says of the manner in which you should play the beginning of the Fugue, "I do not wish to see you facing the beasts in the arena to test your faith, as in Nero's time, but it is in that spirit that you must play." COMI 39.

Work: Symphonic Variations (1885)

Referring to this work Cortot remarks, "'From whence, oh my God, comes this peace that floods my soul?' cries the poet, led by such an ecstasy to the very gate of mystery and revelation. In all music I know of few pages to be compared with these. There does not exist in all Franck's work, even in the compositions essentially religious, the expression of a nobler mood." COFP 85.

Editor's note: Based on Cortot's description in an earlier paragraph, the passage he refers to can only be the exquisite mss. 230-250, or beginning at rehearsal 'M' in the Peters Edition.

Elsewhere, Cortot, speaking in his *Cours d' Interpretation* at the École Normale, and remarking on a student's dry analysis of this work, said,

> If you seem to recoil at the mere thought of a commentary, as you seem to suggest in your first lines, you should have brought me one of those analyses—theme A, theme B, etc—made by vivisectors and anatomists,

who think that by cutting slices out of a dead body they fit themselves to discover the vital principle.

This is precisely what I want to find in a performance—the vital principle. But you cannot be animated by it unless you imagine yourself to be the composer of the work you are interpreting.

If you had been the composer of the *Variations Symphoniques* you would have brought to bear upon your analysis the very factor which you have already introduced in the act of forbidding yourself to do so—the factor of *feeling*. That is what counts in art—*feeling*, not *formalism*.

If we wish to see nothing in a work but its notes and its form let us make a museum specimen of it. Let us put under glass cases the musical scores we must no longer touch. But if we play them let us, even at the risk of making mistakes, try to revive their movement, their action, and their emotion. Only thus shall we show ourselves worthy of our mission. COMI 267.

Grieg

General Observation:

It is well known that the pianist-composer Percy Grainger was a protégé of Grieg. His writings, therefore, on Grieg's pianism and preferences on interpretation of his music, based on first-hand experience and long correspondence, are crucial for the pianist. From Grainger's foreword to the Grieg *Piano Concerto, Op. 16* we read,

> Those that had the good fortune to hear Grieg perform his own compositions, whether as a pianist or as a conductor, are more likely to be alive to the heroic and intense attributes of his art than are those less lucky in this respect, for Grieg was nothing if not extremely virile and dynamic as an interpreter of his own works. Always a poet, but, above all, always a man. As a rule his tempi were usually faster than those heard in performances of Grieg's works by other artists, and invariably the wistfulness and poetic appeal knew no trace of sentimentality or mawkishness. Sudden and strong accents of all kinds and vivid contrasts of light and shade were outstanding features of his self-interpretations, while the note of passion that he sounded was of a restless and feverish rather than of a violent nature. Extreme delicacy and exquisiteness of detail were present in his piano playing and altho the frailty of his physique, in his later years at least, withheld him from great displays of

rugged force at the keyboard, he prized and demanded these resources in others, when occasion required.

Grieg eschewed all "muddiness" or turgid obscurity of tonal effect in writing for the piano or other instruments and the performer of Grieg's music should try to realize the composer's predilection for bright and clear and clean sonorities. GCON.

Work: Ballade in the Form of Variations on a Norwegian Folksong, Op. 24 (1875-1876)

From Finn Benestad we read,

> The *Ballade* was written in the winter and spring of 1875-76 and its creation can be seen as an attempt by Grieg to free himself from the despair of that time. His parents both died in 1875 and this coupled with the realization that he and Nina would never be able to have children, set in motion a period of intense grief and led Grieg to doubt for the first time the Christian faith of his childhood and to wonder where he could turn for reassurance. Grieg said, "No, you can have all the dogmas, but the belief in immortality I must have. Without that everything comes to nothing." In addition there was at this same time a rumor circulating that his wife had had an affair with his brother John. He poured this sadness into his most ambitious piano piece, *Ballade in the form of Variations of a Norwegian Folk Song in G minor, op 24.* He said that it was written 'with my life's blood in days of sorrow and despair.' After finishing the *Ballade* Grieg wrote nothing more for almost a year. GRIE 199-200.

Editor's note: The title of the piece on the autograph is *Capriccio (Ballade) on a Norwegian mountain tune in the forms of variations.* The folk tune on which the variations are based had gone through several metamorphoses over the centuries, but the text with which Grieg found it reads as follow:

> I know so many lovely songs
> Of fair lands throughout the world
> But never have I heard sing
> Of things close to us.
> Therefore shall I now attempt
> To wrote a song so people will see
> That even the North can be beautiful
> Though despised by the South.
>
> GBAL.

Benestad writes,

> So personal was this work, that Grieg never performed it for a public audience. After completing the *Ballade*, Grieg performed it privately for the director of the Peters publishing firm, Max Abraham, in Leipzig,

Germany, in the summer of 1876. According to his friend Iver Holter, who was in attendance at the private performance, after Grieg had finished he was not only drenched in sweat from the physical exhaustion of playing, but was so emotionally agitated and shaken that he was unable to speak for a long time.

In a letter to Frants Beyer from Leipzig dated March 27, 1898, Grieg described a performance of the *Ballade* by Eugène d'Albert in which he played, "so brilliantly that it took the audience by storm. Think what that means! He had virtually all the requirement: with both refinement and grand style he played that mighty passage that increases in intensity until it breaks out in sheer fury. And then after that you should have heard the daringly long fermata on that low E-flat. I think he held it for half a minute. But the effect was colossal. And then he completed that old, sad song, so slowly, quietly, and simply that I myself was deeply moved…" GRIE 203.

Handel

Work: Suite in E major (published 1720)

Speaking with affection of this well-known work of Handel, Cortot wrote, "The current legend that "The Harmonious Blacksmith" was inspired by a French song published by Ballard in the eighteenth century is false. It is more probable, according to another version, that Handel, then teacher of the little princess Anne, daughter of the Prince of Wales, was surprised one day by a storm, and, taking shelter in a blacksmith's forge, heard the man singing while striking the anvil. Delighted by the union of this song and its accompaniment, Handel probably wrote this piece, whose title is not an editor's whim, since the piece was known during the composer's lifetime under the appellation that tradition has preserved for us." COMI 77-78.

Haydn

Work: Fantasia, Hob. XVII/4 (1789)

Haydn had a high opinion of the *Fantasia*, which he offered to Artaria with the following words, "In a humorous mood I have composed an entirely new capriccio for the piano; its good taste, singularity, and careful execution are sure to please both experts and amateurs. It is in a single movement, rather long, but not particularly difficult." HAYD 282.

Work: Sonata in E-flat major, Hob. XVI/49
Second Movement

Haydn considered this movement the climax of the whole work as his letter to the dedicatee, Marianne von Genzinger, illustrates. He called her attention to the adagio and added, "It has a deep significance that I will analyze for you when opportunity offers.' It is a shame there is no record extant of his intended analysis or interpretation! We must use our imaginations. HAYD 281, 94.

Janáček

Work: Street Scene I.X. 1905 (1905)

In 1905, Janáček had composed a piano sonata originally known as *Street Scene I.X. 1905.* This sonata, or what remains of it, was an immediate and passionate response to a contemporary event. On 1 October of that year there was a demonstration in support of the establishment of a university for Czech students in Brno. The Austrian authorities reacted by calling in troops and the following day, during a skirmish, a twenty-year-old worker received a wound from which he later died in the hospital. Janáček was outraged and wrote the sonata as an expression of his feelings. The first movement is entitled "Presentiment" and the second, "Death." JANA 96.

MacDowell

Work: Witches' Dance (1883)

In a December 1922 analysis of *Witches' Dance* by Edward MacDowell, the *Etude* magazine published the following pedagogical suggestions made by Mrs. Edward MacDowell,

> Behind every composition there is always a background which, when understood, contributes much to the proper understanding of the composition. Innumerable people essay to play this composition without the slightest idea of what Mr. MacDowell had in mind when he wrote the work. Indeed, many have a totally different conception of the piece from that intended by the composer.
>
> The first error that most people make about the *Witches' Dance* is that they have a different kind of witch in mind. They think of some old hag, like the witches in Macbeth, or, the witches that the good folk of

Salem feared when they nightly barred their doors to keep them out. That is not at all the kind of sprite that Mr. MacDowell pictured. It was rather the mischievous demons or elves who fly in clouds through the air, like pixies. They were light gossamer nothings, mischievous, but delicate as a feather, wafted by the swift March breezes. Because so many people have pictured a malignant old hag, or crone, in association with *Witches' Dance*, the average student bangs away at the piece and tries to add a kind of morbid or tragic element into it. Mr. MacDowell never had any such thought. He played most of the work as though it were made of thread lace.

Regarding the following suggestions given, I am following the precedents set by him, and in this way I have felt at liberty to do away with one repetition and also to eliminate one extremely awkward passage, which make the whole work needlessly difficult for many students, and has doubtless placed it beyond the grasp of many who would otherwise be able to play it with pleasure. BRJJ 68.

Mozart

Work: Concerto in G major, K. 453 (1784)

Michael Steinberg recalls the famous story behind this concerto: "On 27 May 1784 Mozart paid 34 kreuzer, roughly $10 in today's money, for a starling that could whistle the beginning of the finale of his G-major Piano Concerto- or at least something very close to it. Mozart jotted down the musical notation in his account book with the comment 'Das war schön!', even though the bird insisted on a fermata at the end of the first full measure and on sharping the G's in the next bar... When the bird died it was buried with full honors in the Mozarts' garden on 4 June 1787, the occasion was commemorated with a poem by the composer." CONC 295-296.

Work: Concerto in C minor, K. 491 (1785-1786)

After hearing this work at the Augarten in 1799 the young Beethoven exclaimed to the composer J. B. Cramer, "Ah, we shall never be able to do anything like this!" BEET 209.

Mussorgsky

Work: Pictures at an Exhibition (1874)

It is well known that Mussorgsky based his most enduring and epic piano work, *Pictures at an Exhibition*, on a series of paintings by the Russian artist Viktor Hartmann. Vladimir Stasov, a friend of both Hartmann and Mussorgsky, arranged an exhibition of Hartmann's paintings in 1874 which fired Mussorgky's imagination, and he composed *Pictures* (originally entitled *Hartmann*) in six weeks. Writing to Stasov after seeing the exhibit himself Mussorgsky said, "My dear généralissime, Hartmann is seething as Boris seethed,—sounds and ideas hang in the air, I am gulping and overeating, and can barely manage to scribble them on paper. I am writing the 4th N⁰ —the transitions are good (on the 'promenade'). I want to work more quickly and reliably. My physiognomy can be seen in the interludes. So far I think it's well turned..." MUSS 185.

Vladimir Stasov viewed *Pictures* as an imaginary tour through the Hartmann exhibit. His rarely read programs for each movement follow.

"Promenade"

In this piece Mussorgsky depicts himself "roving through the exhibition, now leisurely, now briskly in order to come close to a picture that had attracted his attention, and at times sadly, thinking of his departed friend." MUCA 172.

"Gnomus"

Stasov comments, "A sketch depicting a little gnome, clumsily running with crooked legs." Hartmann's sketch, now lost, is thought to represent a design for a nutcracker displaying large teeth. MUCA 172.

"Interlude, Promenade Theme"

According to Stasov, "This, and all other Interludes, is a placid statement of the promenade melody depicting the viewer walking from one display to the next." MUCA 172.

"Il vecchio castello" (The Old Castle)

"A medieval castle before which a troubadour sings a song." This movement is thought to be based on a watercolor depiction of an Italian castle. MUCA 172.

"Tuileries" (Dispute d'enfants après jeux) (Dispute between Children at Play)

Stasov comments, "An avenue in the garden of the Tuileries, with a swarm of children and nurses." Hartmann's picture of the Jardin des Tuileries near the Louvre in Paris is now lost. Figures of children quarrelling and playing in the garden were likely added by the artist for scale. MUCA 172.

Bydlo (Cattle)

Stasov says this is "A Polish cart on enormous wheels, drawn by oxen." MUCA 172.

"Ballet of the Unhatched Chicks"

Stasov comments, "Hartmann's design for the décor of a picturesque scene in the ballet Trilby." MUCA 173.

In a footnote to Stasov's comment in the revised edition Gerald Abraham provides the following details: "Trilby or The Demon of the Heath, a ballet with choreography by Petipa, music by Julius Gerber, and décor by Hartmann, based on Charles Nodier's Trilby, or The Elf of Argyle, was produced at the Bolshoy Theatre, Petersburg, in 1871. The fledglings were canary chicks." MUCR 172.

"Samuel Goldenberg and Schmuyle"

Stasov comments, "Two Jews: Rich and Poor." Stasov's explanatory title elucidates the personal names used in Mussorgsky's original manuscript. Published versions display various combinations, such as "Two Polish Jews, Rich and Poor (Samuel Goldenberg and Schmuyle), "Limoges", le marché (La grande nouvelle) The Market at Limoges (The Great News). MUCA 173.

"Limoges"

Stasov comments, "French women quarrelling violently in the market." Limoges is a city in central France. Mussorgsky originally provided two paragraphs in French that described a marketplace discussion (the 'great news'), but soon removed them." MUCA 173.

"Catacombæ" (Sepulcrum romanum) and "Con mortuis in lingua mortua"
The Catacombs (Roman sepulcher) and With the Dead in a Dead Language.

Stasov comments, "Hartmann represented himself examining the Paris catacombs by the light of a lantern." MUCA 173.

The Hut on Fowl's Legs (Baba-Yagá)

Stasov says of this work, "Hartmann's drawing depicted a clock in the form of Baba—Yaga's hut on fowl's legs. Mussorgsky added the witch's flight in a mortar." MUCA 173.

The Bogatyr Gates (in the Capital in Kiev)

Stasov comments, "Hartmann's sketch was his design for city gates at Kiev in the ancient Russian massive style with a cupola shaped like a slavonic helmet. [Referring to the title] Bogatyrs are heroes that appear in Russian epics called bylinas. The title of this movement is commonly translated as 'The Great Gate of Kiev' and sometimes as 'The Heroes' Gate at Kiev.' Hartmann designed a monumental gate for Tsar Alexander II to commemorate the monarch's narrow escape from an assassination attempt on April 4, 1866... The solemn secondary theme is based on a baptismal hymn from the repertory of Russian Orthodox chant." MUCA 173.

Rameau

General Observations:
Alfred Cortot states, "In French art a portion of the beauty is derived from discretion, proportion, perfect equilibrium, exact matching of means with idea. Some effort is required on the part of foreigners in this direction in order to understand us. The beauty of Rameau's art is created by the same qualities that are admired in Racine." COMI 74.

The following images come from the writings of French pianist Alfred Cortot.

Work: Pièces de clavecin (1724)
"The whole of this suite is a stylization of village merriment, except the first piece, which is essentially different." COMI 76.

Le Rappel des oiseaux (The Chattering of the Birds)
"*Le Rappel des oiseaux* is a descriptive piece akin to Couperin's *Gazouillement*, but it permits us to judge the essential difference separating the genius of the two masters. *Gazouillement* is written by a Parisian for very Parisian aviaries. *Le Rappel des oiseaux* breathes the twilight of the woods, the moist atmosphere, and enchanting hour of sunset." COMI 75.

"Here the emotion is so perfectly in agreement with the mysterious and tremulous poetry, with the melancholy of faint bird call in the deepening dusk, that the quality is much more subjective than Couperin's. Rameau wrote that in a dismal town, Clermont-Ferrand. It suggests a desire to retire into oneself in the contemplation of nature and to steep one's mind in its solace." COMI 75-76.

Rigadoun
"*Rigadoun*, for other reasons, is colored by Rameau's sojourn in Auvergne. It has the solid basis of a bourée. We must not be afraid of appearing as

rustic peasants. Play heavily with bold tone. It is poetry in wooden shoes."
COMI 76.

Musette

"In *Musette* a firm rhythmic grasp is necessary, as well as the bagpipe
tone of the musette. The piece is entirely rustic." COMI 76.

La Villageoise (The Villager)

"The next piece [*La Villageoise*] is similar in character to Schubert's
Marguerite at the Spinning-wheel. It is the pensive song of a young girl,
not the work of a dry as dust theorist. Tender and poetical, but essentially
simple, it should be obviously free from violent effects." COMI 76.

Tourbillons (Vortices)

"*Tourbillons*, however, takes us back completely to imitative music. In a
letter to a friend Rameau states very definitely that it represents the whirling
clouds of dust raised by horses' hoofs from carriages on the highroad."
COMI 73.

"A curious detail in the first gigue is that it is inspired by a French folksong *Le Roi Dagobert*. This deliberate borrowing must be emphasized,
resulting for the second gigue a different colouring, the result of a finer more
sensitive touch." COMI 75.

Les Cyclopes (The Cyclopes)

Editor's note: Most of us know that the Cyclopes are a race of one-eyed
giants from ancient mythology. Fewer of us know that their job was to
forge and hammer the steel in Vulcan's furnace. In this marvelous piece by
Rameau one can hear hammers of all shapes and sizes as the Cyclopes go
about their work in the heated atmosphere of the furnace.

Le Lardon (Bacon)

"Rameau's contemporaries had already long ago dubbed these sixteen bars
with the nickname under which the piece has come down to us, *Le Lardon*.
It was a burlesque description of the action of one finger of the left hand as it
interjected a series of detached notes between the fingers of the right hand—
suggestive of a chef running strips of fat through a joint." COFP 197.

Saint-Saëns

Work: Concerto no. 4 in C minor, Op. 44 (1875)

Alfred Cortot, whose 1935 recording of this Concerto, in spite of
some messy moments, is one of the glory moments in the history of the

phonograph, reports that Saint-Saëns had exhorted him to "jouer le solo comme une role," to play the role like a part in a play. CONC 392.

Work: Piano Concerto no. 5 in F major, Op. 103 (1896)

Cortot wrote, "Saint-Saëns has left us no written confidences with regard to this work, but in the time of Diemer,[56] to whom the concerto is dedicated, I remember that Saint- Saëns asked him, as he was preparing to perform it, to enliven the rhythms by constantly evoking a languorous Oriental atmosphere." COMI 234.

Satie

Work: Danses Gothiques (1893)

Fritz Spiegel writes, "In March of 1893 Satie wrote his nine *Danses gothiques* 'to restore the great calm and tranquility of [Satie's] soul.' The restoration of tranquility referred to the termination of a tempestuous affair he had with Suzanne Valadon. Satie recorded the event meticulously, 'On the 14th of the month of January in the year of grace 1893, which was a Saturday, my love affair with Suzanne Valadon began, which ended on Tuesday the 20th of June of the same year.' There are many ways of breaking off affairs of this kind but Satie, ever the original, chose not to inform her that his affections had cooled but instead he told the police, and asked the startled *gendarmerie* to post a guard outside his house to prevent her from visiting him." LIVE 170.

Scarlatti

General Observations:

In the preface to his *Essercizi*, one of the few verbal utterances preserved by Scarlatti and one in which he addresses us directly he says, "Do not expect any profound learning, but rather an ingenious jesting with art." KIRK 104.

In the same preface Scarlatti gently suggests an approach to perusing music when he says, "Therefore show yourself more human than critical, and

---

56 Louis Deimer (1843-1919) was a composer and highly regarded French pianist.

your pleasure will increase…Live Happily." Such an ingratiating attitude suggests much about the personality of Scarlatti and his music. KIRK 104.

"Scarlatti frequently told M. L'Augier," reports Dr. Burney, "that he was sensible that he had broke through all the rules of composition in his lessons; but asked if his deviations from these rules offended the ear? And, upon being answered in the negative, he said, that he thought there was scarce any other rule, worth the attention of a man of genius, than that of not displeasing the only sense of which music is the subject." KIRK 104.

Editor's note: With such opinions, it is tantalizing to speculate on the kind of music Scarlatti might have written had he been born in 1950.

Schoenberg

Work: Concerto for Piano and Orchestra, Op. 42 (1942)

In an explanatory note to this work, Schoenberg paraphrased the events of [the movements of] his piano concerto:

Life was so easy
Suddenly [sic] hatred broke out (Presto)
A grave situation was created (Adagio)
But life goes on (Rondo)

CONC 398.

Schubert

Work: German Dances, D. 783 (1823-1824)

Schumann's ultra-imaginative and highly detailed scenario of the German Dances comes from a review in the *Neue Zeitschrift Für Musick* which reads, "In the Deutsche Tanze, on the other hand, there dances, to be sure, a whole carnival. 'T'would be fine,' Florestan shouted in Fritz Friedrich's ear, 'if you would get your magic lantern and follow the masquerade in shadows on the wall.' Exit and re-enter the latter, jubilant.

> The group that follows is one of the most charming. The room dimly lighted—Zilia at the piano, the wounding rose in her hair—Eusebius in his black velvet coat, leaning over her chair—Florestan (ditto), standing on the table and ciceronizing—Serpentin, his legs twined around Walt's neck, sometimes riding back and forth—the painter a la Hamlet,

parading his shadow figures through the bull's-eye, some spider legged ones even running off the wall on to the ceiling. Zilia began, and and Florestan may have spoken substantially to this effect, though at much greater length:

No. 1 in A major. Masks milling about. Kettledrums, Trumpets. The lights go down. Perruquier: "everything seems to be going very well." No. 2. Comic character, scratching himself behind the ears and continually calling out "Pst, pst!" Exit. No. 3. Harlequin, arms akimbo. Out the door head over heels. No. 4. Two stiff and elegant masks, dancing and scarcely speaking to one another. No. 5. Slim cavalier, chasing a mask: "At last I've caught you, lovely zither player!" "Let me go." She escapes. No. 6. Hussar at attention, with plume and sabertache. No. 7. Two harvesters, waltzing together blissfully. He, softly, "is it thou?" They recognize each other. No. 8. Tenant farmer from the country getting ready to dance. No. 9. The great doors swing open. Splendid procession of knights and noble ladies. No. 10. Spaniard to an Ursuline: "Speak at least, since you may not love!" She: "I would rather not speak, and be understood!"...

But in the midst of the waltz Florestan sprang from the table and out the door. One was used to this in him. Zilia, too, soon left off, and the others scattered in one direction and another. SRMH 843-844.

Work: Grand Rondo in A major, D. 951 (1828)

Of this four-hand work Robert Schumann wrote to Friedrich Wieck on November 26, 1829, "The other day I was playing his (Schubert's) four-hand Rondo, Op. 107, which I consider one of his best compositions; and is there anything to compare with the thunderous calm, the great, self-contained lyrical madness, and the gentle deep ethereal melancholy which pervades this truly great and complete work? I can just see Schubert walking up and down his room, wringing his hands as though in despair, while his mind keeps running on:

Grand Rondo in A Major, D. 951, ms 1-3, Breitkopf and Hartel

He cannot get rid of the idea, and brings back the great pure strain once more at the end, where it seems to breathe its last in a gentle sigh." SCEL 80.

Work: Sonata in A minor, D. 845 (1825)

In an undated review of this work Robert Schumann wrote, "The first part is so still, so dreamy; it touches one to tears; yet so simply, so easily it is constructed, from two ideas only, that one cannot but wonder at the enchanter who so deftly opposes and intermingles them." SCRE 254.

Work: Sonata in D major, D. 850 (1825)

Robert Schumann wrote in the *Neue Zeitschrift Für Musick*, "What a different kind of life wells up from the energetic D major Sonata, seizing us and sweeping us away, stroke upon stroke! Then the Adagio, wholly Schubertian, impulsive, extravagant, scarcely can he find an ending." SCMM 113.

Work: Sonata in G major, D. 894 (1826)

In a letter to Clara dated Dusseldorf, Friday, February 22, 1856, Brahms wrote, "How pleased I was that you played some Schubert. One must do it, if only for the sake of the beloved name, even if nothing is suitable for playing (in public). If I were a moderately respected pianist, and one who commands respect, I would have played a sonata in public long ago (the one in G, for example). It cannot help but enchant people if it is beautifully played." BRAL 122

Writing of this same sonata, which he calls "Fantasia or Sonata," Robert Schumann said, "Though without many words we may describe all three sonatas as 'glorious' [these three being the A minor, D. 845, the D major, D. 850, and G major, D. 894], the "Fantasia or Sonata" seems to us the most perfect of his sonatas in form and spirit. Here everything is organic, breathing the selfsame life. He who has not sufficient imagination to solve the riddle of the last movement, had better eschew it." SCMM 112-113.

Stravinsky

Work: Concerto for Piano and Wind Instruments (1923-24)

Stravinsky described it as "a kind of Rumanian restaurant music." CONC 465.

Weber

Work: Konzertstuck, Op. 79 (1815-1821)

Cortot says the following,

In 1821, on the same day that the first performance of *Der Freischutz* was given, Weber carried the pages of the *Konzertstuck*, still wet with ink, to his wife, to whom in the presence of his friend Benedict he outlined its poetic argument. Benedict wrote out this scheme from memory, for Weber always refused to let it be printed at the top of the work, and this is how it has come down to us:

We all know the enormous extent to which the Romantics were preoccupied with the Middle Ages, and we are not surprised to see Weber's imagination exercising itself upon a medieval subject:

Larghetto. A noble lady in the castle tower has awaited for many years the return of her husband from the Crusades. She has had no news of him. She imagines that he may be dead.

Allegro appassionato. And she has a vision of the knight lying wounded and abandoned on the battlefield. She is in despair; and we are made to feel her regret that she cannot be with him in that far land where she might, at least, died at his side.

Adagio e tempo di marcia. Trumpets suddenly ring out: she sees a troop of armed men approaching. Among the knights she recognizes her husband.

Pui mosso, presto assai. Delirious joy!

[Cortot continues] One cannot deny that this scheme is rococo, nor that the musical plot is rather out of date. Such as it is, however, its materials still provide a basis for interpretative skill. COMI 191-192.

About the Author

The New York Times has written of Neil Rutman that "he won the audience over for himself with exquisite performances of Mozart and Schubert—both commanding and full of character." *The Washington Post* stated that "his playing met the highest standards and his spotless articulation gave the whole program unusual polish and virtuoso marks."

As a young man Neil Rutman distinguished himself as a top prize winner in the Busoni, Kapell, Casadesus, Concert Artist Guild, and International Johann Sebastian Bach Competitions. An active performer on several continents, Mr. Rutman has garnered critical praise for his all Poulenc CD on which Emmy Award winning actor Tony Randall provides the narration of 'The Story of Babar the Little Elephant,' several Mozart Piano Concerti CDs, and an all Chopin CD. He has been a contributing author to *The Piano Quarterly*, *Clavier*, *The Piano Teacher*, and the book *The Pianists Craft*.

A native of San Francisco, Mr. Rutman graduated from the Eastman School of Music and the Peabody Institute. He has studied with Aiko Onishi, Cecile Genhart, and Ellen Mack. Mr. Rutman is Artist-in-Residence at the University of Central Arkansas from where his students have become laureates in the East West Artist Auditions in New York City, the Kappell, and the Clara Wells Competitions.

A former collegiate boxer, Neil Rutman coaches the University of Central Arkansas Boxing Team. Mr. Rutman, who serves as a volunteer Probation Officer and mentor for juvenile offenders in Faulkner County, was honored with the Martin Luther King—President Barack Obama Service Award in recognition of his contribution to youth. Mr. Rutman gains his greatest enjoyment from the association of family, friends, and travel. Visit www.neilrutman.net for more information.

Bibliography

AFPM Howat, Roy. *The Art of French Piano Music: Debussy, Ravel, Fauré, Chabrier*. New Haven: Yale University Press, 2009.

ALBE Clark, Walter Aaron. *Albéniz: Portrait of a Romantic*. Oxford: Oxford University Press, 1999.

ALMA Mast, Paul B. *"Style and Structure in 'Iberia' by Isaac Albéniz."* (Ph.D diss., University of Rochester, Eastman School of Music, 1974).

ALCO Collet, Henri. *Albéniz et Granados*. Paris: Éditions d'Aujourd'hui, 1982. Spanish trans. P. D. F. Labrousse. Buenos Aires: Tor=SRL, 1948.

ANEC Lebrecht, Norman. *The Book of Musical Anecdotes*. New York: Free Press, 1985.

APRC Hinson, Maurice. *At the Piano with Robert and Clara Schumann*. Van Nuys, California: Alfred, 1988.

BAAD Dürr, Alfred. *Bach, Johann Sebastian. The French Suites: Embellished Version: BWV 812–817*. Kassel: Bärenreiter Urtext, 1980.

BACB Badura-Skoda, Paul. *Interpreting Bach on the Keyboard*. Trans. Alfred Clayton. Oxford: Oxford University Press, 2002.

BACF Forkel, Johann Nikolaus. *Johann Sebastian Bach, His Life, Art, and Work*. Trans. Charles Sanford Terry. New York: Da Capo Press, 1970.

BACG Griepenkerl, F. K. *Klavierwerke von Joh. Seb. Bach*. vol. viii (Leipzig: ca. 1835). Qtd. in Badura-Skoda, Paul. *Interpreting Bach on the Keyboard*. Trans. Alfred Clayton. Oxford: Oxford University Press, 2002. 85-87.

BACO "Courante." *The New Encyclopaedia Britannica*. Vol. 3. 10th Ed. 2010.

BACS Schweitzer, Albert. *J. S. Bach, vol. 1*. Trans. by Ernest Newman. New York: Dover Publications, 1966.

BABF Bónis, Ferenc. *Így láttuk Bartókot: ötvennégy emlékezés*. Budapest: Püski, 1995.

BARK Bartók, Peter. *My Father*. Tampa, Florida: Rinaldi Printing, 2002.

BARP Yeomans, David. *Bartók for Piano*. Bloomington: Indiana University Press, 1988.

BART Bayley, Amanda, ed. *The Cambridge Companion to Bartók*. Cambridge and New York: Cambridge University Press, 2001.

BATS Smith, Timothy A. *Fugue No. 4: C-Sharp minor. Well-Tempered Clavier Book I. Sojurn, Soli Deo Gloria*. Last accessed August 10, 2014. http://www2.nau.edu/tas3/wtc/i04.html

BBAL Leitzmann, Albert. *Beethovens Briefe*. Leipzig: Insel-verlag, 1912.

BEAT Albrecht, Theodore. "Beethoven and Shakespeare's *Tempest*: New Light on an Old Allusion." *Beethoven Forum* 1 (1992): 81-92.

BEBR Brendel, Alfred. *Alfred Brendel on Music, Collected Essays*. Chicago: A Capella Books, 1991.

BEBU Beethoven, Ludwig van. *Variations for the Pianoforte*. Ed. Hans von Bülow and Sigmund Lebert. New York: G. Schirmer, Inc., 1928.

BEEC Stanley, Glenn. *The Cambridge Companion to Beethoven*. Cambridge: Cambridge University Press, 2000.

BEEF Fischer, Edwin. *Beethoven's Pianoforte Sonatas: A Guide for Students and Amateurs*. Trans. Stanley Godman and Paul Hamburger. London: Faber and Faber, 1959.

BEEK Drake, Kenneth. *The Sonatas of Beethoven as He Played and Taught Them*. Bloomington: Indiana University Press, 1981.

BEEL Kalischer, A. C. *Beethoven's Letters with explanatory notes*. Trans J. S. Shedlock. New York: Dover Publications, 1972.

BEER Reinecke, Carl. *The Beethoven Pianoforte Sonatas. Letters to a Lady*. Trans. E. M. Trevenen Dawson. London: Augener & Co., 1901.

BEES Schindler, Anton. *Beethoven as I Knew Him*. Ed. by Donald W. MacArdle. Chapel Hill: The University of North Carolina Press, 1966.

BEET Forbes, Elliot. *Thayer's Life of Beethoven*. Princeton: Princeton University Press, 1967.

BEEZ Czerny, Carl. *On the Proper Performance of all Beethoven's Works for the Piano*. Original date. Vienna: Universal Edition, 1970.

BEJC Chang, Josephine. "Josephine Chang Piano Teacher." Last modified December 15, 2015. https://josephinechang.wordpress.com/2013/11/10/2884/

BESK Johnson, Douglas, Alan Tyson, and Robert Winter. *The Beethoven Sketchbooks*. Berkeley: University of California Press, 1985.

BOEN "Bouree." *The New Encyclopaedia Britannica*. Vol. 2. 10th ed. 2010.

BRAB Hinson, Maurice. *Brahms, Ballades, Op. 10 for the Piano*. Van Nuys, California: Alfred, 1990.

BRAJ Swafford, Jan. *Johannes Brahms, A Biography*. New York: Vintage Books, 1999.

BRAK Kalbeck, Max. *Johannes Brahms, vol 4.* Tutzing, Country: H. Schneider, 1976.

BRAL Avins, Styra, ed. *Johannes Brahms: Life and Letters.* . Trans. Josef Eisinger and Styra Avins. Oxford: Oxford University Press, 1997.

BRC1 Litzmann, Berthold. *Letters of Clara Schumann and Johannes Brahms, 1853-1896, vol. 1.* New York: Vienna House, 1973.

BRC2 Litzmann, Berthold. *Letters of Clara Schumann and Johannes Brahms, 1853-1896, vol. 2.* New York: Vienna House, 1973.

BRHN Hinson, Maurice. *Brahms: The Shorter Piano Pieces.* Van Nuys, California: Alfred, 1992.

BRIE Derenburg, Mrs. Carl, a.k.a. Ilona Eibenschütz. "My Recollection of Brahms." *Musical Times* 67.1001 (1926): 598-600.

BRJJ Johnson, Jeffrey. *Performances in the Grand Style - From the Golden Age of the Etude Magazine (1913-1940).* Mineola, New York: Dover Publications, 2003.

BRUH Bruhn, Siglind. *Images and Ideas in Modern French Piano Music: the Extra-musical Subtext in Piano Works by Ravel, Debussy, and Messiaen.* Stuyvesant, NY: Pendragon Press, 1998.

BRVB von Bülow, Marie. *Hans van Bülow, Briefe und Scriften, vol. 7.* Leipzig: Breitkopf and Härtel, 1895-1908.

BUWA Walker, Alan. *Hans von Bülow: A Life and Times.* New York: Oxford University Press, 2010.

CHAD Adorno, Theodore W. *Introduction to the Sociology of Music.* Trans.. E.B. Ashton. New York: Seaburg Press, 1976.

CHCO Cortot, Alfred, "Frederic Chopin: *Les Preludes.*," *Conferencia: Journal de l'Universite des annales* 28(1933/34): 252-262.

CHFL Liszt, Franz. *Life of Chopin.* Trans. Martha Walker Cook. New York: Oliver Ditson & Co., 1863.

CHFN Tomaszewski, Mieczyslaw. "Chopin, Fantasy in F minor, Op. 49." The Fryderyk Chopin Institute. Last modified January 2010. http://en.chopin.nifc.pl/chopin/composition/detail/id/112

CHHE Hedley, A. *Selected Correspondence of Chopin.* London: Heinemann, 1966.

CHJH Huneker, James. *Chopin: The Man and His Music.* New York: Charles Scribner's Sons, 1900.

CHOC Cortot, Alfred. *Chopin Ballades, Student Edition.* Trans. David Ponsonby. Paris: Salabert, 1957.

CHOE Eigeldinger, Jean Jacques. *Chopin, pianist and teacher.* Cambridge: Cambridge University Press, 1986.

CHOM Marek, George and Maria Gordon-Smith. *Chopin.* New York: Harper and Row, Publishers, 1978.

CHOT Opineski, Henryk. *Chopin's Letters.* Trans. E. L. Voynich. Mineola, New York : Dover, 1977.

CHSO Eigeldinger, Jean Jacques. "Frederic Chopin: Souvenirs inédits par Solange Clésinger." *Revue musicale de Suisse romande* 30/5 (1978): 224-238.

COEN "Columbine." *The New Encyclopaedia Britannica.* Vol. 3. 10th ed. 2010.

COFP Cortot, Alfred. *French Piano Music.* Trans. Hilda Andrews. New York: Da Capo Press, 1977.

COGS Lubin, George. *Histoire de ma vie.* In *Oeuvres autobiographiques, vol. 2.* Paris: Gallimard, 1970-71.

COJK Kallberg, Jeffrey. "The Rhetoric of Genre: Chopin's Nocturne in g minor." *Nineteenth-Century Music* 11.3 (Spring 1988): 238-261.

COMI Thieffrey, Jeanne. *Alfred Cortot's Studies in Musical Interpretation.* Trans. Robert Jaques. New York: Da Capo Press, 1989.

CONC Steinberg, Michael. *The Concerto: A Listener's Guide.* New York: Oxford University Press, 1998.

COPR Cortot, Alfred. *Chopin 24 Preludes, Student Edition.* Trans. David Ponsonby. Paris: Salabert, 1970.

CSJB Litzmann, Berthold. *Clara Schumann-Johannes Brahms: Briefe aus den Jahren 1853-1896.* Leipzig: Breitkopf and Härtel, 1927.

DEBA Baudelaire, Charles. *Complete Poems.* Trans. Walter Martin. Manchester: Carcanet Press Limited, 1997.

DEBE Debussy, Claude. *Lettres a son Editeur.* Paris : Durand, 1927.

DEBL Debussy, Claude. *Oeuvres pour deux pianos.* Edition de Noel Lee. Paris: Editions Costallat, 1985.

DEBM Thompson, Oscar. *Debussy Man and Artist.* New York: Tudor Publishing Company, 1940.

DEBS Schmitz, E. Robert. *The Piano Works of Claude Debussy.* New York: Dover Publications, 1966.

DEBU Lockspeiser, Edward. *Debussy.* London: J. M. Dent and Sons Ltd., 1936.

DECA Casella, Alfredo. *Claude Debussy.* Dubuque, Iowa: Nichols Publishing, 1992.

DEDU Dumensil, Maurice. "Coaching with Debussy." *The Piano Teacher* 5 (1962): 10-13.

DELE Lesure, Francois and Roger Nichols, eds. *Debussy Letters..* Trans. Roger Nichols. Cambridge, MA: Harvard University Press, 1987.

DELL Liebich, Louisa. "An Englishwoman's Memories of Debussy." *The Musical Times* 59 (1918): 250

DEBN Ryan, Meg, perf. *Et blanc et noir*. The Los Angeles Philharmonic. Last accessed June 30, 2013. http://www.laphil.com/philpedia/music/en-blanc-et-noir-claude-debussy

DEML Long, Marguerite. *At the Piano With Debussy*. Trans. Oliver Senior-Ellis. London: J. M. Dent and Sons, Ltd., 1972.

DENI Nichols, Roger. *Debussy Remembered*. Portland, Oregon: Amadeus Press, 1992.

DEPR Robert, Paul. *Images: The Piano Music of Claude Debussy*. Portland, Oregon: Amadeus Press, 1996.

DESB Bruhn, Siglind. *Images and Ideas in Modern French Piano Music: The Extra-Musical Subtext in Piano Works by Ravel, Debussy, and Messiaen*. Hillsdale, New York: Pendragon Press, 1997.

DEVA Vallas, Leon. *Claude Debussy, His Life and Works*. Trans.Maire O'Brien and Grace O'Brien. New York: Dover, 1933.

ESCA Dubal, David. *The Essential Canon of Classical Music*. New York: North Point Press, 2001.

ETAH Taylor, Ronald. *E.T.A. Hoffmann*. London: Bowes and Bowes, 1963.

ETPL Johnson, Jeffrey. *Piano Lessons in the Grand Style—From the Golden Age of the Etude Music Magazine (1913-1940)*. Mineola, New York: Dover Publications, 2003.

EWEN Ewen, David. *The Complete Book of Classical Music*. Englewood Cliffs, New Jersey: Prentice Hall, 1988.

FAML Long, Marguerite. *At the Piano with Fauré*. Trans. Olive Sernior-Ellis. New York: Taplinger Publishing, 1981.

FALE Jones, J. Barrie. *Gabriel Fauré: A Life in Letters*. Trans. and ed. J. Barrie Jones. London: B. T. Batsford Ltd., 1989.

FEFE Aggeler, William. *The Flowers of Evil*. Fresno, CA: Academy Library Guild, 1954.

FHFM Hiller, Ferdinand. *Mendelssohn, Letters and Recollections*. Trans. M.E. von Glehn. New York: Vienna House, 1972.

GAQU Quantz, Johann Joachim. *On Playing the Flute*. Trans. Edward R. Reilly. London: Faber & Faber, Ltd., 1966.

GATA Arbeau, Thoinot. *Orchesography*. Trans. Mary Stewart Evans. New York: Dover Publications, 1967.

GBAL Steen-Nökleberg, Einar and Ernst Hertrich. *Edvard Grieg Ballade, Opus 24*. Munich: G. Henle Verlag, 1992.

GCON Grainger, Percy. *Piano Concerto in A minor, Op. 16 by Edvard Grieg*. Milwuakee: G Schirmer Inc., 1949.

GENH Gordon, Stewart. *Cécile Staub Genhart: Her Biography and her Concepts of Piano Playing*. DMA Dissertation, Eastman School of Music. Ann Arbor, MI.1964.

GIEN "Gigue." *The New Encyclopaedia Britannica*. Vol. 5. 10th ed. 2010.

GRAN Clark, Walter Aaron. *Enrique Granados: Poet of the Piano*. Oxford: Oxford University Press, 2006.

GRRO de Larrocha, Alicia. "Granados, the Composer." Trans. Joan Kerlow. *Clavier* 6/7 (1967): pp. 21-27.

GRIE Benestad, Finn. *Grieg: The Man and the Artist*. Trans. William H. Halverson and Leland B. Sateren. Lincoln: University of Nebraska Press, 1988.

GRSA Salvador, Miguel. "The Piano Suite *Goyescas* by Enrique Granados: An Analytical Study." DMA Essay. University of Miami, 1988.

GRVI Granados, Enrique. *Papeles intimos de Enrique Granados*. Barcelona: Amigos de Granados, 1966.

HAEN "Harlequin." *The New Encyclopaedia Britannica*. Vol. 5. 10th ed. 2010.

HAYD Geiringer, Karl. *Haydn, A Creative Life in Music*. Berkeley: University of California Press, 1982.

JANA Horsbrugh, Ian. *Leos Janáček: The Field that Prospered*. New York: Charles Scribner, 1982.

KIRK Kirkpatrick, Ralph. *Domenico Scarlatti*. Princeton: Princeton University Press, 1981.

LIBU Busoni, Ferrucio. *The Essence of Music*. Trans. Rosamund Ley. New York: Philosophical Library, 1957.

LIEN "Jack-o'-lantern." *The New Encyclopaedia Britannica*. Vol. 6. 10th ed. 2010.

LIHA Liszt, Franz. *Harmonies poétiques et religieuses*. Munich: Henle, 2010.

LIHU Johnson, James. "The Tone of Hell: Translation of 'Après une lecture de Dante.'" *Pustblume: Journal of Translation* 1 (Spring 2007):7-11.

LILB Liszt, Franz. *Consolations and Liebesträume for the Piano*. Ed. Rafael Joseffy. New York: G. Schirmer, Inc., 1924.

LIMI da Vianna da Motta, José. *Sonata in B minor and other works for the Piano*. New York: Dover, 1990.

LIPM Ramann, Lina. *Franz Liszt als Künstler und Mensc. Band 1*. Leipzig: Breitkopf & Härtel, 1880.

LIPT Liszt, Franz. *Années de pèlerinage, "Italie"*. Ed. Rafael Joseffy. New York: G. Schirmer, Inc. 1938.

LIS1 Walker, Alan. *Franz Liszt Volume 1: The Virtuoso Years, 1811-1847*. New York: Alfred A. Knopf, 1989.

LIS2 Walker, Alan. *Franz Liszt Volume 2: The Weimar Years, 1848-1861*. New York: Random House, 1983.

LIS3 Walker, Alan. *Franz Liszt Volume 3: The Final Years, 1862-1888*. New York: Alfred A. Knopf, 1996.

LISA Walker, Alan. *Living with Liszt from the Diary of Carl Lachmund, an American pupil of Liszt, 1882-1884.* Stuyvesant, NY: Pendragon Press, 1995.

LISC Sitwell, Sacheverell. *Liszt.* London: Faber & Faber, 1955.

LISF Liszt, Franz. *Années de Pèlerinage, Première Année, Suisse.* Munich: Henle, 1978.

LISG Jerger, Wilhelm. *The Piano Master Classes of Franz Liszt, 1884-1886: Diary Notes of August Göllerich.* Trans. Richard Louis Zimdars. Bloomington, Indiana: Indiana University Press, 1996.

LISL Williams, Adrian. *Franz Liszt: Selected Letters.* Oxford: Clarendon Press, 1998.

LISM Liszt, Franz. *The Letters of Franz Liszt to Olga von Meyendorff, 1871-1886.* Trans. William R. Tyler. Washington D. C.:Dumbarton Oaks, 1979.

LISV Hill, Peter. "Programme Notes." Last modified February 19, 2015. https://oliviasham.files.wordpress.com/2012/05/osham_notes_2011-2.pdf

LISW Watson, Derek. *Liszt.* New York: Schirmer Books, 1989.

LIVE Spiegel, Fritz. *The Lives, Wives, and Loves of the Great Composers.* London: Marion Boyars Publishers, 1997.

LZEN "Mazeppa." *The New Encyclopaedia Britannica.* Vol. 7. 10th ed. 2010.

MEND Jacob, Heinrich Eduard. *Felix Mendelssohn and his Times.* Trans. Richard Winston and Clara Winston. Inglewood Cliffs, New Jersey: Prentice Hall, 1963.

MENL Mendelssohn, Felix. *Felix Mendelssohn: Letters.* Ed. G. Selden-Goth. New York: Pantheon Book, Inc., 1945.

MESC Schubring, Julius. "Reminiscenses of Felix Mendelssohn-Bartholdy." *The Musical Times* 1866: 221-236.

MESS Stratton, Samuel. *Mendelssohn.* New York: E.P. Dutton and Company, 1910.

MOZT Niemtschek, Franz. *Leben des K.K. Kapellmeisters Wolfgang Gottlieb Mozart, nach Originalquellen beschrieben.* Prague: 1798.

MUCA Calvocoressi, Michel D., and Gerald Abraham. *Mussorgsky.* London: J. M. Dent & Sons, Ltd., 1946.

MUCR Calvocoressi, Michel D., and Gerald Abraham. *Mussorgsky.* Revised edition. London: J. M. Dent & Sons, Ltd., 1974.

MUSS Gordeyeva, Ye. *Musorgskiy: Letters.* Moscow: Music, 1984.

MYER Myers, Rollo. *Modern French Music from Fauré to Boulez.* New York: Da Capo Press, 1984.

NABO Monsaingeon, Bruno. *Mademoiselle conversation with Nadia Boulanger.* Trans. Robyn Marsack. Manchester: Carcanet Press Limited, 1985.

PAEN "Pantaloon." *The New Encyclopaedia Britannica.* Vol. 9. 10th ed. 2010.

PEEN "Peirrot." *The New Encyclopaedia Britannica.* Vol. 9. 10th ed. 2010.

POCO Poulenc, Francis. *Francis Poulenc: Selected Correspondence, 1915-1963.* Trans. Sidney Buckland. London: Victor Gollancz Ltd., 1991.

POEL Poulenc, Francis. Élégie pour deux pianos. Paris: Éditions Max Eschig, 1960.

POEN Poulenc, Francis. *Entretiens avec Claude Rostand.* Radio interview with the critic Rostand. Paris: R. Julliard, 1954.

PONC Poulenc, Francis. *Nocturnes pour Piano.* Paris: Heugel & Cie., 1932.

PONZ Poulenc, Francis. *Les Soirées de Nazelles.* Paris: Durand, 1937.

POUL Daniel, Keith W. *Francis Poulenc, His Artistic Development and Musical Style.* Ann Arbor, Michigan: UMI Research Press, 1982.

PORE Leden, Victor and Marina A. Ledin. Liner Notes. *Poulenc, Piano Music.* Oliver Cazal (piano). Naxos 8.553930. 1999. Compact disc.

POWR Radford, Winifred. Liner Notes. *Pierre Barnac—PB1.* Pierre Barnac (vocalist, narrator), Graham Johnson (piano). England: The Friends of Pierre Bernac, 1980.

PRAU Shlifstein, Semyon, edi. *S. S. Prokofiev Materialy, dokumenty, vospominaniya.* Moscow: Gosudarstvennoye Muzykalnoye Izdatelstvo, 1956.

PRBB Berman, Boris. *Prokofiev's Piano Sonatas, A Guide for the Listener and the Performer.* New Haven: Yale University Press, 2008.

PRBM Monsaingeon, Bruno. *Sviatoslav Richer: Notebooks and Conversations.* Trans. Stewart Spencer. Princeton, New Jersey: Princeton University Press, 2001.

PROD Prokofiev, Sergey. *Sergey Prokofiev Diaries 1907-1914: Prodigious Youth.* Trans. Anthony Phillips. Ithaca: Cornell University Press, 2006.

PROF Nice, David. *Prokofiev From Russia to the West 1891-1935.* New Haven:Yale University Press, 2003.

PROK Prokofiev, Sergei. *Prokofiev by Prokofiev: A Composer's Memoir.* Trans. Guy Daniels. Garden City, New York: Doubleday and Company, Inc., 1979.

PRRH Robinson, Harlow. *Sergei Prokofiev.* Boston: Northeastern University Press, 1987.

PRSM Nestyev, Israel and Edelman, G., eds. *Sergey Prokofiev 1953-1963: Staty I materialy.* Moscow: Sovietsky Kompozitor, 1962.

PRTS Schipperges, Thomas. *Prokofiev* London: Haus Publishing, 1995.

QUOT Giddings, Robert. *Musical Quotes and Anecdotes.* England: Longman Group Limited, 1984.

RABM Martyn, Barrie. *Rachmaninoff: Composer, Pianist, Conductor.* Aldershot, England: Scolar Press, 1990.

RACH Seroff, Victor I. *Rachmaninoff.* Freeport, New York: Books for Library Press, 1970.

RADO Ravel, Maurice. *Piano Masterpieces of Maurice Ravel*. New York: Dover Publications, 1986.

RAFP Spiers, John. "Le Tombeau de Couperin." Maurice Ravel Frontispice. Last modified June 20, 2013. http://www.maurice-ravel.net/tombeau.htm

RAKH Wehrmeyer, Andreas. *Rakhmaninov*. Trans. Anne Wyburd. London: Haus Publishing, 2004.

RALM Bertensson, Sergei and Jay Leyda. *Sergei Rachmaninoff: A Lifetime in Music*. Indianapolis: Indiana University Press, 2001.

RAMH Harrison, Max. *Rachmaninoff: Life, Works, Recordings*. New York: Continuum, 2005.

RAMM Cameron, Norman. "Conversation with Rachmaninoff." *The Monthly Musical Record* (November 1934): 201.

RAMS *The Art of the Piano*. Directed by Donald Sturrock. Burbank, Ca: Warner Home Video (NVC Arts), DVD, 1999.

RAOS Riesemann, Oskar von. *Rachmaninoff's Recollections*. London: Allen & Unwin Ltd., 1934.

RAPM Ravel, Maurice. *Piano Masterpieces of Maurice Ravel*. New York: Dover Publications, 1986.

RAVE Roland Manuel, Alexis. *Ravel*. Trans. Cynthia Jolly. London: Dobson Limited, 1947.

RAVV Nichols, Roger. *Miroirs for Solo Piano*. London: Peters Edition, 1996.

RAVL Stuckenschmidt, H. H. *Ravel, Variations on his life and work*. Trans. Samuel R. Rosenbaum. Philadelphia: Chilton Book Company, 1968.

RAOR Ornstein, Arbie. *A Ravel Reader: Correspondence, Articles, Interviews*. New York: Columbia University Press, 1990.

ROSE Rosen, Charles. *The Romantic Generation*. Cambridge: Harvard University Press, 1995.

SAEN "Saraband." *The New Encyclopaedia Britannica*. Vol. 10. 10th ed. 2010.

SAND Sand, George. *Winter in Majorca*. Trans. and annotated Robert Graves. Chicago: Academy Press Limited, 1978.

SCEL Schumann, Robert. *Early Letters of Robert Schumann*. Trans. May Herbert. London: George Bell and Sons, 1888.

SCEU Schumann, Eugenie. *The Schumanns and Johannes Brahms, The Memoirs of Eugenie Schumann*. Trans. Marie Busch. Freeport, New York: Books for Libraries Press, 1927.

SCHI Hinson, Maurice. *Fantasiestucke, Op. 12 for the Piano by Robert Schumann*. Van Nuys, California: Alfred, 1992.

SCHL Schumann, Robert. *Piano Works, Volume II*. Munich: Henle Verlag, 1987.

SCHN Schumann, Robert. *Piano Works, Volume III.* Munich: Henle Verlag, 1976.
SCHU Marston, Nicholas. *Schumann, Fantasie, Op. 17.* Cambridge: Cambridge University Press, 1992.
SCJC Chissell, Joan. *Schumann.* London: J. M. Dent and Sons Ltd., 1967.
SCLL Weissweiler, Eva. *The Complete Correspondence of Clara and Robert Schumann, Critical Edition, vol. 1.* Trans. Hildegard Fritsch and Ronald L. Crawford. New York: Peter Lang, 1994.
SCMM Schumann, Robert. *On Music and Musicians.* Trans. Paul Rosenfeld and ed. Konrad Wolff. New York: Pantheon, 1946.
SCNF Jansen, Gustav. *Robert Schumanns Briefe.* Leipzig: Neue Folge, 1904.
SCNI Niecks, Frederick. *Robert Schumann.* London: J. M. Dent & Sons Ltd., 1978.
SCPB Wolf-Dieter Seiffert. "Robert Schumann, 'The Prophet Bird' (No. 7 from Forest Scenes op. 82)." Last modified 2010. http://www.henleusa.com/files/schumann_prophetbird_en.pdf
SCWD Jensen, Eric Frederick, "A New Manuscript of Robert Schumann's *Waldszenen,* Op.82." *Journal of Musicology* 3(1984): 69–89.
SCR1 Bowers, Faubion. *Scriabin: A Biography of a Russian Composer 1871-1915, vol. 1.* Palo Alto, California: Kodansha International Ltd., 1969.
SCR2 Bowers, Faubion. *Scriabin: A Biography of a Russian Composer 1871-1915, vol. 2.* Palo Alto, California: Kodansha International Ltd., 1969.
SCRE Schumann, Robert. *Music and Musicians, Essays and Criticisms.* Trans. Fanny Raymond Ritter. Freeport, New York: Books for Library Series, 1972.
SCRI De Schloezer, Boris. *Scriabin: Artist and Mystic.* Trans. Nicolas Slonimsky. Berkeley: University of California Press, 1987
SCRR Rimm, Robert. *The Composer Pianists-Hamelin and the Eight.* Portland, Oregon: Amadeus Press, 2002.
SCSL Schumann, Robert. *The Letters of Robert Schumann.* Ed. Karl Storck. Trans. Hannah Bryant. New York: Arno Press, 1979.
SHCA Jensen, Eric Frederick. *Schumann.* Oxford: Oxford University Press, 2004.
SRMH Strunk, Oliver. *Source Readings in Music History: The Romantic Era.* New York: W. W. Norton and Company, 1965.
STFR *The Little Flowers of St. Francis.* Trans. Raphael Brown. Garden City, New York: Hanover House, 1958.
VOLL Czerny, Carl. *Vollstandige theoreticsh-practische Pianoforte-Schule, Op. 500.* Vienna: A. Diabelli u Comp., 1845.
WOLF Wolf, Konrad. *Masters of the Keyboard.* Bloomington, Indiana: Indiana University Press, 1990.

Index to Works Cited